Also by

Sister Gargi (Marie Louise Burke)

Swami Vivekananda in the West: New Discoveries

His Prophetic Mission (vols. 1 and 2)

The World Teacher (vols. 3 and 4)

A New Gospel (vols. 5 and 6)

Vedantic Tales

Hari the Lion

Swami Trigunatita: His Life and Work

A Heart Poured Out: A Story of Swami Ashokananda

A Disciple's Journal

In the Company of

Swami Ashokananda

Vital Breath

A DISCIPLE'S JOURNAL

In the Company of

Swami Ashokananda

Sister Gargi

(Marie Louise Burke)

Kalpa Tree Press
New York

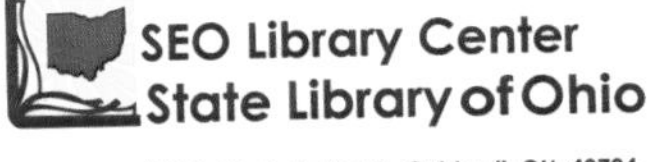

Kalpa Tree Press
65 East 96th Street, Suite 12D
New York, NY 10128

Library of Congress Catalog Card Number: 2003107619

Publisher's Cataloging-in-Publication Data
Burke, Marie Louise, 1912–
A disciple's journal : in the company of Swami Ashokananda / Sister Gargi (Marie Louise Burke). — 1st ed. — New York : Kalpa Tree Press, 2003.
p. cm.
Includes index.
LCCN 2003107619
ISBN 0-9706368-2-2
1. Burke, Marie Louise, 1912– 2. Ashokananda, Swami. 3. Ramakrishna Mission—Biography. 4. Vedanta Society—Biography. 5. Hindus—California—San Francisco—Biography. I. Title.
BL1175.B875A3 2003 294.5′55′092
QBI33-1439

10 9 8 7 6 5 4 3 2 1

FIRST EDITION

Designed by Fearn Cutler de Vicq
Set in Sabon
Printed in the United States of America

CONTENTS

PREFACE

Even if the present reader does not normally read prefaces, he or she should probably read this one. The disciple in this book's title never intended, or even dreamt, that her journal would one day be read by anyone other than her doting older self, so naturally she did not explain in it what she already knew. If, however, the reader is not familiar with the Vedantic tradition or has not read this book's companion, *A Heart Poured Out: A Story of Swami Ashokananda,* he or she will need a little background information. In this case, read on.

Swami Ashokananda (1893–1969) was a monk of the Ramakrishna Order in India. In 1931, when he was thirty-seven years old, he was asked by his monastic seniors to serve as assistant minister in the Order's affiliated center in San Francisco. He arrived there July 4, 1931. The following year, because of the illness of the swami then in charge, Swami Ashokananda became the Society's spiritual leader.

The Vedanta Society of San Francisco was founded in 1900 by the renowned Swami Vivekananda (1863–1902), a direct disciple and chief apostle of Sri Ramakrishna (1836–86). The Society was housed in a temple built by Swami Trigunatita (another direct disciple of Sri Ramakrishna) in the Marina district of the city. Completed in 1908, the Temple was (and still is) a narrow, three-story frame building, Victorian in style, with towers on top that were primarily, but not incongruously, Hindu. When I knew it, the building's ground floor consisted, front to back, of a small library-reading room, Swami's office, and the Society's "back office" at the end of the hall; beyond that, with its main entrance from the street, was a large auditorium that included the shrine. The second floor was given over to a monastery, and the third or top floor housed the quarters of the swami-in-charge. Although the Society was spiritually affiliated with the Ramakrishna Order in India, its membership was entirely American. It was regulated by the laws of California and was financially autonomous.

I first came to the Vedanta Society's Temple at the close of 1948. By that time Swami Ashokananda had expanded the work of the Society to include a center and temple in the city of Berkeley, across San Francisco Bay, and was developing a retreat on two thousand acres of rolling, wooded land he had bought in Olema, Marin County, across the Golden Gate Bridge. Yet another center and temple were under construction in Sacramento, the capital city of California, and plans for a large new temple in San Francisco were being contemplated. The San Francisco Vedanta Society (by then named the Vedanta Society of Northern California) had about 150 members, most of whom worked for a living. After learning of the Society's expansion, I wondered, indeed marveled at, how so much work could have been done by so small and modest a congregation.

As I came to know Swami Ashokananda, the answer to that question became clear. Here was a man to whom the word *impossible* was anathema and whose character could be defined by the words *faith, sacrifice, determination*, and *strength*. Those qualities were, moreover, contagious; they entered into the heart of the membership and imbued it with the conviction that nothing—*nothing*—was impossible in the service of God. And thus everything was, of course, possible, despite the sometimes virulent opposition that Eastern religions came up against in the West during the first half of the twentieth century.

Vedanta is not a proselytizing religion. It says what it has to say to whomever wants to listen, but it does not wave flags or blow trumpets. While its teachers know that its message is life transforming, they also know that very few people want their lives to be transformed—however miserable and painful those lives may be. When a person is ready for change, he or she will come to the right spiritual teacher in his or her own time and way. That is all. Vedantists believe that there is a sort of cosmic law about it and that the teacher will wait for the student to come of his or her own accord. When the student finally does come, generally the greeting is, "What took you so long?"

Vedanta has been on this earth for thousands of years. It is the philosophical basis of Hinduism and, in its breadth and depth, encompasses all the great religions of the world. It was born in the forest retreats of ancient India, where sages and seers had retired to seek the utmost reality of existence. Now and then, one or another of those seers (*rishis*) would find through inward search what he (or sometimes she) sought and would proclaim that indescribable truth to his or her disciples in approximate words that could be easily memorized, for those were days before writing was known. A teacher's terse revelations were collected and became known as the Upanishads, a Sanskrit word meaning, roughly, "a teaching given to one sitting near," that is, to a disciple. The Upanishads form the last books of the Vedas, the earliest extant scriptures on earth. The Sanskrit word *Vedanta* means "the end of the Vedas"—"the end" in the sense of the culminating truths as well as the last books. Those Upanishadic, or Vedantic, utterances have survived intact through millennia. So highly have they been revered in India that to change a single word would be sacrilege. India's history is aglow with commentators on and teachers of the Upanishads, great shining souls who have realized the truths discovered and sung by the Vedic *rishis* and who have taught them to others with meticulous accuracy. Thus Vedanta has flowed in unbroken streams from teacher to disciple down through countless generations.

In our own times, Sri Ramakrishna, an untutored priest and a disciple of an enlightened Vedantic monk, manifested in his life and words every aspect of Vedantic wisdom. He followed, one after another, each religious path that was known to him, and at the end of each he experienced the same essential truth—thus verifying once and for all the ancient Vedic saying: "Truth is one; sages call it by various names." Christians, Muslims, and of course Hindus of various sects sat at his feet, as though at the feet of their own prophets and saviors, and there found the reality and the peace they sought.

Sri Ramakrishna's illustrious monastic disciple, Swami Vivekananda, was the first Hindu monk to bring Vedanta (which he equated with the universal message of his Master) to the West—not as a missionary, but as a teacher of spirituality. Swamiji (as Swami Vivekananda is usually called) came first to the Parliament of Religions, held in Chicago in 1893, and stayed for two or three years to lecture in America and England. Four of his brother disciples followed in his wake. Then, in the early decades of the twentieth century, came the next generation of monks, to which Swami Ashokananda belonged. Today there are thirteen Vedanta societies in America, many with retreats, and others throughout the world, each headed by a monk of the Ramakrishna Order.

That is essentially what the reader needs to know. When I was a disciple of that great, powerful, and loving Swami, I kept an informal diary of the things he said and did, in order to pin them down for myself before the wind blew them away. That diary, *A Disciple's Journal,* is not by any means a complete record; it is a sketchy reflection of my experience of a great man. Just the same, it rounds out the story that I tried to tell in *A Heart Poured Out,* my biography of Swami Ashokananda published earlier this year. My journal entries are like small details of a large canvas. They tell of magic days and years that once took place in this sorry world, days that will never return, never again in the same wonderful way. It was the Swami's presence that gave them light and life—and if *A Disciple's Journal* has captured even a little of that presence, it will have achieved much more than its author could have dreamt.

I want particularly to give my thanks to the editor and publisher, Dr. Shelley Brown, whose expertise, know-how, hard work, and meticulous care gave these two books their shape and style. No amount of gratitude could ever balance those gifts; and for her laughter, continuing friendship, and loving encouragement, the very idea of thanks is absurd.

Gargi

San Francisco
April 14, 2003

CAST OF CHARACTERS

We felt a warm and comfortable delight in being together—the women students of Swami Ashokananda. Whatever our ages or backgrounds, and they both ranged widely, there was a camaraderie between us that made any of our gatherings, large or small, seem like a reunion of compatriots in a foreign land, or, more to the point, a get-together of aliens on planet Earth. We spoke the same language, which was not understood in the slightest degree by our everyday associates; we used the same currency to assess the value of the things around us; and we understood not only why some things were valuable and others were not, but why some things were hilarious and others stupefyingly dull.

Over and above these cultural likenesses, and perhaps at the root of them, was the fact that we loved the ideal of Vedanta with all our hearts and pursued it without compromise and without rivalry among ourselves. Swami Ashokananda's teaching molded our lives and gave them meaning, and it was broad enough to encompass and sustain us all. Nothing needed to be said about belonging—one was either a dedicated worker of the Vedanta Society or one was not.

It is true that the Society's workers were appointed by Swami Ashokananda, but this happened only after their own inner drive and ability became apparent. An organization of energies formed as though by itself. Josephine Stanbury, for instance, oversaw all work connected with the altars (and was incidentally the Society's treasurer); Anna Webster was in charge of the crew of women that worked at the retreat property at Olema, turning a virtual wilderness into something almost parklike; Edith Soulé, the Society's secretary, took care of the office and all that that entailed; Mara Lane was the Society's librarian; Helen Sutherland did the interior decorating of the temples under Swami Ashokananda's direction; Nancy Jackman taught a class in Western philosophy; Kathleen Davis, one on the Gita; and Jeanette Vollmer, one on Sanskrit—and so it went.

During the period covered by this journal, the Society's workers formed a nucleus that seemed to have an evolving life of its own, a nucleus that could perpetuate itself from generation to generation. Each student in that nucleus had a voice, as though in a celestial choir, or, in Hindu terms, a role in a divine *lila* or divine play.

I knew many of those workers very well and admired all of them. The glimpses I give of a few of them in this journal do not even faintly limn their extraordinariness—their strength, generosity, capacity to love, and burning loyalty to the ideals of Vedanta. They were very different one from another, and yet each was lit from within by the same steady glow. I cannot reproduce that glow, but at least I can tell very briefly who they were—those shining women (and two men) who enter the conversations in this journal, say a few words, and then disappear. Here are some thumbnail sketches to pin them down.

(First names in alphabetical order)

Alfred T. Clifton (Swami Chidrupananda)
From 1933, Al Clifton was Swami Ashokananda's student and right-hand man, laboring with unwavering dedication at every task. Early on he joined the monastery in San Francisco, and he took *sannyas* (the final vows) in 1962. He served as the president of the Vedanta Society for many years.

Ann Myren
A high school teacher in the East Bay town of Richmond and later a teacher in Alameda Community College, Ann became Swami Ashokananda's student in 1958. During the 1980s and 1990s, Ann was the president of the Vivekananda Foundation, which she co-founded to help spread Swami Vivekananda's message.

Anna Webster
A forthright Bostonian, down to earth and extremely devoted, Anna was of great help in designing the altar for the New Temple. As the much loved, no-nonsense leader of the women's work crew, Anna energetically drove a truck around the rugged acreage of the Vedanta Retreat at Olema.

Bobbie Day
A close friend of the author's from high school days, Bobbie became interested in Vedanta and eventually, in the 1960s, took initiation from Swami Ashokananda.

Dorothy Madison
As a brilliant and dynamic high school teacher in the town of Richmond, Dorothy steered many students toward Vedanta. With Ann Myren, she was co-founder of the Vivekananda Foundation. A talented writer, she contributed a number of articles to the Ramakrishna Order's journals.

Dorothy Murdock (Pravrajika Madhavaprana)
Dorothy came to Vedanta as a high school student, urged by Dorothy Madison. She later graduated from the University of California with a degree in history and taught in an East Bay middle school. She was a valued worker in the Berkeley Vedanta Society before she joined the San Francisco convent in 1962.

Dorothy Peters (Pravajika Nirbhayaprana)
Presently the senior *sannyasini* of the convent in San Francisco, she was one of the first four nuns to take monastic vows (*brahmacharya*). Dorothy was a leader in landscaping the many beautiful gardens of the Vedanta Society and worked with Swami Ashokananda on the sculptures for the altar in the New Temple.

Ediben (Edith Benjamin Soulé)
Ediben was one of Swami Ashokananda's first students. She had a pure and beautiful voice and, before coming to Vedanta, became well known locally as a concert singer. Spirited and outgoing, with a loving word for everyone, she was the Society's secretary from 1942 until she resigned in 1972.

Edna Zulch
A diminutive and congenial widow with three grown sons, Edna was a hard working editor of *The Voice of India,* the Vedanta Society's high-quality magazine that was published during 1945–46 and later revived with trial issues in the early 1950s. She was an amusing and loving friend.

Elna Olsen
One of Swami Ashokananda's first students, Elna was a dedicated and tireless worker of the Vedanta Society in many fields. She had been trained to drive by the racer Barney Oldfield. Although gentle and soft-spoken, Elna alarmed other devotees

when she drove Swami Ashokananda in record time to and from Berkeley.

Ernest C. Brown
A disciple of Swami Trigunatita, Mr. Brown joined the monastery in the Old Temple in 1908. Later he left and married, but was readmitted by Swami Ashokananda when his wife died. In the 1950s he served as president of the Vedanta Society until, in his eighties, he made a pilgrimage to India, where he lived for the rest of his life.

Eve Bunch
Eve was a registered nurse who joined the Vedanta convent in San Francisco in 1961. She was one of the first four nuns to receive *brahmacharya.*

Florence Wenner
Florence joined the Vedanta Society around 1940 but, to Swami Ashokananda's dismay, she left it in 1946. She was the chief editor of the Vedanta Society's journal, *The Voice of India,* during 1945–46.

Helen Sutherland
Helen was the decorator of the interior-decorating firm of Sutherland and Stanbury, while Jo Stanbury kept the accounts. For many years they furnished and decorated at cost all the temples and retreat houses of the Vedanta Society of Northern California. Helen and Jo were inseparable friends as well as business partners.

Jeanette Vollmer
Jeanette was an active member of the Vedanta Society who held classes in Sanskrit. She performed her most essential service by recording Swami Ashokananda's lectures and classes.

Jo (Josephine) Stanbury
Jo was a beautiful young widow when she joined the Vedanta Society in 1933. She was in charge of the exacting ceremonial preparations for worship at the Society, which included the preparation of offered food. She also cooked for Swami Ashokananda, who required a special diet, and for any devotee who was ailing or in need of a good meal.

Kathleen Davis
Kathleen was one of the first students of Swami Ashokananda. A grammar school teacher in San Francisco, she spent all her spare time at the Vedanta Temple. She did a great deal of literary work for *The Voice of India* and in later years was of indispensable assistance in the preparation of volumes 3 and 4 of *New Discoveries* for publication.

Luke (Mary Lou) Williams
A brilliant and caustic thinker, Luke was an active worker in the Old Temple and at the Vedanta Retreat at Olema. Austere and strong-willed, she was nonetheless a highly entertaining and humorous companion.

Mara Lane
A much loved grammar school teacher in San Francisco's Chinatown, Mara was one of Swami Ashokananda's first students and a lifelong practitioner of Vedanta. For many years she served as librarian at the Old Temple, where she was a cheerful presence with a halo of golden hair.

Marilyn Pearce (Pravrajika Vishuddhaprana)
A high school student when Dorothy Madison introduced her to Vedanta, Marilyn graduated with honors from the University of California in Berkeley before joining the convent in San Fran-

cisco—one of the first four nuns to take *brahmacharya.* Now a senior *sannyasini,* she is in charge of the bookshop at the Vedanta Society.

Marion Langerman
A member of the Berkeley Vedanta Society, Marion remained an ardent devotee throughout her life. Although she was an efficient office worker, she had a penchant for either quitting her secular jobs or being fired from them. This habit allowed her free time to devote to temple work.

Miriam Kennedy (Pravrajika Nityaprana)
The Vedanta Society's troubleshooter and assistant to the secretary, Miriam was an extremely efficient and dedicated worker. She was one of the first four nuns to take *brahmacharya* and was a lifelong member of the permanent convent in San Francisco.

Miriam King
A loner, Miriam was independently undertaking the practice of meditation and austerity when she discovered Vedanta. She joined the San Francisco convent but left it after a year or so, and her subsequent attempts to be a nun were also temporary.

Nancy Jackman (Professor Nancy Tilden)
While completing her doctorate in philosophy in the late 1940s, Nancy became Swami Ashokananda's disciple. She introduced many students of Western philosophy to Vedanta, several of whom also became students of Swami Ashokananda. She was co-secretary of the Vedanta Society from 1972 to 1998.

Sally Martin (later Mrs. John Hoffmann)
Sally was one of the college students introduced to Vedanta by Nancy Jackman. She was a madcap and eventually a dissident.

Virginia Varrentzoff (Mrs. John Varrentzoff)
Virginia became the joint secretary of the Vedanta Society with Nancy Jackman in 1972. Since the death of her husband in 1964, Virginia has lived within the Vedanta convent in San Francisco as a lay member. Her daughter, Chela, became a student of Swami Ashokananda when she was a young girl.

A Disciple's Journal

In the Company of

Swami Ashokananda

PROLOGUE

For almost twenty years I sat at the feet of Swami Ashokananda. I learned from him, was amazed by him, enchanted by him—and often left in profound awe.

I had my first appointment with the Swami in early 1949. I had been attending his lectures for several months and had found, almost at once, that the philosophy and religion of Vedanta accorded with and clarified my own way of thinking. I knew without any doubt that Vedanta was a way of living that I wanted to follow. Yet, I had taken months to ask Swami Ashokananda for an interview because I feared he would sense, with his unfailing insight, the dark and bottomless pit within me and turn me away. I could not have been more wrong: he did not turn me away; he was kindness itself.

After my first interview, I had an appointment with him every two weeks for several months. He came to know me, and I came to feel that his words were the voice of my innermost being.

He once asked during one of my sessions with him what I wanted. I thought to reply, "I want to realize God," but such an answer seemed too pretentious, too grand, and also too glib and not altogether true. What did I want? I wanted simply to be myself as truly as I could be. Finally I said, "I want to be a real person." He nodded; he was satisfied with that. I remember that he told me in connection with the life I was then living, "You are riding on the crest of a wave; it is bound to crash." On another occasion, he said, "You gild everything with a veneer of beauty; real beauty comes from deep within things." Sometimes, after I had expressed some opinion, he would remain silent, and my own voice would come back to me like an echo of a braying donkey. Those silences were far more effective in pointing out my failings than anything he could possibly have said. I squirmed under them. But also he listened to my opinions and my dreams with deep attention, as though there were nothing more important and fascinating on earth. I felt his compassion and his understanding flowing out to me and over me, like a healing balm.

"Do you believe in God?" he once asked me. "Yes," I replied. "I believe that if God did not exist, nothing could exist. I believe He is existence itself." I did not know how very Vedantic that reply was, but his eyes shone with what I had come to think of as "Swami light."

I trusted his words implicitly, even in mundane matters. I remember once telling him of a worldly dilemma I had. He gave a clear answer and then said, "Anyone could tell you that; you don't need a spiritual teacher for that." "Yes," I said. "But I believe *you*"—again the Swami light. Every day I prayed with all my heart that he would be my teacher.

For some reason that I don't remember (perhaps it was for no particular reason), in the spring of 1949 my husband and I went to New York for a week or so, between my appointments with the Swami. While we were in New York, we walked one night to our customary restaurant, choosing on a whim to take an unfamiliar street. Suddenly a voice behind us called out my husband's name, and a man whom I did not know caught up with us. "My God," he said to Jackson, "I was just thinking of you. I had no idea that you were in New York. It's a miracle!"

It was indeed. Jackson's friend went with us to dinner, and it turned out that Jackson was the only person on earth to fill an important job at the top of his profession at the Merganthaler Linotype Company in Brooklyn. Of course, we would have to live nearby—perhaps forever. Jackson was at loose ends at the time, and the offered job seemed to fall straight out of heaven at his feet. There was no question of his not taking it, and when he asked me if I would be willing to live in New York, there was no way to say no.

Back in San Francisco, sitting across the desk from Swami Ashokananda, I told him that I had to go to New York for good, perhaps in July.

"Ah!" he said. "I had wanted to teach you!"

"That is what I want," I said.

"Why did you not say so?"

Flabbergasted, I whispered, "I thought it should come from you." I had indeed thought that disciples were chosen like adopted children, only the most worthy picked and cherished. It had never occurred to me to ask. Swami laughed. "No," he said. "You have to ask. But never mind. I will teach you. You can come back from New York twice a year to see me." He leaned forward in conspiracy. "Now, don't tell that *I* asked *you*." I do not remember a happier day in my life. When I got home I did cartwheels across the lawn in my joy—and to Jackson's prescient dismay.

That summer we went to live in Manhattan. Before I left San Francisco, one of the devotees at the Temple asked me what I was going to do in New York. "I don't know," I had answered, and she said, "Why not try to find things about Swami Vivekananda in the old newspapers there." And that is what I did. I made a resolution to go to the New York Public Library on Fifth Avenue and Forty-second Street every day and search through the huge volumes of yellowing newspapers for the name Swami Vivekananda. The task seemed hopeless.

In those days, I was absorbed in reading *The Life of Swami Vivekananda by His Eastern and Western Disciples* (Advaita Ashrama, 1949), but I found very few clues in that wonderful book about what Swamiji was doing or when he was doing it. When, exactly, was he in New York? When did he lecture there, and when did he hold classes? The pages of the *Life,* when read for exact dates, or even for approximate dates, were of no help. I once asked Swami Nikhilananda, head of the Ramakrishna-Vivekananda Center in New York (whose Sunday lectures were to me like water in a desert), how one could learn about Swamiji's stays in the city, for I thought that someone must have done this work before. He said, "Nothing is known. You have to do it the hard way, but give me whatever you find." Although I thought that all swamis were God Himself, I did not reply. Whatever I might find would be a surprise gift for Swami Ashokananda; no other eyes would see it first.

I kept on turning the huge, crumbling pages of the New York newspapers from 1895—at least I knew that he had been in New York that year—looking up one column and down the next for the magic words *Swami Vivekananda.* Nothing. I was beginning to think he had never really existed. Then one afternoon I saw it! VIVEKANANDA! I do not remember now what news article I found first, but it was like a bolt of lightning. He was *real*; he was there in New York. After weeks of searching those old newspapers, I had come to feel that I myself was living in 1895 Manhattan, buying the goods that were advertised, attending that year's performances at the Metropolitan Opera House, and being aghast at the news that a bicycle (newly introduced) could whiz along at nine miles per hour. And lo! There was Swami Vivekananda, *real,* in the newspapers, walking the same streets as I in my own 1895 world.

After that, things grew easier. One date led to another and I found more reports and articles. I went to the public library in

Brooklyn, and there found yet more. Fortunately, I had a good friend who had worked for many years in the New York Public Library and who could readily get things done there. He arranged to have the library make photostatic copies of the articles I had discovered (xeroxing was far in the future).

I bought an album with plastic sheets, between which the photostatic copies could be inserted, and made a compilation of news articles from the New York and Brooklyn papers, articles that as far as I knew had not been discovered before. (Indeed they had not been.) I took this album with me when I returned to San Francisco in late December and presented it to Swami Ashokananda—a Christmas gift.

His delight astonished me. I had not thought the newspaper articles were anything very special, aside from being curiosities. But to him they were as wondrous as they had been to me when I had first found them. And all those tedious afternoons when my searches had yielded nothing were a thousandfold rewarded by the sight of his joy. He told me that Josephine Stanbury (another student) had recently found an advertisement in some obscure decorators' journal that offered for sale some items that had belonged to Swami Vivekananda. On inquiry, it had turned out that Swamiji had stayed with a family in Salem, Massachusetts, before the Parliament of Religions in 1893.

"When you return to New York," Swami said to me, "you must go there and find out all you can."

And so, of course, that is what I did, with results that have since been published as the first volume of *Swami Vivekananda in the West: New Discoveries* (initially titled *Swami Vivekananda in America: New Discoveries,* Advaita Ashrama, 1958). When I brought my meager findings to Swami in the summer of 1950, his delight was again the greatest reward I could ever have wished for. But much later, his reaction to those findings came as a shock to me. One day, leaning forward slightly in his chair, he said, "You must write about Swamiji." He might as well have told me to fly to the moon (when such a thing had not even been dreamt of).

"I can't," I said.

"You must!"

"But I can't! How can I write about Swami Vivekananda?"

He looked at me sternly. "I would not ask you to do something," he said quietly but with the firmness of finality, "if I did not know you could do it."

I went on making sounds of protest, but I knew I was defeated. What I did not know was that a great gift had been given to me, pressed upon me, and that I should have been dancing with joy and gratitude, just as I had on the day he said he would teach me.

I visited San Francisco from New York a few more times. My recollections of those sojourns run together, but I took notes. On June 15, 1950, I began to write the journal that starts with instruction in meditation and continues for the next two decades with the ups and downs of spiritual life under the eagle eye and guiding hand of Swami Ashokananda.

I

CARTWHEELS

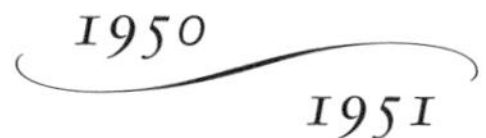

In the summer of 1949, Swami Ashokananda had said he would be my teacher. Although I didn't know exactly what that meant, I didn't care; I was overjoyed. Whatever it was, it was what I wanted. That much I knew.

A few months later, I had to move with my husband, Jackson, to the East Coast, a whole continent—and a whole world—away. In the sweltering July and August of a Manhattan summer, I wrote several letters to Swami, telling him of some dreams I was having. He wrote back to say that they were "significant." A little later, he sent me some instructions in meditation, which I followed to the letter and also with my whole heart and soul. After a few weeks my brain did a series of what felt like somersaults. I reported these cerebral acrobatics to Swami.

Alarmed, Swami sent a series of telegrams: STOP MEDITATING AT ONCE. WRITE TO ME DAILY. He told me the brain ("like an old jalopy") had to catch up with the meditating mind, particularly when the meditation was on the philosophical side. He said he would tell me more when I returned to San Francisco for a visit.

It was not until the summer of 1950, during one of my

frequent visits to San Francisco, that his instructions became more specific. My journal entries for that year all took place in Swami's office in the Old Temple, the first Hindu temple in the Western world.

June 15, 1950

Swami told me to meditate on two specific holy people.
Me: Can't I also meditate on God?
Swami: Just do as I tell you. They are God.
Me: Yes—but with form.
Swami: What is wrong with form? I like form.
Me: Yes. But I don't understand God with form.
Swami: Do you have to understand?
Me: Sometimes I like to understand.
Swami (more kindly): Do you understand how food is digested, how vitamins are absorbed into the body? Must you know all that before you will eat?
Me: No.
Swami: Meditate as I tell you. It is food. It is not necessary to understand.

June 16, 1950

Today Swami said I must never be impatient about realizing God. If there is quiet determination, it will come. It is not alone through meditation that one grows in spirituality; one absorbs it throughout the day. One must just go on breathing; one cannot stop breathing. Breathe like a fish. He imitated a fish and looked exactly like one—a great benevolent fish in an ocean of spirituality, breathing in and out effortlessly and blissfully. I could not laugh; it was such a beautiful picture. (As I was to learn later, he was a marvelous mimic, particularly of animals—lions and cobras and birds. And also of people—though I never saw him imitate any person except to his or her face, and then hilariously and often devastatingly.)

Buddha's Birthday, June 18, 1950

I have never seen the altar more beautiful, or Swami more beautiful. I was overwhelmed that I was alive, that this beauty existed, and that I was my particular self to see it just as I saw it. Buddha surely was there and because of that it was so extraordinary. I was seeing something of him.

Later I spent the afternoon in the Temple, reading Swami Vivekananda and meditating. My mind is calming down now, and I feel like the fish swimming in blissful waters.

June 19, 1950

Swami explained to me at length why it is that one should meditate on God with form and how one can realize the Absolute through form. I cannot remember his exact words, but this is the way I understood it:

All form is God. He is incarnated in everything. But it is because one associates some forms with ugliness or grossness that we cannot see Him there. It is our own minds that obstruct and distort the view. The thief is also God, but to meditate upon him would have disastrous results because of all the other associations we make.

Meditation on a pure and subtle form, such as the *Ishta* [Chosen Ideal], is an approach to the Absolute; if one meditates on such a sublime form, one will be able to see through it to the Absolute as it really is.

Then he said another reason for my meditating on the *Ishta* was that my emotions had to go somewhere. "You love your husband, you love your sisters, and so on, but you are like a flowing stream. They will say, 'Stay here; we want you.' And you will say, 'Oh, you want me? Then I will stay.' The stream will become a pool of stagnant water. You must keep flowing toward the ocean. It is because streams flow toward the ocean that they are fresh and good. I am telling you only because you would not understand and would get impatient. It isn't really necessary to know."

THE SUBSTANCE OF MY MEDITATION was settled, but there was something called "initiation" in which one receives from the teacher a mantra—a word or group of words that one is supposed to repeat and which is an all-important step in spiritual life. Initiation is like taking a first sacred vow; it commits both guru and disciple, not with mere words but with a sort of ignition spark that jumps from the teacher and awakens, as though with a touch, something deep within the disciple. In return, the teacher takes a good deal of garbage from the disciple's mind. The greater the power of the teacher, the more garbage passes over to him or to her.

When I heard about this, it did not seem to me to be a fair exchange—an incomparable treasure for a heap of bad karma—but the giving of initiation is an act of grace, and grace has nothing to do with fairness or with justice, or, for that matter, with exchange.

I had also heard that initiation constituted the "second birth"—that is, the birth of the soul into spiritual life. I did not know if I had been really initiated or not, and I did not like to ask. I thought that I had probably not been. I had gathered that the procedure involved a small ceremony before the altar in the auditorium. The disciple was forewarned, wore clean clothes, and offered flowers. There was a lot of excitement about it, as though a new era had begun in the disciple's long—lifetimes long—spiritual evolution. Nothing like a ceremony had happened to me. Although I was practicing meditation, I was not initiated, not born yet, perhaps not yet spiritually worthy of birth.

Then one day in August of 1950, when I was sitting in Swami's office, he said: "Go and wash your hands and rinse your mouth." When I returned, he gave me two mantras, and I knew that I had been initiated. Just like that.

My journal the following year reveals another kind of spiritual instruction from Swami Ashokananda. While instruction in meditation and the giving of a mantra lie at the core of spiritual guidance, there is a lot more to spiritual life than meditation and the repetition of one's mantra, or *japa*. Presumably, the rest will come of its own accord, fueled by the living treasure that one has received and that one keeps alive and aflame by practice. Slowly that flame will change one's entire outlook on and reaction to the world. It will also change one's features, the sound of one's voice, the look in one's eyes, and the way people respond to one's presence in their lives.

In India, where often the disciple never again sees the initiating teacher, the age-old traditions of the country support and guide him or her. The entire continent is geared to a spiritual life, and there is no one who does not sympathize with what a spiritual aspirant is trying to do. There is no strong current opposing a newborn seeker.

In the West, on the other hand, a spiritual tradition does not permeate the air, the water, and the dust. It is not as natural to the people as breathing, or as expected as the next beat of a heart. The only place in the West where one can learn the ways of spiritual living and devote oneself to adapting to those ways is in the company of the holy—preferably, if one is so lucky, in the company of the teacher himself, or herself, who knows one's quirks inside and out. The teacher takes the place of a millennia-old culture of spiritual thinking and living, of spiritual being.

I had a great deal to learn, a great deal to change within myself. Aside from teaching me how to meditate, Swami Ashokananda taught me how to think and act and be. It was a secondary instruction, but it was no less important than the primary one. Fortunately, I never thought otherwise; and although I often resisted Swami Ashokananda's guiding hand, I never for a moment regretted having come under it.

Thus, my journal in 1951 tells largely of Swami's "secondary" instruction, his day-to-day bolstering of my strengths and his squashing of my weaknesses—sometimes with a smile, sometimes with a wallop, but mostly just by his presence and example.

January 14, 1951

Swami: Do not be small. If there are torrents of rain, one must be ready with a large vessel. Open your heart; then when the *Ishta* comes you will be ready. Be big. Write every day. Dash off articles. Lazy bone!

Me: I always think I will do that next week or tomorrow.

Swami (smiling): Do it today. Why don't you write stories? Write stories of incidents in the lives of Swamiji [as Swami Vivekananda is familiarly called] or Sri Ramakrishna. Make them come to life. Can you do that?

Me (dubiously): Yes . . .

January 28, 1951

Swami: Everything is steeped in sweetness, as in syrup. It is everywhere permeating everything. You should all be sitting in front of Sri Ramakrishna—then you will get this, not sitting here [with him in the back office]. The veil of time hides Eternity.

March 1951

Swami came downstairs late in the evening, about ten. He looked tousled, as though he had been asleep. His hair stood up in a tuft in front. Kathleen, Jo, Mara, and I were in the back office. I was editing a lecture of his and asked him if a certain Sanskrit phrase meant "suddenly free." This started a most wonderful talk about freedom, only a little of which I can remember. It was as though he had come down expressly to say these things to us and needed only an opening.

At the end he said, "That is what all of you should be—suddenly free. But you don't want it; you like your misery. All of you here have freedom. I can see that Sri Ramakrishna is carrying you, but you like to be miserable. You are like tadpoles in a pool wagging your tails. If God should suddenly take the rags of your personality from you, you would run after Him to grab them back. The least little thing that the ordinary worldly person would take in his stride, you make a terrible fuss over. None of you has any problems. God has made it easy for you. Someday you will look back and see there was all happiness here."

Swami was radiant during all this. There was much more that I have not remembered, but the general purport was that God is very close if we would but give Him a chance and not cling to our "rags of personality" or "wag our tails" like tadpoles that do not want to become frogs.

Another time that spring he said, "Sri Ramakrishna is willing and anxious to push you all to the top, to give you the highest. I know this for certain."

One should be able to live a spiritual life anywhere, under any circumstances. If one does so, one will not only satisfy one's own spiritual longing but also bring peace and harmony into the lives of all those with whom one comes in contact. That is the theory, and I believe it is valid. I also believe that one has to be a realized soul to start with if such a life is going to work. In my case it didn't work. I found it impossible to swim with a whole heart on the surface of the ocean and, at the same time, to swim down with all my might into the ocean's infinite depths.

My soul was crying. Perhaps the human soul is always crying for God, but when that cry is conscious and unceasing, there is no way that one can attend to anything else. I knew without any doubt that I needed to plunge headlong into a spiritual life. I knew that that was not an easy thing and that I needed spiritual direction, and I knew that my spiritual teacher was in San Francisco.

After much discussion, Jackson and I came to the conclusion that our different goals and different ways of life were harmfully pulling against each other and that however painful a break between us might be, to separate was the only way either of us could survive. We had both tried to compromise, but a life of compromise was not what either of us wanted. And so, in mid-July of 1951 and in the friendliest of ways, we agreed to live apart. I returned to San Francisco permanently. We said it was a trial separation, but I think we both knew it would be forever.

On August 1 of that year I moved into an apartment two and a half blocks from the Temple. I had determined, with Swami's consent, to try to be a Vedantist, living as best I could in accord with Vedantic ideals, practicing renunciation, meditation, and the rest of it. There was no other life I wanted. But I cannot say that the plunge was not a shock. I remember well the first time I returned from an excursion downtown to what was now my home neighborhood. I came by bus, not by the family limousine, and alighting in that unfamiliar and, in those days, lower middle-class district of the city, I wondered with dismay what I was doing there. Then I walked up a hill to the small house where, second-floor rear, I had an apartment to my liking and where I was starting the spiritual life that I had longed for. Dismay vanished.

It was a nice enough apartment. There was a living room that looked out onto an untended garden and a line of drying underclothes, a large kitchen I could dance in during moments of joy, a bedroom that I turned into a shrine, and a small breakfast-laundry room off the kitchen that I turned into a bedroom. I furnished the rooms with pieces I had brought from New York and with odds and ends from my family's home, which I robbed of what I needed. All in all, except for the occasional wood louse and the noise that arose during the night from the landlady's quarters below, it was a comfortable and, I thought, attractive place to live. Even my two sisters liked it, though when I first pointed out the house to my sister Leila, she exclaimed, "Oh, my God, you can't live *there.*" My brother was equally affronted.

To be sure, it was a glaring change from the East Side of Manhattan where Jackson and I had lived in an apartment building equipped with a doorman and an elevator boy (and definitely no lice). If at times I felt displaced in my top rear flat on Fillmore Street in San Francisco, I reminded myself of why I was there, and any threatening depression lifted.

As I remember it, several years passed before I got down to serious work. Meanwhile, I tried to follow a schedule of studying Indian history and philosophy and of writing, meditating, and attending Swami's lectures and classes. I had an appointment with him not every two weeks but every day at one o'clock.

After about a month of this, one of the old-time students told me that I really shouldn't come to the Temple every day—the implication was that Swami did not like my coming so often and that she was conveying his wishes to me. But had he not told me to come every day? I wasn't sure. So the following day I went downtown on a shopping spree (a habit I had not yet dispensed with), and the day thereafter I was still in a quandary of indecision. Should I go to the Temple at one o'clock or not? The best thing do to at such times, of course, is to pray for a definite sign, some spectacular happening that clearly says yes or no. No such sign was forthcoming; so I thought, I will go downtown. Just then the ceiling light in my shrine room exploded. Clearly, I should not go downtown. So, it being nearly one o'clock, I hurried to the Temple.

"Where were you yesterday?" Swami demanded.

"I thought I shouldn't come so often," I said, or perhaps whispered.

"Who told you that?"

I told him who had told me, and he looked thunderous. "Do you do what I tell you or what others tell you? Don't listen to other people!"

Well, that was definite. I now knew that he expected me every day at one o'clock, and after that I never missed the appointment, until, in a few months, there stopped being a regular time for me to see him. Almost always, I was either inside the Temple or less than three blocks away in my apartment.

My daily routine started with my rising at 7:00 a.m.—for me an unthinkably early hour. I showered, meditated, had breakfast, and then sat at my desk to study Indian history. All I remember of this endeavor is my charts of the early Aryan tribes that inhabited North India thousands of years (estimates vary) before Christ. These tribes, from which the Vedas—the world's earliest scriptures—arose, were, to my mind, an unruly bunch. They split up, intermarried, joined forces, had offshoots, and altogether complicated themselves beyond all orderly reckoning. After struggling with them for two hours, I turned to the six systems of Indian philosophy, which in their own way were no less complex. After an hour or so of skullbreaking study, I had lunch and walked to the Temple for my appointment with Swami.

In the afternoons I tried to write, sitting at my desk with cotton wool for a brain. No ideas came, let alone words in which to couch them. I wrote in longhand on large, wide-ruled, spiral-bound notebooks and rarely filled a page a day. Now and then a wood louse would distractingly crawl across the paper, coming from where I did not know. I would kill it.

Swami Ashokananda had told me to write sketches of the swamis (his contemporaries) who had briefly visited the Society since my permanent return to San Francisco. This was a project that had a particularly paralyzing effect upon my mind, and, as will come clear later, never fully rose from the ground.

When I first returned to San Francisco, there were wonderful gatherings in the Temple, initially only after the Wednesday night lectures and Friday night classes, but later almost every evening. Five or six of us, sometimes nine or ten of us, would congregate in the "back office" (next to Swami's office), which was where all the business of the Society took place. There was a large desk and, next to it, Swami's chair. Other than that, the room contained a number of straight-backed, wide-seated wooden chairs lining two walls and three small tables for typing. One of these was used by Miriam Kennedy, who kept the Society's books (before finding Vedanta, Miriam had been personal secretary to a big-shot movie producer in Hollywood, so she knew her way around).

In the evenings, we would sit in the straight-backed chairs, sometimes two to a chair, and Swami would talk to us more often than not of spiritual things, his face glowing. It was also a time for scolding. Invariably someone would say something that revealed to him some quirk of character, and, if he saw fit, he would take that opportunity to tear the unfortunate—or fortunate—person to shreds. For the most part, though, he spoke to us in reply to a remark or a question that poked the overflowing beehive of his spiritual knowledge: he spoke of God; of philosophy; of the great saints, ancient and modern; of Vedanta; of the place of Vedanta in the modern world; of anything that rose in his mind. We sat spellbound for hours.

Anyone was welcome to those gatherings, but only relatively

few students came. For some the talk was too intense; others could not bear to witness the scoldings that could erupt at any moment, and still others somehow felt uncomfortable or out of place. I was told by the old-timers that a devotee from out of town who seldom came to the Temple had once fallen off her chair in a faint when Swami said that most of us would spend this life working out our karma.

One never knew what would unnerve some students. Well aware of this, Swami would temper his talk in the presence of those who were not seasoned. He would, for instance, speak in detail about the preparation of Indian food, the beauty of the flowering trees in Bengal, or the current political scene in the West. Whatever he spoke of had about it the nimbus of spirituality, but it was not always the naked thing. At any time, however, there would come invaluable observation or advice.

Those were blissful days, but from time to time they were also difficult. I wrote the following entry in my journal a little more than two months after my break with my old life. This and many other private conversations were held in Swami's office.

September 27, 1951

Swami: Have you been happy? Do you feel that you will want to continue this kind of life, or is it too soon to tell?

Me: I think I like it.

Swami: Have you felt despondent?

Me: No.

Swami: Well, that is very good.

Me: But I have felt that if you did not come back at all, I would not stay here. (Swami had been to Tahoe for four days in August.)

Swami: What nonsense! Why do you think that?

Me: I know it is wrong. I was examining how I felt, how much enthusiasm I had, and I came to that conclusion. There is a lack in me.

Swami: You have seen the other swamis; they are great men. If I should die, someone greater will come.
Me: I didn't think that far. You would want me to stay here and work for Vedanta?
Swami: Certainly. Devotion in itself shows highness of heart. Life here will not always be pleasant. There will be hardship, but hang on!

Later that day

Me: I feel awfully unspiritual when I wake up.
Swami: Don't pay attention to that. Attend to your conscious moments. When a man has to catch a bus, he doesn't stop to think how he feels or whether he has a good or bad sleep—he just runs to catch the bus. In worldly life a person goes to work no matter how he feels; it should be the same in spiritual life. Just go ahead. After you wake up, lift your consciousness.
Me: Yes. But it takes a little time.
Swami (sternly, lest I regret the breakup of my marriage): Do the best you can. There is nothing in mutual love, because neither person is perfect enough, and after a time each finds the other empty. It is when two people love a third thing—have another thing together—that they find satisfaction. With ordinary people the third thing is children, but even this is no good. After a time the children develop their own selfishness; they cause trial and heartbreak. Love God. If you are inclined spiritually, that is the thing to do. All this marriage business is no good. Pray to God.

For many years, as soon as I got home, I would write down a little of what Swami had said during the wonderful evenings in the back office. Often the hour would be late and I would simply jot down a few notes in speedwriting, promising myself to write it out in full later on. I seldom did, and now those notes are indecipherable. Thus many evenings of inspired talk are forever lost. This was before the days of tape recorders, and, in any case, it would have seemed out of keeping to record those informal, semi-private talks. Several notes from those years, full of my early frustrations and anxieties, are given here.

October 15, 1951

Swami: How is the article [about the swamis] coming?
Me: Slowly.
Swami: Why is it so slow? Because your mind does not focus. Why does your mind not focus?
Me: Why, Swami?
Swami: It is *tamas* [sloth].
Me: What can I do about it?
Swami: Fight it! The mind should always be profitably employed. Why do you find the article so difficult?
Me: I don't know.
Swami: Do it this way: take each swami chronologically as he came here. Make a list of everything about them. Then relate them each to a larger thing—their work in the United States, the work of Swami Vivekananda; then relate that to a larger thing—to Sri Ramakrishna; then relate that to a still larger thing—the universal. You seem dispirited.
Me (after a prolonged silence): The thing is that I know nothing of those swamis.
Swami: An anthropologist builds a whole skeleton from a single bone.
Me: I just write a lot of nonsense.
Swami: Don't be afraid of writing nonsense. You must write. You are not playing any more. Write as though your livelihood depended on it. If you do not do it, you will never become established in this way of living. There will be nothing to fasten on to. Your life will become empty and meaningless. What will you

do? You say, "Oh, I will meditate." For how many hours can you meditate? And do you think that your meditation will always be inspiring? No. There will be long periods of time in which you will meditate and nothing will happen. If you do the thing now that is difficult for you, you will not be afraid any more.

Me: Swami, I find it difficult to study when I am trying to write.

Swami: You are to do the difficult thing.

Me: I do not know whether to write first or study first.

Swami (crossly): I thought you had a schedule. You were to write in the afternoons.

Me: Yes; that was before I started to write.

Swami: Do that. Write in the afternoon.

October 21, 1951

Swami: Are you feeling happy?

Me: Yes, Swami.

Swami: How is your apartment? Do you like it?

Me: Yes. It is fine.

Swami: What will you do when you become restless and unhappy here? You will take off to New York.

Me: I do not think so.

Swami: Do not become too isolated. You study and write at home all day or come and sit here in these dingy rooms. Your mind will become tired and dissatisfied. Do you see your friend Miss Day [Bobbie, my friend since high school days]?

Me: No. I haven't seen her for some time. I have talked to her over the phone.

Swami: Well, see her. Do not lose contact with your friends. What other friends have you? There is that one who is crazy. How is she?

Me: She is all right. She is in Okinawa now. I have another friend who lives in San Mateo. I see her now and then.

Swami: What does she do?

Me: She is married and has children and goes to a psychiatrist.
Swami (laughing): Well, see your friend Miss Day.
Me: Bobbie and I always had a wonderful time together, but even the most unworldly of worldly life seems empty and boring to me now.
Swami: That is all right as long as *this* life holds interest for you.
Me: It does, at the moment.
Swami: That is good. Worldly people deplete themselves until they become like dry fibers. They run around filling in their lives with this and that—art, music, entertainment, social life—so that in the end there is no energy left. They spend their whole lives filling in time.
Me: It is terribly sad.
Swami: Yes. In spiritual life one grows quiet and tastes real joy. One learns to be quiet. The mind grows still and one finds real happiness.
Me: That is a great art, the art of living.
Swami: It is *the* great art. The whole world becomes joyous, filled with sweetness and festivity. Wherever one goes it is festive, dripping with honey. One sees everything that way—stars, sun, moon, a dung heap.
Me: Does one see it that way always, all the time?
Swami: Yes, nothing can change it. Sickness, old age, nothing can touch it. But don't look at me to see a person in that state. I used to see everything that way. Well, it will come again.
Me: Don't you see it always?
Swami: Do I look like a man full of joy?
Me: Yes.
Swami (smiling): My mind is so full of bricks and buildings and figures! When one is so busy helping people, how can one just be blissful?
Me: Does one cancel out the other?
Swami: It is a different state of mind. I cannot just sit here exud-

ing joy and sweetness. People would come; "Oh, what a wonderful man!" they would say.
Me: That would help people.
Swami: Yes, but how many would come for that? People do not want that joy.
Me: They would if they knew what it was.
Swami: But there must be a house to come to—a retreat, roads, buildings. There has to be a cook. It is all fine to enjoy the dinner, but somebody has to cook it.

October 22, 1951

Swami Ashokananda and the assistant minister, Swami Shantaswarupananda, went with Ediben Soulé and Anna Webster, two devotees, in the afternoon to see *The River,* a movie made in India by the great French director Jean Renoir. Somehow the women seemed to be done up in furs and jewels, off to the matinee. As he was leaving the Temple, Swami put his hat on in the hall and, seeing me there, took it off very formally and bowed his head slowly toward me. I laughed and looked at Swami Shantaswarupananda, who was standing by the front door and witnessing the whole thing. There was a look of baffled horror on his face. He does not understand these games.

When they had left, the air of festivity went with them. The place seemed to be empty and forlorn.

I said to Miriam Kennedy, "We are left behind."

"One gets very used to that," she said.

"I guess I will just go back to my little hovel," I said.

"And I will go back to my bookkeeping," said Miriam.

October 23, 1951

Swami: How is the article?
Me: I cannot write more than a page a day—two at the most.
Swami: There is no excuse for that.

(Silence. I grew hot and flushed while Swami turned the pages of a magazine. At length he looked up and smiled somewhat slyly.)
Me: What can I do about it?
Swami: What do you do? Does your mind just wander off into a daydream?
Me: No, I don't know what I do. The time just goes by.
Swami: You daydream. Your mind just wanders off, wool gathering.
Me: It doesn't get off the subject.
Swami: Pah! You are not even aware that it gets off the subject. Do you cook your own meals?
Me: Yes, Swami.
Swami: All your meals?
Me: I cook my dinner. (He asked me what I usually eat.)

Swami went back to looking through his magazines—the *Saturday Evening Post, Country Gentleman, Sunset, The New Yorker.* He turned the pages casually, glancing at them. Sometimes something caught his eye and he read it more carefully, such as an article on converting a garage into a dance hall. This he then read aloud to me. "My, how wonderful," he said in genuine appreciation.

Later, Swami went into the hallway and started to talk to Ediben about India. I stood in the door of the library and overheard him express some of his long-standing opinions of Mahatma Gandhi's role in Indian history.
Swami: Gandhi was a very holy man; there is no doubt of that, but he was a stupid man.
Me: Politically stupid?
Swami: I said a stupid man; I did not qualify it. He had a hobby, and he put his hobby [ahimsa] before the good of his country. What India needs is what Swamiji taught. Strength! They have been grass eaters for too long.

October 1951

Jeanette Vollmer was sitting on the floor of the library trying to unravel a billowing mass of recording wire that the students in Sacramento had managed to get tangled. Luke (Mary Lou Williams) was helping.

Swami (coming into the room): What are you doing?

Jeanette: I am trying to save some of this wire. We can use it over again.

Swami: Everyone here is a crazy person. I have come to that conclusion. You are all crazy people. Something is wrong up here (touching his head). You ask and ask if you can record lectures. The next thing I know there is just tangled wire that you spend hours and hours untangling. Then you ask again to record lectures; again the tangle.

(To Luke and me) Once Jeanette insisted upon recording a lecture. She played it for me, and there was nothing—silence. You go to all this trouble and expense. What for? I do not know. The only conclusion I can come to is that I am surrounded by crazy people.

October 28, 1951

A number of disciples were gathered in the back office of the Temple after the Sunday lecture.

Swami: No one here need worry about progress. You are being pushed. Everyone who came to Sri Ramakrishna attained spirituality. It is the same even now. That force is still working and will go on working for a long time. Those who kindled the fire may be gone, but the fire is still roaring. You can warm yourselves by it. Just do what you have to do; you will go ahead. But you do negative things and hold yourselves back.

Disciple: What are negative things?

Swami: Well, hating others, comparing yourself with others, not being contented—those are negative things.

November 3, 1951

Eve Bunch, a novice in the convent, said to Swami that she was discouraged by his lecture on the kundalini.

Swami: Discouraged—I hate that word—only fools and cowards are discouraged. Do you think the practice of religion is easy? Did Sri Ramakrishna ever say that anything was easy to follow? Don't be cowards; be strong! On the one hand, you accept Sri Ramakrishna as an Incarnation; on the other hand, you act as though you are weak, miserable creatures. You are a jumble.

If you want to attain to the highest, practice Vedanta. This is the way: think of everyone as God Himself and serve Him. But you do not do that. You hate this one and that one. You are hurt; you shrink from others. You cling to your own idiosyncrasies. See the Divine in all.

November 16, 1951

"The subtle desires of the senses cling even after the gross desires are gone," Swami said to Mara. "The monks, after their physical desires are gone, will want to hear a woman sing—the voice of a woman. It is the sex desire in its subtle form. One is never truly rid of it until realization, complete purification of mind."

Sometimes, homesick, I drove down to the "Ranch" near Los Gatos, sixty miles south of San Francisco. The thirty acres my family owned was called the Ranch, although it was a country home and not a ranch in the true sense of the word. My parents had no intention of growing crops or raising livestock, although my mother had a fancy for hens of various breeds and for turkeys that strutted when provoked, dipping their wings in the dust and making a "pfutt" sound.

It had once been a large Spanish holding owned by the first governor of California, who gave shelter to a famous daring-do bandit named Joachim Murietta. His large hacienda had long since burned down, leaving only a two-story adobe dwelling. This building, about twenty-five feet square, was a landmark and boasted a bronze plaque that attested to its age and historic prestige. Its roof was covered with the branches and flowers of ancient rose vines, whose thick trunks seemed to support the roof itself.

Enchanted, my parents had bought the thirty acres, extended the adobe house, and built five other houses around it. Under the property's huge and ancient oak trees, my mother created extensive, informal, and luxurious gardens. I spent every summer at the Ranch from the age of eight—swimming, playing tennis, riding horseback. Best of all, I liked wandering alone on its uncultivated hill, from the top of which one could see to the east the vast orchard-filled Santa Clara valley, which was a mass of white blossoms in the spring, and, to the west, the low coastal mountains, where every tree and bush seemed placed by a master artist. During my childhood and youth, the presence of God was exceedingly, sometimes unbearably, strong on that hill. Once, when I was fifteen or so, I flung myself upon the earth and vowed to dedicate my life to that presence, to God. I believed He, or She, took note.

At the Ranch, I saw beauty wherever I looked. I loved the place with my whole heart, not just for the wonderful, flawless summer days I and my family and our friends spent there, but for the solitary hours of peace and inner happiness that I whiled away just looking, just being. A stranger once told my brother-in-law that he used to park his car on the public road that ran alongside the Ranch and listen to the bursts of laughter that filtered through the trees. Those moments of eavesdropping, on what he rightly assumed to be heaven, made his day.

My mother died in 1941 when I was twenty-nine, and the gardens began to go to seed. My father died ten years later. Most of the Ranch was sold off and subdivided. My sister Leila and her husband, Holloway, took possession of the main house and its immediate surroundings. The Ranch died. I felt that its presiding deity had forsaken it, and when I asked Swami Ashokananda if that could be true—if there had really been a presiding deity—he did not deny the possibility. He just strongly recommended that I put all that behind me. Actually, I had no choice. But nostalgia dies hard, and from time to time, with Swami's reluctant consent, I drove to the Ranch at Los Gatos for a day or two.

November 26, 1951

Swami: How are you?

Me (having just returned from the Ranch): Not so good.

Swami: Why?

Me: I am upset because I get upset.

Swami: Los Gatos is no place for you. Whether you know it or not, that life is not based on the same thing on which you are basing yours.

Me: I cannot be away from here for two days without getting upset and depressed. It does not seem to be a very strong state of mind.

Swami: It is as it should be. When one comes down from a high altitude, it is very depressing. You are used to being here in rarefied air. Naturally you feel it when you leave. Just be cheerful. Everything is all right. You have no problems. The situation with your husband is still unsettled; but just wait. This life may be difficult now; but it will be gratifying later on.

Me: Will I ever be spiritual?

Swami: Why not? Don't expect it within one year or five years. Plod on.

Me: It is difficult to be patient.

Swami: Don't use that word in my presence. This is your life. There is no alternative. Face it. The mind must be trained.

December 7, 1951

Swami: God became man so that He could sacrifice Himself and thus be redeemed. People participate in that sacrifice and redemption through communion. It is the great drama.
Me: I can see that it must be all for fun. What other reason could there be? It need never have started. It starts in order to get back to where it was in the first place. Everything was just fine.
Swami: But we see the world. Here it is. No sense in asking why. The thing is to know what to do now. Yes, it is all a play. It is a great fun. See it all as a game He is playing. Welcome the thunder and the lightning. Welcome the storm and the quiet before the storm. Welcome pleasure, welcome pain—Brother Pain, welcome to you! Stand aside as the witness. See sweetness in all. When you can do that, you will be free.

The great swamis [direct disciples of Sri Ramakrishna] were like giant redwood trees. The ones you know today are like bay tree saplings compared to them.
Me: Could one know their greatness just by seeing them?
Swami: When you see the ocean, you know it. They were a vast ocean, but filled with sweet water, not brackish.
Me: I think you are like an ocean.
Swami: I am the very least of the swamis of today—a tiny little lake, and stagnant.

December 1951

Swami: It is extremely important that you become established in this life. You cannot go back to a married life. Even if you had the opportunity, you could not live that life. Do you want a social life, going to dinner parties, entertaining, and so on? Do you want that?
Me: No. I don't.

Swami: Well then . . . this is a competitive life. In worldly life one competes against others; in spiritual life one must compete with conditions. Work, work, work. Otherwise depth cannot be reached.

10:30 p.m., December 31, 1951

Swami (on his way upstairs, to all who were there): Happy New Year to you all! A brave New Year! A courageous New Year! A strong New Year! No weakness, no pampering. Stand strong, straight, unafraid!

2

A HACK WRITER

1952

In the years before I discovered Vedanta, I had written poetry and short stories. The poetry came in a flood, welling up, it seemed, from some subterranean lake. I somehow drowned myself in that lake and from there dictated the words and lines to the hand that wrote them down. It was not that I did not chisel the phrases and lines as they arose, but there first had to be a total absorption in a deeper, wiser consciousness than that which ordinarily informed my mind. Otherwise I did not call the result writing. To me, the act of writing required an immersion in another world, another mind below the surface. What trickled or flooded up was not necessarily good—the surfacing water could be muddy or brackish. Nevertheless, it had come from a subliminal source and was *writing*.

Short stories and poetry flowed most easily from the submerged lake of rhythms and cadences. Nonfiction that required research flowed not at all, unless it was a tirade of some sort, to be at once destroyed. To write essays on the visiting swamis, as Swami Ashokananda had asked me to do in 1951, was to seek water in a block of solid rock that extended to the center of the earth and beyond. In fact, it was not to seek water at all, but to access my brain, which, as I said earlier, was a mass of cotton wool, steeped now in the smoke of innumerable cigarettes. The page of my notebook remained blank—well, not altogether blank; I wrote some nauseating descriptions of godlike men who had huge, glowing eyes and elongated hands.

The difficulty was that Swami Ashokananda's contemporaries from other Vedanta societies in America seemed to me to be beings who walked with God Himself, spoke with God, and perceived the world with the eyes of God. They had come to the Temple, had talked with the devotees in thick Indian-accented English that might as well have been Sanskrit, and had then vanished into the upper regions of the monastery. I was awed by these visitations. How was I to write anything but reverential, besotted goo? And that is what I wrote.

January 3, 1952

Swami (looking at my manuscript): After all these years you have written only sixteen pages.

Me: There's more, but it all has to be rewritten.

Swami (to others present): She is a master. She must polish and polish. A Hindu story tells of the Master Artist in Heaven. He polished everything; he was a great artist. It came time for his son to marry, and so he decided that he himself would fashion the bride, as then she would be perfect. So he set about it. She was never just right. For years and years he worked on her, polishing and polishing, until at last, what did he have? A small mole.

Me: Yes. That is the way it is.

Swami: That won't do. Be a hack writer!

Me: I am a hack writer. But it takes me a long time to hack.

Swami: Well, keep on. I don't want to make it too hard for you.

January 8, 1952

Swami: Worldly people are no good. They are just rotten. That is my opinion.

Me: Oh, do you think so?
Swami: Yes, I think so. Why should I not think so?
Me: They try to be good.
Swami: Pah! They are good when it suits their purpose. They would not draw one breath if they thought it would do good for others. There is no hope for worldly people.
Me: That is terrible.
Swami: Why is it terrible?
Me: I know worldly people. I feel sorry—
Swami: Why should you feel sorry about them?
Me: I don't know. I can't help it.
Swami: There was a man in the *Gospel of Sri Ramakrishna* who could not sleep in his bed because he thought of all the people who did not have beds.
Me (laughing): Yes, I should just worry about myself.
Swami: You are out of the world. Don't get sucked back in. Go forward, race ahead! You have been led out of the forest into a clear field. Don't just stand in the field and think, "Oh, how good God is to have saved me, how beautiful the field is," and write a poem about it. The tigers will creep out of the forest—run! Renunciation is the thing. You cannot see what is real if you do not renounce the unreal; that is the only way.

Tighten up. It is a question of how you spend time. You spend your time in work for God. Work as worship. When you write or study, always think of it that way. Of course, I know it is hard. You stay at home all day doing what does not come easily. But as I said in my lecture Sunday, spiritual life is really not hard when one considers how long it takes for the ordinary person to change. They change very little in one lifetime—imperceptibly. In spiritual life the problem is that they change so fast that one must think how to channel those changes. That is the problem here.

The average person should live 70 percent of his life in austerity and 30 percent in pleasure—but that pleasure should be in accord with what is right. Most people are self-indulgent; that is the worst troublemaker. In the early part of a person's life, one should be trained in moral and spiritual virtues, not in the development of talents. Talent is not important; it is character that is important. Later, talents will develop as they should.

January 12, 1952

I went with Jo Stanbury to a nearby market for Swami's dinner. Jo mentioned that his diet is extremely restricted—a combination of diets for high blood pressure, diabetes, and stomach ulcers, leaving him practically nothing to eat. Yet he eats as he pleases.

"If only he would follow doctor's orders," Jo said.

"Maybe he feels the matter is predetermined," I suggested.

"If that is the case," Jo said, "he is not consistent. He does sometimes take some care about his diet. But, of course, swamis are never consistent. One just doesn't know and can't judge. He might just pop off or go back to India. Then where would we be?"

Jo had hinted to me to come to the Temple that night. I brought along my manuscript to work on in the back office, in case Swami wasn't there.

Swami: What have you there?

Me: The article about the swamis.

Swami: Let me see it. (I gave it to him, and he read here and there, smiling as though amused and pleased.) It is very uneven. You have written so much on Swami Pavitrananda. If you are going to have infatuations, how can you be a good writer? But do it in your own way. Finish it, and we will see. Finish it soon. Of course, I don't want to nag you too much.

Me: I will finish it next week.

Swami: Good. If it is ever published, the swamis will cut your throat.

(The article turned out to be, as Swami would say, "a miserable failure" and was never published.)

January 1952

Swami (teasing Kathleen about her newly permed hair): You look like a Fiji Islander. Can't you do something? Put oil on it.
Kathleen: When it grows out it will be all right.
Swami: Well, in the meantime, I am sure you can do something.
Kathleen (mournfully): When I was a baby, I wanted to be bald like my uncle. My hair was a nuisance even then. I had to have it put up in curlers at night. I always slept on lumps.
Swami: You give such importance to small things. Other people have had hair. It is the art of the dramatist to build up the insignificant until it has immense importance.

January 16, 1952

Swami has put a stop to the evening meetings in the back office. He wants to make us independent of him. This has caused a lot of woe. To some he was brusque about it: "Go home!"
Swami (to me): I am sorry I spoke the way I did. Some arrangement must be made. All of you will have to learn to be independent. I am an uncertain person now. That is one reason for it. Also, I cannot discriminate between students. There are many who would like to be here. They see all of you here and do not see why they cannot come. They should come. I am a man of good will (his face shining with good will).

This place is so small, but that is not the only reason. It is really not good for some to be here too much. I have noticed that they become unbalanced. They are not strong enough to hold the impact of spirituality.

I must have seemed downhearted. Swami went on to console me, "You come during the day, don't you? Come at lunchtime.

And then you come anyhow on Wednesday and Friday nights. Of course, there are five more nights in the week. Make your house attractive so that you will like to be in it. Read or study or write, if you feel like it, in the evenings.

"There will be times of depression and discouragement. Think then of Sri Ramakrishna and Swamiji. You are doing their work. You have come to Sri Ramakrishna. Whether you understand that or not, it is a fact. You have come from a rough sea into a calm harbor. The world can never buffet you again.

"A little effort and the path is made clear. Look at your own life. Have not all obstructions been removed? Be a worker. Devote yourself to the Lord's work. That is the way to come close to God and to become a source of great good to the world."

(Happily, soon all of us were back in the evenings, and things went on as before.)

January 19, 1952

A large crowd, which included students from Berkeley, was gathered in the back office after Swami Vivekananda's birthday celebration.

Swami: What you call idolatry is the worship of the living God. I know of a man who had been away from home for a time. On his return he saw the picture of Sri Ramakrishna just shake from head to foot with joy. It was the figure, not the picture itself, that shook like that. [The man he spoke of was a monk, Swami himself, on his return from New York in 1932.]

Another monk touched the feet of the statue of the Divine Mother and felt not stone but warm, living flesh. [This monk was Swami Nirvedananda.]

Mr. E.C. Brown, the president of the Society and a monastic, came downstairs. It will soon be Mr. Brown's eighty-second birthday.

Swami: Well, what is it, Mr. Brown?

Mr. Brown: I was just wondering if you might consider the hour.
Swami: It is said that there are three things one should not keep even the remnants of: a serpent, a disease, and an Englishman (referring to Mr. Brown). Of course, I just made up the last part.
Mr. Brown: Mrs. Soulé could express my sentiments better in song, but I will sing them.

(In a croaking voice)

Oh, father, dear father, come home with me now,
The clock in the steeple strikes one.

Swami: He is getting a little crazy. Look how flushed he is!

(With the backing of others, Mr. Brown was finally able to convince Swami that he should go upstairs.)

January 22, 1952

Swami: How is meditation?
Me: Very good.
Swami (referring to the tumult that his order to stay away in evenings had created): Mind is pacified?
Me: Yes, Swami, but sometimes I am very emotional during meditation.
Swami: Emotion can be good. What kind of emotion?
Me: Good emotion.
Swami: That is all right. But suppress it during meditation.
Me: Sometimes it is so strong, I cannot.
Swami: If Hitler were standing alongside you with a stick, you would be able to suppress it. If you were compelled to suppress it, you could suppress it.

January 23, 1952

Swami was about to go upstairs as I entered the front door.
Swami: Well, how is the writing?
Me: I finished, but I find it is not good. The part about Swami Pavitrananda is really not good.
Swami: That is just puerile! Finish it and then change it. Do the

big thing first, like a sculpture; later chisel and refine. Have you written the conclusion?

Me: No, Swami. I thought I would type the rest first.

Swami: No. You are just afraid of the hard part. Face it! Typing is just mechanical work. Write the conclusion. (Swami put such power behind all this that I felt myself shaking.)

January 26, 1952

Swami (as I entered): Well, how is the article?

Me: I finished it. I wrote the conclusion.

Swami (trying not to look pleased, and succeeding): Now write a summary—a synopsis of the introduction and conclusion and give it to me.

Me: Yes, Swami.

Swami: You are doing well?

Me: I guess so.

Swami: If you feel all right, then you are all right. (He went upstairs.)

January 29, 1952

Swami: Be strong and be happy. Without happiness nothing can be done. Learn how to write just as you learn how to meditate. Write as worship. Understand that you are living a dedicated life. You are people of little faith. Think of Swamiji—he gave his life for America. You have the privilege of participating in his work. Do you feel that? (His eyes were burning when he asked me this.)

Me: I feel it more and more.

Swami: Feel it! Work for him! When you can do that, I will know you are a human being.

Me: I cannot believe that he wants me to.

Swami: That is a flimsy excuse for not doing it—"Oh, Lord, I am so unworthy." Sri Ramakrishna once asked a devotee to fix him some tobacco. But the devotee said, "Oh, no, sir, I am too unworthy to do that." And he didn't do it. Don't commit that sin.

Later that day

Swami: I think we will start a magazine. The editorial offices could be in Olema. I might live over there.
Me: How wonderful that would be! When?
Swami: You ask when? Look how long it has taken you to write one article. After you have finished the article, you can write poetry. You can also write the lives of great men, reflective and poetic articles. Also, you can write one-act dramas of incidents in the lives of saints. You could also do summaries of books. The magazine needs the sort of thing you can do. It needs a light touch.

One must have a purpose—an ideal purpose, of course—but there must be a practical purpose along with it; otherwise the ideal has nothing solid to grow on.

February 12, 1952

Mara Lane says that Swami used to suddenly come downstairs in the evening, stand in the doorway, and deliver a few statements that would hit the bottom of one's soul and revolutionize one's life. Then he would depart as suddenly as he had come, leaving one with one's mouth hanging open.

February 14, 1952

The guru and the disciples—worlds apart, and yet, because his genius is the genius of compassion, he reaches across the apparent gulf and draws us to him, much as a mother draws the child to herself. The mother understands its baby talk and its needs and gives it strength and guidance along the steep, winding road to adulthood. The guru will sometimes give the mature disciple a swift fatherly kick up the hill, which can be painful. Swami told us, "A man of illumination can be as hard as flint; his mind rejects the relative. Or he can be as soft and tender as a flower. When he sees God in all forms, he is the soul of compassion; he will give his life for others. Those two attitudes are two phases of the same thing."

February 18, 1952

I had been complaining that Dr. Chaudhuri's class on Indian philosophy at the American Academy of Asian Studies was sometimes repetitive and boring.
Swami: Boredom is the privilege of fools and the rich. It is a habit. You must get over it.

February 1952

Me: Will I ever realize God?
Swami: If towards the end of your life you see God everyplace, maybe sometimes more vividly than at other times, but always feel His presence, then you will be safe.
Me: Is it possible that that will be?
Swami: I expect that from all of you. But it is necessary to work.

March 1952

Me: I have been trying to write poetry, but I cannot.
Swami: Train your mind to produce. In the past you wrote only when the mood struck. Spirituality means the ability to produce at any time. Then inspiration is really yours. Otherwise it comes and goes; it is never truly yours. You have not written for a long time so your mind has to get into practice. Be a hack writer. That is the way to clear the obstructions; then that exquisite thing will come. I am convinced that there are wonderfully beautiful things within everyone. All that is necessary is that the obstructions be removed. You are to grow into a writer, a reader, and a meditator. That is my job, and I will take no excuses. Be a soldier in the field.

March 1952

Swami (to Ediben, laughing): Mrs. ——— asked me if she would have to give up skiing. I was very surprised. I would never have thought she was a skier. I told her she would not have to give that up.

Me: Oh! You mean one does not have to give up skiing?

Swami: Was I talking to you?

Me: I mean in general.

Swami: Austerity for you! (He chanted in Sanskrit and then translated into English.) "Through austerity one knows Brahman."

Me: I am not very austere.

Swami: You are not anything at all yet. You are becoming.

March 26, 1952

Swami (to Edna Zulch): Conflict is good. Each time you fall and get up, you are a little stronger. Through struggle comes strength. God gives His blessings, but first He makes you worthy of receiving them, just like a king who trains his sons so that they can rule the kingdom. Do not be afraid. As long as you have fear, you will never attain to God. You may fail yourself time and again, but God will never fail you. Never. He will always stand behind you and give you strength.

April 17, 1952

There was a meeting of the Society's members the night before about building a new temple to accommodate the overflowing crowds in San Francisco, to which all said, "Aye."

Swami: Are you enthusiastic about the new temple?

Me: No, not very.

Swami: Why?

Me: I am not very interested in buildings. It is because I am too selfish. All I want is to realize God.

Swami: What will you do when you realize God? Pinch Him?

You will serve Him. So serve Him now. That is the way to draw close to Him; there is no other way. Act as though you had realized Him. The bad man becomes good by acting as though he were good. In that way his mind gradually changes. Serve God through all beings. Devote yourself to His service. Well, you know all this; you also do it. But learn to do it more and more.

April 18, 1952

Swami (in regard to giving money): Why must you plan your whole life now? Plan each year as it comes. That is the way to be practical. Before you buy anything, think if it is really necessary. I do not say that so much because of the money as because of the mind. Buy only what is essential. On the other hand, don't get fanatical about it. Have a wholesome attitude. The most important thing is the spirit of renunciation. Keep that.

April 24, 1952

Swami (apropos of the new temple): I get into one mess after another. It is very unusual.

Me: You are very unusual.

Swami: What makes you think I am unusual?

Me: All great men are unusual.

Swami: You think I am a great man because you see me here in these surroundings, lecturing and all that. In other places I would be just an ordinary man. It is the place.

Me: Wherever you would be, there it would be.

Swami (after a little time): Vedantic truths are wonderful. They make men great who embody them. Look at Swamiji—wherever he was, people recognized him for a great man. People who embody Vedantic truths understand the human heart. They know how to prod people toward their own light. They understand all sides of a person, yet they are cautious; otherwise harm could be done. They have deep understanding for everything.

Great musicians used to want to play before the swamis at

the Madras Math [monastery], because they knew their music would be best appreciated there. The aesthetic sense of spiritual men is keenly developed, but most important is their understanding of the human heart. Look at Holy Mother—what a wonderful understanding she had. *(With great kindness)* Somewhere there is a Mother Heart that loves you, no matter what you are or think of yourself. It is hard to believe, but it is literally so. Holy Mother was an embodiment of that Mother Heart. It is literally true.

May 14, 1952

Swami: The greatest thing that could happen to mankind today is the spread of spirituality. There must be spirituality of the kind that will not create dissension among men but will unify them. That is Vedanta. It is a spirituality that will coordinate and give meaning to all the greatest achievements of men. The swamis should be contemplative and not busy laying bricks and putting up buildings.

Me: Why?

Swami: That is what people want.

Me: But someone has to lay the bricks, and it seems that only the swamis can do it.

Swami: When there are enough people trained to do the work, then the swamis can be contemplative.

Later, talking to a devotee, Swami said how much meditating the monks have to do. "Meditation requires largeness; to become large, one must learn how to work for others, to work unselfishly. One thus becomes big of heart. Without this, true meditation is impossible."

May 15, 1952

When I came into the library Swami was talking to Jeanette and Edna about meditation.

Swami: When there is consciousness of subject and object, that is not true meditation.
Jeanette: Is there a time when one feels that it is someone else who is doing the meditation, and you are just watching?
Swami: No. If that happens, there is something wrong with the head. You should never observe your own meditation. Some people in the beginning watch every little thing that takes place within them. They get caught in that trap. Maybe that is what you do.
Jeanette: No. My meditation isn't that good. There is nothing to watch.

(The conversation turned to the subject of suffering and the presence of evil.)

Swami: Well, why should there be evil and suffering? Why did God create the world like that? One should ask that question. Of course, you do not suffer, so you don't ask it.
Me: No, but I guess if I suffered, I should ask it.
Swami: You should.
Me: But then, who am I to say that my suffering is wrong? If I had never suffered, I would not be here.
Swami: Do you think that one has always to suffer to come to God?
Me: Not always.
Swami: Why should it ever be that way? Why should one suffer at all?
Edna: Because of our mistaken ideas.
Swami: Why should people have mistaken ideas in the first place? Why shouldn't we realize the truth here and now? Why suffer? Why should God have created a world in which people must have mistaken ideas and suffer and struggle in order to realize Him? Why did He create it at all?
Me: Maybe He didn't.
Swami: Ah! That is closer to the truth.

Edna: You said in one of your lectures that nature, if left to itself, does not always take one to the goal.
Swami: That is my opinion of it. Nature is like a river. The current sometimes flows straight to the ocean or in devious routes —but sometimes the water gets caught in an eddy and swirls around and around, always coming back to the same place.
Me: What is nature?
Swami: She is very smart. Well, answer the question yourself. You tell me what nature is. Go on!

The talk became light and joking. It has been a long time since Swami has been in such fine good humor, relaxed and liking to talk with us, with his mind for a few minutes away from the problems that press upon him from all sides. The air seemed to sparkle.

May 17, 1952

Swami: Well, how are you?
Me: I am very happy, but I do not work hard.
Swami: Do you think that is cause and effect? You are happy because you do not work hard?
Me: No. I know that if I don't get to work, my happiness won't last. But Swami, I would do anything in the world, anything at all, rather than write. I can watch my mind figuring out things to do.
Swami (regarding me during this speech with extreme disapproval): Do you think you have any choice about it? Lay it to your heart that you have no choice. You are doing the work of Sri Ramakrishna and Swamiji. Once you break through the dam, the water will make its own channel and cut it wider and wider.

I had no reply to that, but I had other problems. Like most beginners in spiritual life, I had reached a state in which the enticing come-on of spiritual experiences and dreams had stopped, and I felt doltish and singularly unfit for a life of spiritual striving. I did not know quite how to put this to Swami without whining. I was not unhappy; I was just flat—a surface that neither gave off nor took in light. Everything around me looked as ordinary as I felt. I approached the subject in a crablike manner, from the side.

Me: Swami, what you spoke of in class last night—seeing the world as excruciatingly beautiful—I have seen it like that a little bit. But I do not see it like that any more. Why is that?

Swami: When one is spiritual, one sees that.

Me: Am I less spiritual now than then?

Swami: There is no endeavor more fruitless than thinking about the past. The wonderful thing about it is that when the inside changes, the outside changes also. It is as though a curtain were rolling up off the face of the universe, revealing a wonderful reality behind. And through that, one can see the pure Spirit shining.

Me: It is really always like that, isn't it? Right now it is like that. It is *here*.

Swami: Yes. He, not It. "It" is living, a living Being.

Me: I know that I do not really believe it because when I meditate, I try to focus on It—Him—with my thought. If I really believed He were real, I would not think so much; I would stop thinking, and It—He—would be there.

Swami: Yes, but it is better to think of God than to think of worthless things, even if you cannot always feel His presence. Love is the thing. Without love, nothing can be accomplished. Love Sri Ramakrishna.

Me: How can I love him if I do not know him?

Swami: You do know him. He is the Soul of your soul. If that were not true, you would have some reason in saying that you cannot love him without knowing him. But you know him; he is the Life of your life.

Me: I do not identify the two.
Swami: They are identical.

May 27, 1952

When I sit in Swami's office, it is mostly in silence while he reads the newspaper or some book. Sometimes he sings or whistles a devotional tune that has a plaintive air about it. Miriam comes in and out with information about buildings and architects. Ediben comes and goes, or the phone will ring and there will be long conversations. Sometimes it is very quiet, sometimes very active. Whatever way it is, I always feel that I want to sit there forever.

Sometimes Swami looks up at me questioningly. I feel that I should say something or ask some question, but I have nothing to say. If there had been anything on my mind, it loses all significance or I cannot remember what it was. Often I feel stupid (is there nothing in my head at all?). Swami will ask, "Yes?" And I will say, "Nothing."

Today Miriam tried to get hold of Mr. Gutterson, the architect for the new temple, to change some plan and cancel an appointment. The architect's secretary told her that Mr. Gutterson had gone home in order to find absolute quiet in which to do his work for Swami, as he had a deadline to meet. Upon hearing this, Swami said, "Oh, golly! Mr. Gutterson is beginning to act just like a student!" I was smiling at this and smiling also in delight at Swami's greatness—not because of the architect, but just because of his greatness that one cannot help feeling. It is like a light shining.

"What are you thinking?" Swami asked me.

I replied, "Nothing."

"Yes, you are thinking something."

"Well," I said, "I was thinking how wonderful you are."

"Am I wonderful because I can talk about plans?" he asked.

"No," I answered, "it is not that."

He went back to reading. Then later he looked up and said, "Think of the Lord: as a mother broods over a distant child, think of Him with that same love." Then very kindly and almost sadly he said, "There is no happiness in time." He means he will die, I thought, and he knows it will be hard for me—hard for us all. "Go beyond time," he said.

"But it takes time to go beyond time." I said.

"Yes," he replied. "Use time to undermine time."

June 1952

Swami (to a group of devotees): When the lion roars in the jungle, the jackals are quiet. When the voice of Advaita roars out, all the other philosophies are stilled. It is like the sun overpowering all other lights and engulfing them.

Devotee: Even one of those little lights would be enough, if one could only see even that!

Swami (suddenly majestic and furious): You people all hang on to your little miseries. You are milksops, weaklings, cowards! To show you sympathy is a sin. Go out into the world—go anywhere and see how worldly people suffer. What terrible suffering they endure, and what strength they call up from within themselves, while here you whimper at the slightest thing, all of you.

This was a long and magnificent speech. I cannot remember it all. These things are delivered with such power that one shakes inside. Often I feel like laughing; his phrases are so apt, so telling, that there is something glorious about them, however much they may strike home—like flashes of lightning, direct and uncompromising. Laugh or cry, one cannot ignore the jolt.

June 12, 1952

My life was still chugging along on a plateau, which I suspected was taking a downhill turn. This lackluster mood probably extended to my face and manner, obvious to Swami. I did not have to open the subject or sidle into it.

Swami: You are trying to change your whole way of living, your whole mind. It needs time. What is the sense of drastically ripping off the old? You do not know what effect that might have on your mind. It is a law that when the young bud grows, the old leaf falls off by itself. When you become established in the new, the old will just fall off. It is not good just to rip off the old leaf prematurely. Are you game to live a life all alone?

Me: Yes.

Swami: Spiritual life is a lonely life. One goes from the alone to the alone. Are you game?

Me: Yes.

Swami: You could still go back . . .

Me: I feel that would be suicide.

Swami: Yes, that is true. Well, do you think you will like this life?

Me: I think that will be up to me, won't it?

Swami: Yes. But do you think you can find what you want in it?

Me: That also will be up to me, but I don't know what horrible things are within me that will come up and spoil everything or make things difficult.

Swami: Sooner or later one has to get rid of them.

Me: Yes.

Swami: Spiritual life is always a risk. It is like digging where you think you will find diamonds. Maybe there will be nothing there, but take that risk. No effort is lost—are you game to take the risk?

Me: Yes. I am afraid of only one thing.

Swami: What is that?

Me: Of when you will no longer be here.

Swami: Go to Sri Ramakrishna and Swamiji. Turn to them. They will always be here, and Sri Ramakrishna will always come. But if you are looking the other way, what can he do? Make a practice now of turning toward him. You will feel his presence. Whenever you need help, he will talk to you and you will talk to him. Sri Ramakrishna and Swamiji will always stand by you; they will always be here. Know that it is they whom you have come to.

Me: And to you, too.

Swami: Yes, but they are the main root; we are just the branches.

June 16, 1952

Me: Is it because you think I might want to go back to New York that you want me to stay married?

Swami: What I advise is caution. Spiritual life is like mountain climbing. To exert caution is part of it. You must be very sure-footed. That doesn't imply fear or retreat. Do not think whether you are happy or unhappy—just be.

July 1952

Swami (to me): Work that is not consciously done for the Lord is nothing. Fortunately, there is a great Soul presiding over all. Do everything unto Him. It may seem just imagination at first, but later on you will feel His presence tangibly. You will really know that you are doing everything for Him and that He is pleased with what you do, very pleased.

Swami (to the devotees): You people should not worry. Sri Ramakrishna can push the cripple across a mountain. The explosive power of Sri Ramakrishna is behind you. He turns everything to good use, even your mistakes.

August 25, 1952

Swami: Do you think you are going to like this life you have chosen?

Me: I think so.

Swami: There is a long way ahead. Have you considered your prospects for the future?
Me: I haven't thought of it that way.
Swami (smiling): Oh, you haven't?
Me: If it's the way it is now, it will be all right. I will just grow older and older.
Swami: That is one way of looking at it.
Me: Presumably I will get more and more spiritual, and that will help. If I don't, it will be too bad.
Swami: Too bad for whom?
Me: For me.
Swami: That is right. That is one way of looking at it.
Me: What other way should I look at it?
Swami: It is a good way. Hang on! When things grow difficult, hang on!
Me: What will happen when all spirituality goes?
Swami: That is the very time to hang on, when everything seems dry. When a sailboat goes out to the ocean, it is all smooth sailing at first; it is easy. But when the boat hits rough waters, the sailors must hang on and push ahead. The difference is that with the sailboat, one is not sure of the end. Here one can be sure. Be a hero! Are heroes made by success or by their failures?
Me: By their failures.
Swami: That is right. Hang on through thick and thin, in spite of everything.
Me: Yes.
Swami: Are you afraid?
Me: No, I am not afraid.
Swami: I am going away in a few days for two or three weeks. Carry on with your work, and write to me frequently.
Me: Yes. I hope you will get a rest.
Swami: I hope so too. If not, I will get stale. The presence of a tired man and a sick man is not good.

Me: That is not what your presence is.
Swami: Yes, I'm a tired and sick man.

August 27, 1952

Today, Swami announced that we will revive *The Voice of India,* the Society's disbanded magazine, starting with trial issues. The board of editors will be Edna Zulch, Kathleen Davis, Luke Williams, and me. The magazine will have to be first-rate. The general concept will be the same as it was originally: it will represent all aspects of Vedanta—devotional, philosophical, historical, hagiographical, and even fictional.
Swami (pointing to me): She has the time but not the talent of Florence Wenner [the editor of the Society's original magazine in 1945–46]. She hasn't the versatility. She is a meadowlark poet. Meadowlarks sing in the spring when they feel like it, but at the first sign of autumn they are heard no more. No one knows they exist.

September 25, 1952

Swami (to a group of devotees): You are all cowards. You just mew—you should roar!
Devotee: We should be lion cubs.
Swami: You are not even kittens. Sorry kittens!

3

ALL IN GOOD TIME

The trial *Voice of India,* of which I was the editor-in-chief, was not to be taken lightly. The issues that we produced every two months were supposed to contain our best efforts and to constitute a backlog of articles that we could draw upon if we ever went public and sold the magazine. I not only had to work hard writing brainy articles but also had to put together a comprehensive, varied, and readable journal. Deadlines rushed at us like a steaming train bent on running us down. To write thoughtful articles on Indian philosophy, or simply meaningful essays on Vedanta, was a form of torture to me. My mind could not adapt itself to an outline or even draw one up in the first place. There was, however, no way out. I had to write a couple of articles, a short story, and some poetry every two months or fail ignominiously—an eventuality that was not an option.

We met the publication deadline for the first bimonthly trial magazine of January 1953 at the end of December. The second deadline of mid-February already loomed large at the opening of 1953. I spent the first six weeks of the New Year hard at work preparing a story ("Shankara and the Outcaste"), an article ("The Vedantic View of Healing"), and two poems ("Night" and "Thirst") for the upcoming March issue. Writing articles was still difficult, especially with a new deadline bearing down.

January 5, 1953

Me (apropos of Vicks VapoRub): I wish there were something one could rub on the brain to make it work.

Swami: When a starving man begs for food, do you think he has to rub something on his brain to make the sentences come? His desire forms the right words. If you have the desire to say something, the right words will clothe it. Create the desire within yourself. Why haven't you written down what I have just suggested?

Me: I thought I would remember it.

Swami: Do you think writers remember everything? Always write down everything. Haven't you a notebook? Where is it? When you read, jot down references and ideas. They will be valuable to you. *(To others)* It is going to take years to teach her method!

January 7, 1953

Swami (to a devotee): Do you think Sri Ramakrishna, Holy Mother, and Swamiji will ever let you go? They will never let you lose your way. Theirs is an eternal guarantee. There are ups and downs, but they make you strong. The man who has crossed many mountains is the strong man. Hang on!

Later that day

Swami: When I did the worship in India—offering all the different elements to God—I felt that each had been absorbed back into the Infinite. The whole world seemed to disappear, to dissolve into a vast silence. I did not have to philosophize about it. I actually felt it. That is worship. You can actually offer a flower to the Infinite. When the mind becomes subtle, everything is seen as a symbol of God or of some aspect of spiritual life.

January 8, 1953

Swami: When ritual is just a matter of form, it becomes binding. It is good only when there is meditation and devotion along with it.

Me: Psychologically good?

Swami: Psychologically and spiritually. In spiritual life all psychology is spiritual psychology. One feels the presence of God during worship. I used to take Sri Ramakrishna's picture into his bedroom after performing the worship in Madras. We did that so he could rest. I put the picture on the cot and went away. When I went back into the room it was just filled with his presence. Such a thing is so much better than one's own consciousness that one knows it is not imagination. One could not imagine it.

Me: Would Sri Ramakrishna know that he was there in a picture?

Swami: Of course he knows. How could he be there and not know? It is not the same as saying he is everywhere. A spiritual manifestation like that is objective.

Me: But one has to be spiritual to feel it.

Swami: No, it is not one's own doing. He comes. There are many fish in the sea; if you go deep you might catch one, but when the fish comes up to you, that is the fish's own doing. It is like that. Of course, I will admit a certain susceptibility is necessary. A polished surface catches the rays of light better than a rough one.

Me: It seems to me that only very spiritual people see him. He comes to them. But he wouldn't come to me, for instance.

Swami: Who told you were not a spiritual person?

Me: Well, not enough.

Swami: It is a matter of unfoldment; it is not something added. One does not have to be especially spiritual. Many people coming here for the first time have felt it. They have remarked upon it.

Me: I do not feel anything. That is, it doesn't knock me over.

Swami: That is because you are here all the time. You have become accustomed to it. If you were to go away, you would know

that you had felt it. You would feel the lack; you would miss it.
Me: Yes. I know.
Swami: Grow in devotion. Love Sri Ramakrishna, Holy Mother, and Swamiji. They have form only when they are far away, but as you grow close you see they are the formless Brahman. It is like looking at a brilliant light through a small aperture in a wall from a distance. You think it has form—a small round spot of light. But as you grow close and put your eye up to the hole, you see the infinite light beyond the wall. Love Sri Ramakrishna. He is our own. He is infinite joy and love, infinite peace, our very own, the Life of our life, the Soul of our soul. He is also Brahman, *Satchidananda* [the formless, absolute God]. Don't analyze it. When you think of him, these things will come to you. They are just there. You know enough about him to have all these things revealed when you think of him.

January 10, 1953

Swami came downstairs and seemed for a time restless. "I want you to do something for me," he said. "Come into my office."

I followed him and stood in the door of his office while he jotted down something on paper; then, with an air of conspiracy and looking like a little boy who is up to no good, he said, "Come closer."

I went to his desk, and he whispered, so no one could hear, "Now, there are some nuts. I think they are called Macadamia." He showed me what he had written: Makadamia. "Get a medium-size jar of these. They are round and creamy colored and come, I think, from Hawaii. Maybe Tony's [a grocery store] will have them."

He took out his wallet and from it took a crisp and clean five-dollar bill, adding, "Then also there are cans of almonds. Get two cans." He smiled a little sheepishly as though we were partners in crime.

I got the nuts and returned to the Temple. Swami, happy as a child who has gotten into a forbidden jam pot or a co took them upstairs.

Later that day

Swami told us about Suresh Babu [a lay disciple of Sri Ramakrishna] and of how he carried curd to Swami Vivekananda for many miles on foot so that it would not curdle and be spoiled by the jostling of a carriage. When Swamiji learned of this, he was deeply moved and said, "Whomever he [Sri Ramakrishna] touched, he turned to gold."

Swami (speaking of the direct disciples of Sri Ramakrishna): Twenty thousand saints and mystics could spring from the dust of their feet! Such people come only with Divine Incarnations. It was all so natural. No fuss, no long faces—it was a different world.

January 15, 1953

Swami: Gandhi's ideas were far from perfect. Yet he put them into practice. He was a great power. Our [Vedantic] ideas are more perfect, yet we do nothing. We should become powerful, so that many will follow us. How? By living up to our ideals. Live it! Well, it will happen, but not in our time. Maybe you will do it. You have renounced for God. Through renunciation a power is generated. Once you break through the dam, the water will make its own channel and cut it wider and wider.

January 17, 1953

Swami: I see so much suffering and sorrow in the world that I no longer want to prevent anyone from finding happiness where he can. If something helps him, whether it be truth or not, let him follow it.

Me: But if it is not true, he will find no happiness in it.

Swami: That is the trouble. But even if he finds temporary relief, that is something.

January 21, 1953

Swami talked in the back office to a group of devotees until after 11:30 p.m. Suddenly, in the midst of a sentence, he said furiously, "Go home! All of you go home. Why don't you go to a nightclub? You just sit here for pleasure; you are not doing anything!" He got up and strode majestically out of the room, brushing by Mara and me.

Mara (sotto voce to me): Look out! You will get scorched.

January 31, 1953

Swami was looking at blueprints, whistling, making faces, nodding, pretending to explain the pros and cons to an imaginary architect, looking up at me, and laughing or frowning. There was purity in his face like that of a baby. This went on for a long time. Then something broke the spell, and he was tearing into someone like a lion.

February 3, 1953

Me: Is it all right for me to stuff cotton in my ears when I meditate?

Swami: No, better not to use external aids.

Me: It's very noisy in the morning in my apartment. The people below start getting up.

Swami: Use willpower. Do you know willpower?

Me: No.

Swami: Become acquainted with it. Balanced strength is the true strength. It is like the serene surface of a calm lake. It goes deep, deep. One feels one can give oneself to it and be held securely. If necessary, serene strength can raise waves mountain high.

February 4, 1953

Swami: If one boosts the students' self-confidence in their accomplishments, their ego grows—the accomplishments become associated with the ego. Then they cannot stand the least little criticism; they will go away. Self-confidence has to be crushed for a time, yet accomplishments must grow. When they are no longer associated with the ego, they become acts of worship. It takes a long time.

February 5, 1953

Me: I wrote a letter to Luke this morning in a rage. Perhaps I had better not send it.

Swami: No, don't do that! Wait three or four days. You should write, but don't be small. You are thinking of only your own hurt. She has been sick and has a dying father on her hands. I do not say she is right, but don't be small about it. Be great. You can't do great things through smallness. Don't react that way. When you see something wrong, you should redress it, of course, but be strong.

February 6, 1953

Ediben, Jo, Mara, and Kathleen were in the back office after Swami's lecture.

Me (apropos of Yahudi Menuhin's hatha yoga practices, as pictured in Life *magazine):* Why don't we do that?

Swami (furiously): Why do you want to do that?

Me: You said it was good for the health.

Swami: Get health through your mind. Meditation will tone the whole body. If you practice things like hatha yoga, you will become a slave to the body. You will become bound in it, looking at your face in the mirror twenty times a day and at the face of others. Sri Ramakrishna forbade any such practice. If any of our monks have practiced hatha yoga, they are discountenanced as going against Sri Ramakrishna.

It is time all of you made a plan for your lives. What do any of you do? You are middle-aged, sagging women. You have been hearing about Vedanta for twenty years, yet you cannot answer a question about it. (He imitated us looking off into space, pondering, hemming and hawing, and finally saying wisely, "Yes.") All you want to do is play and have little conversations. Organize your thoughts and your life. I have heard you answer questions on the phone; you do not make any intelligent replies. You just giggle. It is no wonder that Vedanta has not caught on. There is good reason for it. You just play. (He stretched his legs out in front of him, lolling back in his chair with an utterly silly look.)

It is not that you are not good people. You all have many fine qualities. If that were not true, it wouldn't matter. I would think, "Well, they will do something in their next life." No! You can now. But you won't. You are no longer young girls of twenty. It is time you thought about what you are to do.

February 26, 1953

Swami: Infinite care, infinite pains—that is the only way, Marie Louise. Work for the Lord as though He were your father, your mother, your friend. He is the all-pervasive Spirit, infinitely good. He is so subtle that the slightest tinge of grossness gives Him pain. That is why we must take such care in His work.

(The phone rang and Swami talked with Mr. Gutterson, the architect, about the new temple.)

Me: That was magnificent! You were so tactful.

Swami: No, not tactful. I have deep respect for man. Man is divine.

March 1, 1953

Swami: Did you finish the account? [He had asked me to write an account of the dedication of the chapel at Sacramento, which had taken place on February 28.]

Me: No. I couldn't find my glasses.

Swami (with disgust): If you were not a good person you would be an awful person, you have such bad habits. You didn't come to the Gita class and you didn't write the account.

March 11, 1953

Swami: Did you hear the minutes? [Minutes I had edited of the Sacramento annual meeting of 1952 and which had been read the previous day.]
Me: Yes. You made some changes and they were good. I should have thought of them.
Swami: Aren't you ashamed? Or are you just happily ashamed? You should be ashamed! If I have to make changes, the burden is still mine. I should be able to say, "If Marie Louise has done it, it is all right. I don't have to look at it." But you didn't take the burden from me. (Abrupt exit.)

March 14, 1953

Swami (now referring to the 1952 San Francisco minutes that I had also edited): This is sloppy work. What does "Berkeley members" mean? Simply because Ediben had it that way does not mean you should not question it. Put it in good English. *(Pointing out more mistakes)* I cannot stand work that needs to be checked; it turns my blood cold. (He made a gesture of consummate disgust and irritation.) You "think," you "guess"—how can you meditate if your mind is in a state like that? It is the same mind that does this work and that sees God.

Later Swami asked me to take some dictation. It was the first time he had asked this. I got my research case, in which were two spiral notebooks. The wire spirals had become entangled. I fumbled with them desperately for several minutes and then looked up to see Swami nearly bursting with suppressed laughter, whereupon I laughed also.

Swami (after reading the re-edited minutes): You have done a good job. It's all right.

March 28, 1953

Swami (in regard to the magazine): If you think that writing comes spontaneously, you are very much mistaken.
Me: I do think that. If one can write, then one just writes.
Swami: I am telling you differently. Just swallow it! Go to the source of a big river. What will you find there? Just little trickles—one here, one there, half-hearted, sometimes blocked, sometimes going underground—but all together they eventually make a mighty river. If you are the poet you thought you were, or think you are . . .
Me: I don't think I am.
Swami: Oh! That makes it very easy for you. Humility makes things very easy. "I can't do anything." Then no one expects anything from you; you don't have to make any effort. Just lie back.
Me: It is not humility. It is just a fact.
Swami: It is humility, laziness. There is so much going on here. You could make an article every two months about it.
Me: I am not good at remembering accurately. I always wish I had a recording machine. My brain is not a good recorder.
Swami: You could learn that. There was a man who used to always take notes at the Math. The monks didn't like it because some of the things he wrote were personal but he went on until he had volumes. Most of them were lost, but one or two were intact. I translated one of them. There was a great deal of valuable material. Just jot things down. That is all you have to do.

The doorbell rang. Kathleen Davis and Jeanette Vollmer came in from the retreat at Olema, where a women's crew had been working all day long in a gale. Soon other devotees arrived. It was seven o'clock.

Swami (to me): You had better go now and do your evening

work—meditate, eat dinner, write about Ananda. [At that time I was writing a story about Buddha's chief disciple.] Forget you are living in the twentieth century. Live in the time of Buddha. Tell how the people live and talk. Go with Buddha on his travels. Learn about that period.

April 13, 1953

Swami (to himself): What a mess the world is in. He who tries to improve it is a fool. He who tries to get something from it is a fool. *(To me)* The only thing is to leave it behind.

April 14, 1953

Swami: Sri Ramakrishna is the form of Formlessness. As one grows closer to that form it melts into the Formless. Not all forms do that. One can meditate on him to know the Formless God.

April 22, 1953

As Jo was binding the trial magazine and I was trying to help her, I touched wet ink on the cover and smeared it.
Swami (at once noticing this): Take care. In India a diamond cutter will spend months studying a stone. He explores it from every angle, determining all the stresses and strains and flaws. If he hits it in the wrong place, it can fly to pieces. Then finally, after months of study, he gives one little tap, covered with perspiration; it could spell ruin for him. You should take such pains.

April 23, 1953

The May issue of the trial magazine was offered in the shrine. That evening, in Swami's office, many devotees were present.
Swami (glancing through the trial magazine): It could be published now if we wanted to be premature. Maybe it could be printed in India cheaply.

Sri Ramakrishna and Swamiji are behind you. If you sincerely want the magazine, they will help. If you don't want to do it, Sri Ramakrishna will say, "All right, all right." (Swami raised his hand as though comforting a child.) You have to show your desire to do it. A man came to a crossroads and asked directions of a sage who was sitting there. He received no answer. He asked several times—silence. Then he chose one road and started off. At this, the holy man opened his eyes and gave him the directions. The man asked, "Why didn't you tell me before?" And the sage replied, "I wanted to be sure you really intended to go."

April 26, 1953

A large group of devotees was in the back office after the Sunday morning lecture.

Swami (to me upon my arrival): Oh, are you just coming to the lecture, Mrs. Burke?

Me: I am sorry, Swami.

Swami (sternly): If you had any honor you would not come to my lectures at all. You think so little of them and of me that you cannot come on time? What was the matter? Did you sleep all morning?

Me: No. I really had no idea there was this daylight saving. Nobody told me.

Swami: Nobody told you! Does anyone owe it to you to tell you?

Me: No.

Swami: Do you want a servant? Perhaps you would like a personal secretary, some miserable companion. "Nobody told me"—that is the most hateful sentence I have ever heard.

(To Sally Martin) He who burns for knowledge is an ascetic. Hunger burns—it is like a fire, burning away all dross. That is asceticism.

May 3, 1953

Swami (in answer to Phiana, a devotee from Sacramento): The mind should not be tense, but it should not sag. Tell the mind when to rest. The mind should not do as it pleases. In that way you bring it under control. Give work your full attention when you are working. Then turn to something else. Go from one thing to another so that the mind never has time to think wrong thoughts. Everything should be done at the right time. I have no use for people who neglect their duties because they want to talk about God instead of cooking dinner; that is not spiritual. Fight with the mind, wrestle with it. In that way you become strong and gain self-confidence, not only within yourself but also outside.

May 5, 1953

Swami (to me, sternly): How many cigarettes do you smoke?
Me: I don't keep track.
Swami: Keep track. Tell me how many.
Me: At least a pack.
Swami: You are to cut them out altogether. You cannot afford to smoke. There has been a lot written about smoking causing cancer. You have to stay healthy for the magazine. It was because of Florence Wenner's illness that the magazine was stopped before.
Me: What is the best way to stop—all at once, or petering off? (Swami's tone was nothing to argue with.)
Swami: You can peter off. Smoke three a day for a few days.
Me: Can this be six a day to start? (Ediben intervened on my behalf, so that six was the number for the time being.)

May 6, 1953

Jackson arrived in San Francisco without warning. He wants a divorce—*granted.*

May 16, 1953

Swami talked to me or just sat quietly with me for a long time, in case I was upset by Jackson's decision. ("You will be upset," Swami had said earlier. "That is only natural after so many years of marriage.") If I was disturbed, the condition vanished and never returned. Perhaps that was because he reached into my mind with his healing thought and squashed whatever seeds of regret or depression may have been there waiting to sprout. At one point he said, laughing, "It is ludicrous that losing cigarettes and losing a husband are about on a par." Actually, losing cigarettes was at the time far more agonizing.

Swami's office, 1:30 p.m., May 19, 1953

Swami: Come in for a minute. (I went in and sat down.) When do you have to appear in court?

Me: I don't think I have to at all.

Swami (sharply): You live in a fool's paradise. You will have to. Find out about it.

Later that day

Talking with a group of us, Swami said that those who are not anchored in God drift on and on, around and around. They may seem for a time to find an anchor, but it is only temporary. They cut loose again, like a leaf on a stream; sometimes it catches against a rock or a stick, but the current is too strong, so it is only a matter of time before it is dislodged and swept on again. "I hope you people know how lucky you are. You have Sri Ramakrishna and Swamiji."

Swami (to me): Become a scholar. Grow up!

Me: How can I grow up?

Swami: Up, up. Think of Sri Ramakrishna. Pray to him. *(Very softly)* Pray to him.

May 20, 1953

Swami: Convince yourself that you are of the nature of Spirit, and then practice devotion. That is all. That strength and devotion is what I felt in Swamiji's *arati* [music composed by Swami

Vivekananda for evening vespers] when I first heard it at Belur Math—strength, no fear.

May 31, 1953

After his Sunday evening lecture in the Berkeley Temple, Swami was scolding the devotees. Even in the scolding there was an indescribable tenderness and sweetness—a kind of liquid radiance that shone through his eyes. (How can one ever write about Swami?)

Swami: Give up smallness. You all cling to smallness—"This one said that, and that one said the other thing. She was given this to do, and I wasn't." Where there is smallness, God cannot come; God is great. Maybe it is because I am getting old and tired, but to see smallness is unbearable. Vedanta, my eye! As long as you are small, you cannot know God.

June 2, 1953

Swami: It is a nice day. Why don't you take your car and sit at the Marina. Go on. You can take your work. You can watch the water and the hills, but not the people—people are God, but worldly people are poison to you.

Me: The fault probably is in me, because I see the poison and not the God.

Swami: You have to take a practical, human view if you want to talk sensibly. You wouldn't drink ditch water and argue that it is really pure and only poisonous because your stomach is so weak. But it is also good to remember that what you say is true. Vedantists keep the real truth in the back of their minds and act according to the present state of their mind. That is realistic.

Me: Is it all right to watch people on television?

Swami (on the way upstairs): Not too good. Why?

Me: My sister asked me to watch the coronation of Elizabeth II. I don't especially care about it.

Swami: Yes. You can go. See what Nehru does and report to me. See if he bows and scrapes.

June 10, 1953

Swami gave a small tea party in the library for Dr. Sarvepalli Radhakrishnan, whom he had known in India.

July 22, 1953

Edna, Kathleen, Mara, Jeanette, and others were in the back office after the Wednesday evening lecture. Someone asked if the devotees would have to clean the new temple.

Swami: I think it will be too much for them. We will have to get a man to come in.

Devotee: Will there be a daily worship?

Swami: Yes.

Kathleen: Who will do it, the monastic caretaker?

Swami: The caretaker will be taking care. (A gleam came into his eye.) If I find the caretaker not in his rooms, I will hang him upside down from the rafter until all the blood rushes into his head. In fact, if I find any sloppiness, I will hang you all from the rafters by your feet. And if there is still sloppiness, you will be thrown out into the cold. There will be other workers.

(More seriously) You people are getting sloppy. You will have to run the new place yourselves. I won't be there. I cannot keep running back and forth from here to there. I won't be prodding this one and that one. But I will not tolerate sloppiness. I will stand like the angel Gabriel. (He sat up straight and majestic, looking like the angel Gabriel.) Didn't Gabriel stand before the Lord? No one will get by me. The Lord has to be comfortable and happy there.

Edna: What will make Him comfortable and happy?

Swami: Devotion. Sri Ramakrishna couldn't stand dissension. He wanted harmony and peace. Then he was happy. Why should there be any dissension? No one should do any shouting but me.

Your devotion is the strength of the movement. People will come and say, "Yes! This is what we want." They will find serenity, depth, and forbearance. Why should there be jealousies?

Sri Ramakrishna told Holy Mother about Uncle Moon. He is reflected equally in each pool. Each one's relationship with Him is complete. There is just you and God. There is no third person. Although on the outside it is necessary to cooperate with others in your work, still each one works directly for God, and He receives that work. You will have to learn to work directly for God. Here you are always waylaid by the swami.

There was discussion as to when the new temple would be ready and if enough money would come. Kathleen started playing with the pendulum she and I had made out of my ring and a piece of string before Swami came into the back office.

Kathleen: It is swinging to yes.

Swami: She is in her dotage. (Kathleen continued with the pendulum.) Stop that! The older you people get, the more infantile. (Swami spoke of how tired he was.)

Mara: My brother said he did not see how you could give interviews after such a lecture.

Swami: Well, I had forgotten all about those people. They came all the way from San Jose to see me. They were an awfully nice couple. (He had talked with them until nearly eleven o'clock.)

July 26, 1953

I came to the Temple around 8:00 p.m. I felt I should not be there at that hour, but nothing was said; so I sat on a chair with Mara and listened to Swami talk.

Swami: In the Himalayas there are fierce bears. The swamis at Mayavati had to kill several of them.

Kathleen: It seems horrible how one thing has to kill another.

Swami: What is horrible about it? It is nature. It is only horrible when you see it from a small viewpoint. Don't get addle-brained

[ab]out nonviolence. Think deeper. Pacifism is very good if it is the doctrine of a few. In that way the ideal that one should not kill is held before man. But if the majority takes it up, the country becomes a prey to aggressive nations. It will be subjugated, the worse degradation possible.

Look at India. Centuries of pacifism weakened her. She became nothing. Now she is divided into three parts. She didn't know how to prevent it. She was too weak-willed to stand up to the Muslims.

Life is sacred, but there are more precious things than life. If you cannot protect them, it is cowardice. The Hindus make a virtue out of cowardice. I do not say you should kill, but when it is one's duty to kill, one should do it. Be strong! That is what Sri Krishna taught Arjuna in the Gita: do your duty with the knowledge that the Self slays not nor is slain. Be strong and be soft. That is Swamiji's way. This is the age of man, not animals. You know the vision Sri Ramakrishna had of a pregnant woman who gave birth to a child and then ate the child? That is nature. Go deeper.

July 27, 1953

Me: Professor Spiegelberg is giving a course on the recent works of Carl Jung at the American Academy of Asian Studies. Shall I take it? It starts tonight. It is a sort of discussion course.
Swami: Very good. Yes, you can go, but you will have to give me a report of it.

July 29, 1953

I was sitting in the library. Swami was having an appointment in his office. Soon he accompanied his visitor to the front door.
Swami (seeing me): Hello. What are you doing?
Me (as I followed him down the hall to his office): I am reading Carl Jung.
Swami: There was another lecture last night?

Me (in his office now): No, it is tonight, but I don't like to miss your lecture.
Swami: You have heard so many of my lectures.
Me: They are always new.
Swami: That must be because your memory is poor.

That evening

I came to the Temple from Professor Spiegelberg's class. Swami Aseshananda, the head of the Vedanta Society of Portland, Oregon, had stopped in on his way from Yellowstone National Park with two students and was talking to a group in the library.
Swami Aseshananda (to me): How are you? I remember you drove me all around last time. I cannot forget that; it was very nice. You and Mrs. Vollmer. *(To Anna Webster)* How is the truck driver? I saw you driving at Olema better than any man.
Swami Ashokananda (trying not to smile): Don't praise her.
Anna: Oh, Swami, I can bear with praise.
Swami Ashokananda: You horrify me! You do your work as an offering to Sri Ramakrishna.

August 2, 1953

After the Sunday lecture, in the back office, Miriam King asked about the theory of teaching through love and gentleness.
Swami: Of course, love. But there is a point where the guru watches the disciple closely. Sri Ramakrishna did that. He noticed everything. Otherwise, the mind has a tendency to slide back into its old ways. You think, "Oh, what does it matter?" Soon you become submerged under the old habits. The guru is always alert to every little thing. It is not really painful; but because of its intensity, it becomes unendurable. Even grown-up, strong men will howl crying, but I have noticed that whenever I have watched anyone that closely, they have benefited and deepened. Do you think you can grow if you are not thrashed? On the other hand, Vedanta never asks that the disciple accept

everything about the guru. There is always a great deal of individual freedom.

Later that day

Mara: What is the benefit of worshiping in a congregation? I mean what is the sense of worshiping with a group, as they do in the [Hollywood] center?
Swami: Why do you feel you are worshiping with a group? You go to the Temple to worship individually—what if there are a few other people there?
Mara: Then why not worship at one's own shrine?
Swami: What is your own small shrine? How much devotion have you that you should have created any atmosphere in your own shrine? You people have a little bit of devotion, and you want the big thing! Be realistic. Where the Lord is worshiped by many devotees for years, an atmosphere is built up. You can benefit from that. It is also good to be with others who are thinking good thoughts. The mind is collective. My idea is that one should meditate once a day in one's own shrine—that is also beneficial—and once a day in a temple, where the presence of the Lord is strong. Only a fool and an egotist wouldn't go to a public shrine; the Lord is there! Even after years you can build up only a small thing in your own shrine.
Mara: But often you speak disparagingly of "bell-ringing" [a traditional part of Hindu ritualistic worship].
Swami: You are only trying to rationalize your own laziness. You know that we have daily worship upstairs in the monastery. How can you think I disparage bell-ringing? Lazy people!

That evening

The conversation turned to the belief prevalent in India that when a person dies in Benares he or she is liberated—that is to say, illumined.

Me: Why doesn't everyone in India go to Benares and shoot themselves?

Swami: Why don't you?

Me: I haven't the faith.

Swami: Oh, in India they have the faith, but they don't want liberation. They think, "By and by. Right now I have my wife and mother-in-law and cousin and aunt to take care of. Later, perhaps, but not now."

Mara: But would suicide work as well?

Swami: Yes, that would be all right. You people should buy a house in Benares and go and live there. Be sure the house is within the limits of Benares on the right bank.

Mara: But if Sri Ramakrishna has promised to come for us when we die, why do we have to go to Benares?

Kathleen: Isn't that the same as liberation?

Swami: Sri Ramakrishna will help you. It will certainly mean a great deal.

Jo: Swami Yatiswarananda [who had visited San Francisco in 1941 and 1942] said not to count on Sri Ramakrishna coming or on seeing the great ones.

Swami (seriously): You can count on it. It is the word of Holy Mother. He will come to you at the time of death.

Me: And then what?

Swami (sternly, as though it were a flippant question): You will have to make a contract with Sri Ramakrishna.

Me: I mean—will he stay?

Swami (more gently): Yes, he will guide you. *(Suddenly very stern)* Go home. It is eleven-thirty. Go home, lazy people! You don't want to do anything but sit around listening to stories.

(On my way out, I saluted Swami from the doorway.)

Swami (to Jo, who was in his office): She has heard how they take the dust of Swami Prabhavananda's feet in the south. Now she does that *(putting his palms together)* as the next best thing.

Me (protesting): No, I have always done that. I would like to take the dust of your feet, but I know you wouldn't permit it.
Swami: No! Don't do that! You are an American.

August 6, 1953

Swami was discussing plans for the temple with Helen (Jo, Mara, and I were spectators). A discussion followed about the coat that I bought and did not like.
Swami (to me): Shopping has become the main meaning of your life?
Me: Since I cannot smoke, I have taken to shopping.
Swami (not smiling at all): Isn't it time you started to work on the magazine? Or have you forgotten all about that?
Me: No, Swami. I haven't forgotten.
Swami: Very good.

August 8, 1953

I went home to clean my house and returned around seven. Swami was in the library with Helen and Kathleen, working over the color scheme for the interior of the new temple.
Swami: Well, did you get your house clean?
Me: A corner of it. I got tired and stopped.
Swami: Please come in. Sit down. Did you have your dinner?
Me: Partly.
Swami: I see. A preview.
Helen (to me, laughing): A preview! You are a character.
Swami (beaming upon me with a beautiful light in his eyes): A good character.

The discussion regarding the color scheme continued for almost an hour. Then Helen, looking white as a sheet, asked to go home. Swami went into his office with Jo, Mara, Kathleen, and me following. Swami looked at Indian magazines. The dusk deepened—silence and peace, with a remark only now and then.

Me: Shall I turn the light on? (I was sitting near the switch.)
Swami: No. The dusk is peaceful.
Me: I did not want to ask, but your eyes—
Swami: Better to sacrifice the eyes than to sacrifice the peace of the dusk.

August 9, 1953

Swami was working in the library with Helen, choosing samples of glass for the auditorium windows. Kathleen and Mara were there. He asked me to come in. As usual, everyone was staring at him, watching his every gesture and facial expression. He was utterly unselfconscious of their attention, at times whistling meditatively, sometimes looking severe or withdrawn so that no one dared speak. He listened to Helen's every suggestion, concentrating his full mind on the problem at hand, yet never missing an opportunity to drive a lesson home. This endless going over of plans was like a great drama, something stirring and alive.

August 10, 1953

Swami: Are you going to clean another corner of your house today?
Me: No, I have given up.
Swami: You will put it off for another century?
Me: Yes. I think I had better get to work.
Swami: That is good. Don't let your mind stall. Even if it works slowly, keep it moving. Sometimes it will work slowly, sometimes fast; but never let it stall. (Swami was silent while he read six or seven letters from students. A small child raced by the window, screeching like an animal. He looked up in mock amazement.) What is it?
Me: A wild creature.
Swami: A manifestation of vital energy.

August 12, 1953

Swami: Please come in. How is everything with you?
Me: Fine. My friend Bobbie is coming to my apartment to dinner tonight. She is going to bring the dinner. Then we are going to Dr. Chaudhuri's class on Sri Aurobindo.
Swami: Ah! Your friend is becoming really interested in Vedanta. How did she like Chaudhuri last week?
Me: She liked it. I myself didn't go to it. Professor Spiegelberg was still having his class on Jung.
Swami: What did you learn about Jung?
Me: Last time it was about alchemy. Jung says that the alchemists were actually projecting their psychological problems into the laboratory and working them out there. The time before, the class was about synchronicity versus causality. The whole thing seems highly complicated and confused.
Swami: Jung is confused. He draws upon all sorts of things—Indian mysticism, yoga, alchemy—it impresses people.

See how it is: when a Divine Incarnation comes, there is a great upheaval and stimulation of thought in all fields. Everything begins to sprout and become activated—spirituality, materiality, art, science—everything flourishes.
Me: People will become confused with so many ideas.
Swami: Yes, but the worthless will die out, and the right things will last.
Me: I guess it works the same way on an individual level. The individual becomes energized in every way when he becomes spiritual.
Swami: Of course. Do you think it could happen collectively if not individually? See, Marie Louise, how it is—things are moving: Sri Aurobindo, the Academy of Asian Studies, the East-West Gallery. Indian ideas are beginning to spread. Only we lag behind.
Me: Vedanta can never be popular.
Swami: That is true.

Before I left, I told Swami that I had heard from Jackson, who had said that gloom permeated his soul. Swami looked deeply concerned. I was, of course, deeply concerned myself.

August 14, 1953

Swami: So Mr. Jackson isn't happy? (I told Swami of a traumatic experience Jackson had had as a child.) Yes; that could be it. Do you know what his real trouble is?

Me: No.

Swami: It is the outward tendency of his mind. The mind seeks enjoyment in the outside world. That is bound to bring frustration. It will go on and on. Only when the mind tunes inward to God do all those things clear up. The whole mind then becomes free.

It is a matter of *prana* [vital energy]—the energy goes into outward desires. Animals crave enjoyment; that is their whole life. Then there is the subhuman stage and the beginning of group life; the group makes laws that restrict the individual. If nature does not frustrate him, his own laws do. These frustrations twist the mind. Finally, man sees that there is no use in any of it and he stops striving for enjoyment through the senses. When that happens, no experience can affect his mind.

Look at people who are spiritual. Often they are poor, their bodies are sick, they go through miserable conditions, and yet they remain unaffected. It is not the experience itself that twists the mind, but the way one reacts towards it.

Me: Can't psychiatry help a little in clearing things up?

Swami: No. To see the experience that brought about the trouble doesn't help. The mind goes on the same way. What is one to do about it?

Me: I thought it might be like removing a cloud. Then one could turn to religion.

Swami: No. The terrible thing is that after discovering the cause of the trouble, it is still there. The person is the same person.

But Jackson is a good person. He will be all right—sometimes happy, sometimes unhappy.

(Referring to my sister) How is Mrs. Jones?

Me: She is all right. She is coming to town today. She and her husband are going to Hollywood for a vacation.

Swami: What is it they have been doing in Los Gatos?

Me: Well, this will be a vacation within a vacation.

Swami (laughing): Do you see your position? If you had not become embroiled in Vedanta, you could be taking vacations within vacations—and the mind becomes vacant.

Me: The trouble is, it doesn't; it stews.

Swami: No. It becomes vacant.

Me: My sister really has pulled herself out of that state she was in—or was pulled out of it. I think you helped her.

Swami: I am nothing. I haven't the power to help people.

Me: Not even Sri Ramakrishna had the power to help people.

Swami (shocked): Who told you that? He helped everyone. He liberated people with a touch.

Me: Only those who were ready.

Swami: No. He helped everyone.

Me: Why doesn't he do it now—for Jackson, for instance?

Swami: How do you know he doesn't? Do you think God should do things the way you think they should be done? You want things in a hurry and think, therefore, that God should do them that way. That is cheap. It is blasphemy to think that God should act according to the way you think He should act.

Sri Ramakrishna helped everyone. A Divine Incarnation comes for the sake of the whole world. It is true that his special mission was to train a group of close disciples—those special few who came with him—so that they could spread his teachings to the world. He told Holy Mother to look after the people of Calcutta; he left them in her care. You know how he scolded Swamiji for wanting to spend the rest of his life in *nirvikalpa samadhi* [absorption in the Absolute; oneness with Brahman]. He said to him, "I didn't know you were a small-minded person. I had hoped you would be like a great banyan tree under which people scorched by the world could seek shelter—and now you are thinking only of yourself." You know the story of how he went to call Swamiji down to the earth. He said, "You must come! The whole world is burning in misery!"

You want things to happen your way. How do you know Jackson is not being helped? Go on praying. Do your part. You stand on a mountain peak and want to pull him up by force, drag him up over all the jagged rocks. That would tear him to pieces. The compassionate thing is to point out the path that slopes gently around the mountain.

He wants enjoyment, but pain is also enjoyment. You see it subjectively, but look at it objectively, as in a play. All emotions must be there. You would not want to have a dinner composed of nothing but dessert. Don't you know that people enjoy their misery? If you take it away from them, they become more miserable. Pleasure and pain are both necessary to the mind—it thrives on them. To pull someone away quickly from the world is not good. The mind becomes blank. I have seen that happen. The mind loses its stimulus. You will have to learn these things.

(Mr. Clifton appeared in the doorway with an armload of maps.)

Swami (to me): All right, now. Please excuse me.

Despite all that Swami said, my heart still grieved over Jackson's gloom.

4

SWINGING UP INTO FREEDOM

I used to meditate in the late afternoons in the Temple auditorium, sitting cross-legged before the huge oil painting of Sri Ramakrishna. My meditation was a bumpy procedure, frequently interrupted by a heart heavy with concern over Jackson, who used to phone me now and then from Brooklyn Heights, where he was then living. It was clear to me that he was depressed and perhaps lonely.

On some days, my entire meditation hour was filled with prayer to Sri Ramakrishna that he take care of Jackson, give him happiness. I never experienced a reassuring response to this request. On the contrary, I seemed to hear Sri Ramakrishna say quite firmly, "Why are you thinking of such things now? You have renounced all that. Meditate."

I struggled to put my concern for Jackson out of my mind, but it seemed to hover in the Temple auditorium like a cloud, waiting. The moment I arranged myself before the altar, it descended upon me, dark and damp. I did not have the faith to simply place the problem in Sri Ramakrishna's hands, knowing he would do whatever needed to be done. I wanted an answer, loud and clear—a flashing of brilliant light. Nothing happened.

Then, one afternoon, there came from the wall on my left, where hung of portrait of Sri Sarada Devi—the spiritual consort of Sri Ramakrishna, best known to her devotees as Holy Mother—there came not fireworks but a gentle whisper, "Ask me." I turned to Holy Mother, knowing, as I should have known all along, that it was she who cared. I placed the problem before her mother's heart and at once felt the weight of it lift from my own heart and mind. It was as though she had said, softly, simply, "Will I not take care of my child?"

After that, I no longer worried about Jackson's state of mind. A few months later, I learned that he had married a cultured young woman who had every asset he could wish for, and, for all I knew, he lived happily ever after. I was free inside and out.

It never bothered me that in the monistic philosophy I believed in, there was room for prayer and answers to prayer. The level on which I lived and found to be real was a level on which God also lived and about which He—She—cared in abundant ways.

I did not tell Swami about my prayer, and it was years before I wanted to talk about it.

August 19, 1953

I came to the Temple at 10:00 p.m. after Dr. Chaudhuri's class at the American Academy of Asian Studies. Swami was working in the library. Two tables were drawn together. As usual during these sessions, the tables were covered with plans and samples of tile, paint, and so forth. Helen, Kathleen, Mara, and Jo were present.

Swami (seeing me): Come in. (He showed me the designs of chandeliers for the auditorium and then the tile for the rest rooms.)

Mara: Oh, I wish I had a bathroom like that.

Swami (furiously): What would you do? Wallow in it? Have a clean bathroom and clean water. That is enough.

August 21, 1953

Mr. Allan's funeral was held this morning. [Mr. Allan, a disciple of Swami Trigunatita, had been the president of the Vedanta Society of San Francisco when Swami Ashokananda arrived fresh from India in 1931. After a strained beginning, Mr. Allan came to deeply love and respect Swami Ashokananda and to support his work in every way.]

It was the first Vedantic funeral I have been to. It was very simple. There were no eulogies. Swami chanted from chapter 2 of the Gita in Sanskrit and translated the verses. He read Swamiji's poem on Goodwin's death. [J.J. Goodwin was a young Englishman who became Swami Vivekananda's disciple and secretary in America, taking down his lectures in shorthand and transcribing them for publication. Most of Vivekananda's *Complete Works* are due to Goodwin's devoted service. He died in India, much to Swamiji's shock and grief.]

Later, in Swami's office

Swami: Well, did you like the funeral?
Me: Yes. It was beautiful. I hope I die soon, so I can have one.
Swami (smiling): Someday someone will say services over me. Or maybe no one will. Maybe I will die alone by some mountain stream.
Me: However it is, I hope I die first.
Swami (kindly): Oh, no. Remember that the soul never dies. Always remember that the soul never dies. Well. That is that.

(He looked at temple plans and then at catalogues of bathroom fixtures. I took courage and interrupted to explain my theory of a silent toilet. This required diagrams.)

Me: I had them at the house on Chestnut Street.
Swami: What make were they?
Me: Oh, I don't know. Well, maybe Kohler and Kohler.
Swami: You are so unobservant. When you look at something you should see the whole thing—everything about it at a glance.

Me (getting up): I think I will go downtown to buy a coat.
Swami: All right. Better luck this time.

Mara, Kathleen, and I went downtown. I bought a coat. When we returned, Swami was in his office talking to Ediben. I stood in the doorway with the coat box.
Swami: Let us see it. Take it out of the box.
Ediben (laughing): Which one is this?
Me: Number six. *(Laughter.)*
Swami: That is all right. Nothing great is accomplished without a lot of commotion. (I modeled the coat. There was much discussion among devotees as to its pros and cons.) Keep it and wear it. Later you can buy another coat if you find this one doesn't suit the purpose. People will turn around and say, "Vedantists dress very smartly. My!"
Me: My brother-in-law thinks Vedantists look very stylish. He said he didn't see any signs of renunciation here. Everyone looked as though they had come straight out of I. Magnin [San Francisco's most expensive store for women's clothing]. (Swami laughed and put his head in his hands, as though chagrined.)
Swami (thinking of Mr. Allan): Life here is misery. We will never, never see him again. Each soul goes its own way. Anyhow, Sri Ramakrishna said that he would stand by all his devotees at their dying hour. That is certain. Holy Mother said that he gave his word. He also gave his word that none of his devotees would ever lack the bare necessities of life.

People who are growing old try to act like callow youths. Nothing could be more disgusting. If people as they grow older would sit back quietly, then others would see that they have really a vitality and vigor; their eyes would shine with an unquenchable and ever new youth and fullness from within. Well, I won't go on; I shouldn't talk about it until my own eyes shine.
Ediben: They never do anything else.

Swami (to Ediben, who was worrying about her daughter, Anne): How old is she now?
Ediben: Twenty-six.
Swami: Isn't she a little old and large for you to still carry in your womb?
Ediben: It *is* uncomfortable.
Swami: You all should have your dinner now. Go and have your dinner.
Me (upon leaving): You have trained me so well, Swami, to take the keys out of my car, that I took them out when I parked in a garage. They charged me $2.25 for having to move the car.
Swami (sternly): You will also learn to leave them in when you park in a garage. You will also learn that there are parking lots where you park the car yourself and take the keys. You will learn all those different things. *(Smiling)* That is civilization.

August 22, 1953

Swami (on his way upstairs): You look very happy. You must like the coat.
Me: No, I don't think I like it very much. I am happy anyhow.
Swami: Good. That is true happiness.

I decided I did not like the coat at all and took a bus downtown to Saks, where I returned it and finally found a coat I liked. This I took back to the Temple and left in its box, after modeling it for Mara, Jo, and Kathleen. Swami was not downstairs. I did not go to the Temple that evening but learned later that everyone wanted to show Swami the coat. He said, "No, let her show it herself."

Swami liked the coat; I kept it and wore it for many years.

August 24, 1953

Miriam Kennedy told Swami that Mr. Allan's relatives, who had come from the South to attend his funeral, were very much impressed by the concern and consideration Mrs. Allan's Vedantic friends showed her. One man said that his faith in human nature was restored and that no one he knew—not one of his friends—would show such kindness.

Swami (looking out the window, to himself): In the long run that is the important thing. *(To us)* It is genuine feeling that people appreciate. If you feel for them, they will listen to philosophy. If you don't feel for them and yet talk philosophy, they won't listen; it will even seem repugnant to them.

Later that day

Me: I have been reading a review of the Kinsey Report in *Life* magazine.

Swami: What did you learn from it?

Me: It seems that men have much more sexual energy than women. Have they, then, more spiritual energy?

Swami: No. Why would you think that would follow?

Me: Well, energy is energy. Sexual energy is transformed, transmuted into spiritual energy.

Swami: No. Sex is a manifestation of the outward tendency of the mind and senses. It is the strongest manifestation. I also have read reports of the book. I will read the book itself, or look through it, when it comes out. The findings seem quite revolutionary. I think Kinsey has missed a main point. Women find sexual satisfaction in more subtle ways than men. Psychologists know that now. They find it in such things as possessiveness, making a home, and so on. It is a more subtle form of the same thing.

Me: They use as much energy?

Swami: Yes.

That night

Mara and I came in at 10:30 after dinner at Edna's to celebrate Mara's birthday. Swami was in the library talking with Marion

Langerman, who was staying a few days in San Francisco. Kathleen and Jo had gone to get some ice cream. Swami welcomed Mara and me.

In the course of general conversation, Swami said, "Everything in the world that is not connected with spirituality becomes contemptible, futile, and ludicrous. But when even the most common thing is connected with God, it becomes fraught with meaning. If you accept the world as it is without criticism, it will contaminate you; and if you try to understand it, it will also contaminate you."

Mara: How will it contaminate you if you just accept it?

Swami: It will swallow you up.

My interviews with Swami were seldom private. Although he did give private interviews to new students and to old ones in need of overhauling, the general situation in his small office (which was sandwiched between the library and the back office) was that of a midtown clearinghouse. The activities of the Society in all their complex permutations passed through his hands for clarification, untangling, and solution. The problems of Olema, which included everything from erosion control to fierce boundary disputes with the neighbors, were legion and seemingly unending. In addition, the construction and landscaping of the new temples in San Francisco and Sacramento were complicated matters of constant concern.

The phone rang incessantly; people walked in and out of his office carrying rolls of blueprints, swatches of upholstery, or pieces of floor tile; financial questions needed his attention and letters his approval—there was, in fact, nothing connected with the work of the Society that did not pass through his office. In spite of all this, he himself seemed never disturbed or at a loss.

His decisions, his actions, and his reactions were instantly informed by the light of inner being—that divine light common to all life, but which in the crystal-clear mind of the yogi shines unobstructed. He seemed always centered in that light; his mind was always refreshed and replenished by it. He was a serene and clear reservoir from which one could draw buckets of knowledge and unconditional love.

At one time, Swami thought of delegating responsibility to a trained group of workers, but this proved to be premature. His students, however well intentioned and capable, acted with minds driven largely (as human minds generally are) by egotism and intellectual calculation, not yet by steady wisdom. Intellectual brilliance in itself comes to very different conclusions in its operations than does the mind of an illumined soul.

Swami's students were not stupid. They could have been successful in any worldly endeavor. But a religion that purports to be a means of communication between the world of matter and the world of spirit requires a different kind of leadership. The brunt of the work fell always upon Swami Ashokananda. Although this did not consume his spirit, the ceaseless and critical demands upon him took a severe toll on his physical health, which had never been robust, and of which he took little care.

August 25, 1953

I was in Swami's office for half or three-quarters of an hour. In the course of this time, he discussed with Miriam Kennedy the problem of finding a nursing home, at once inexpensive and good, for Mrs. Allan. The telephone rang, bringing to Swami's attention many other problems. I do not listen to these phone calls with enough attention to know all the complications and snarls that Swami deals with and solves.

Swami: What are you smiling at?

Me: Nothing. I feel happy.

Swami: I do not know, Marie Louise, how we will wind up this season. Pressure, pressure, pressure. It is not right. Can you get me that box over there? (In the box were the color schemes that he and Helen had chosen for the new temple lobby and auditorium. He showed them to me and tried out different colors against wallpaper samples of solid tones.)
Me: And you should be having a vacation!
Swami (smiling): Marie Louise, you are very kind and thoughtful, but what can I do?

Later, in the library

Swami: Worship of the Impersonal is looking upon others as Brahman, recognizing them as such. Then all smallness and pettiness are burned out. Our miseries all come from the thought that others are human beings—inferior or superior. Service, discrimination, reasoning—*(softly)* that is great worship.
Kathleen: We were reading that Holy Mother said that if one did *japa* 15,000 to 20,000 times a day one would attain God realization. Marion and I were figuring that that would take about five hours.
Swami: Yes. But what is five hours? Think of how you spend your day. You waste at least five hours. You could be saying *japa*.
Marion: But the mind gets tired.
Swami: Hup! You make a little effort and grow tired, so you give up. It is true that the brain gets tired, but you train it—a little more each day. If you were taking physical exercise, at first you would get tired and you would stop. Then the next day, you would do a little more, gradually increasing. You can say *japa* in snatches through the day—on a streetcar or bus, for instance, when there is nothing else to do. Do it for five minutes, then the next day increase it a little. That's the way. Through the day the mind grows calm; all the spaces are filled up.

Me: Should it always be said with concentration?
Swami: When you say *japa* during meditation, it should always be with full concentration; but when you are working, of course you cannot concentrate on it so much. There should always be some concentration; the more, the better.

(Swami then turned to Marion and asked her where she had had her dinner.)
Marion: At home.
Swami: Very good. *(Teasing her)* You are a holy person. *(To us, seriously)* Never eat in restaurants, unless you can't help it. If you want to keep your mind subtle and sensitive, you should eat at home. There are two kinds of people whom food in restaurants won't hurt: those who are worldly, whose minds are gross to begin with, and those who have realized that all is Brahman—nothing can affect them. Then there is the middle group who must be practical about it; eating out is poison to them.
Me: Is it because of the people in restaurants or because of the food?
Swami: If you had psychic perception, you would see that food touched by an impure person changes color. It poisons your whole system; your mind becomes clouded.

(I asked Swami if there would ever come a time when the world will know a period of peace and become stabilized.) Yes. I believe that we are entering into such a period. There will be peace and understanding between nations. People's minds will turn to spiritual things. After that, there will be degeneration, an age of darkness and small wars, in about one thousand years. After a rapid climb, there comes a hard fall.
Me: Is that what Sri Ramakrishna meant when he said, "Only the grass and bamboo will be left"?
Swami: Yes, that is right.
Me: Then there is a kind of balance between dark and light in time as well as in space?

Swami: There is a balance, period. When nations exist as separate units, they rise and fall separately; that is why at any given time there appears to be both good and evil in the world at the same time. One nation will be up, while the other is down. When the world becomes unified, it will rise and fall as a whole.
Me: From a great distance, would the times of depression appear to be beautiful, like parts of a rhythmic movement?
Swami: Why not think of your own life that way? After millions of lives of bondage, you are now swinging up into freedom—into the Absolute. If even in the small, daily things that happen you could take the position of observer, you would live in that Reality. The thing is to have the feeling that *It* [Absolute Reality] is. (Swami shone, as though he had this feeling.)
Me: In that way, one would live always in the present and therefore in eternity?
Swami: Yes. That is right.

August 28, 1953

I was asked by a devotee if I would drive her and another to Berkeley. I was none too eager and asked Swami if I should do it.
Swami: Don't ask me questions like that. Ask me metaphysical questions but not things like that.
Me: It is somewhat metaphysical.
Swami: Not enough. The point is that you people must learn to decide those things for yourselves. Otherwise, you become dependent and unable to make your own decisions. If you cannot make small decisions, then you will not be able to make big ones. One grows strong through small things. Decide it for yourself—but do not do anything under compulsion. You are not obligated to anyone. Always remember that! Never do anything under compulsion.
Me: What about service to the devotees?
Swami: You can find your own ways of serving them. If you feel

you have to serve them whenever you are asked, life will become unbearable.
Me: That is all I wanted to know.

August 29, 1953

Swami: We must have a place at the Olema retreat for old people. As it is now, they are just at the mercy of nurses. It is heartbreaking. A place like that would also give others a chance to serve. The only difficulty is that people would join the Society simply for that benefit in their old age. But we will have to do something.
Me: What is the use of old age? Is it so one can learn that the body is no good?
Swami: Yes. In spiritual life attachment drops away in old age.
Me: One shouldn't wish not to have it, then?
Swami: Why think about it at all? Live in the present. Remembering the past and anticipating the future is bondage.
Kathleen: What about people who suffer from amnesia? That doesn't make them free.
Swami: When one loses one's memory consciously, deliberately, and voluntarily, that is heaven; but when it just happens, it can be hell. When one just falls asleep, that is nothing; but when one consciously withdraws consciousness from the mind, body, and senses, that is *samadhi* [ecstatic trance]. It is easy to have *samadhi,* but you don't want it; the mind wants variation.
Kathleen: Well, God created variety too.
Swami: Don't talk rubbish!

September 1, 1953

Swami sent Jo for some ice cream. We ate it and chatted lightly. Then in the hall on his way upstairs, Swami said, "I think it is time for me to retire."
Jo: What will happen to us if you do that?

Swami (standing in the doorway): If you stay with Sri Ramakrishna and Swamiji, you will be all right. (He beamed at us radiantly.) If you stay on here and do as you are doing, you will have nothing to worry about; you will reach the highest.
Jo: I wish we could have that in writing.
Swami: What I say is gospel truth.

September 3, 1953

Swami told me that daylight saving time was going off—this after he had scolded me for being one hour late to the lecture. He had said, "Do you want a miserable companion to advise you of these things?" As I left, I pressed my palms together in salute.
Swami: Don't do like that! You are an American. Follow your own customs.

October 8, 1953

I was talking to Swami in his office when Nancy Tilden and Sally Martin came in. I rose to go, but he told me to stay.
Swami (to Sally): God is with form and He is also formless, isn't it so?
Sally: I don't know.
Swami: She wants to swallow the ocean, so she won't drink at the stream that is always running by.
Sally: I would be happy for even one cupful.
Nancy: I am glad the new temple work is going ahead.
Swami: It is a struggle, but I like struggle. We are lionhearted. Nothing great is accomplished without struggle. Eh? Roar like a lion! (He looked like a lion.)

(To Sally) If you can't see God, see the greatness in living men. There is greatness in nature—in huge mountains, in thunder and lightning—but it is an inanimate greatness. Think of the great poets and musicians, the great engineers. Learn to appreciate what is before your eyes; then you will learn to see more.

October 12, 1953

Swami: We will sign the contract for the new temple today.
Me: My, aren't you glad?
Swami (smiling wanly): I am too tired to be glad. If I were feeling normal—yes, I would be glad. What is needed are more friends. If we had money, it would ease everything.
Me: Maybe somebody will come along with lots of money.
Swami: Not in my time, but it is terrible to leave people with so great a burden.
Me: You have lifted the real burden.
Swami: No. Think of those boys in Sacramento who are doing all that backbreaking work. That is not what they came here for. They came to meditate and to grow spiritually.
Me: People say that those monks have progressed tremendously through working like that. Just from seeing their faces, people have said that.
Swami: Who?
Me: Well, Helen, for instance.
Swami: Even so, Marie Louise, that is not what they came for. Such terribly hard work! I think that is what weighs so heavily here (putting his hand on his heart).

Later that day

Swami (severely scolding two devotees): You think of nothing but yourselves. To me it is exactly as though you had rolled in the gutter and covered yourselves with filth. It tears me up. When, after all these years, you still think of yourself, comparing yourself with others and feeling sorry for yourself, I feel as though I had been stabbed in the back. Think of others. Do something for others.

(There was much more. When he had finished, he turned to me. I had been standing in the doorway, transfixed.) Hello! Please come in. Please sit down.

(In a more gentle way, he continued talking to the devotees.) If you do not know what to do for others, help them by your very being. Just the tone of your voice, the look in your eyes, can help people tremendously. If you have the right feeling in your heart, every word you say, the simplest word, will lift people.

One time when I was in the south of India I came to a temple. There was a monk standing there. He looked at me so kindly and said, "Where did you come from?" I will never forget it. There was such sweetness in his voice. In those simple words he imparted such love. When you can get that quality in your voice, you will be doing something. You can't force it; the feeling behind it is the thing that counts. If you could feel for others, Swamiji would be well pleased with you.

I have said these things so often. I shouldn't say them any more. You have given your whole self to God; don't you see that when you turn around and think of yourself, you are taking back your gift?

October 14, 1953

In the morning the offices, it seemed, were crowded with women, coming and going, talking, or milling around. Finally, I was told, Swami blew up and said he could stand it no longer. After laying everyone out, he went upstairs. There had been no magazine work just then, but a few days before much typing and bustle had been going on. Swami had said to me, "All this clacking of typewriters and flapping of papers. Why don't you move the magazine into Luke's apartment? You can divide some of the rent between you. She is leaving in a day or two and her apartment will be empty. Talk it over; make an independent decision." (Independently, we decided that we did not want Luke's apartment. However, it became obvious that Swami could not stand any more fuss and noise. We moved to Jeanette's place, to everyone's joy.)

That evening, after the lecture

Swami (to everyone in the back office): I can no longer stand crowds of people. There is nothing left in this body; it is drained out. My vacation did no good at all this year; it didn't make any change.

Ediben: It wasn't long enough.

Swami: In former years just a week would refresh me. This time nothing happened. I have been a monk all my life. I have never been accustomed to meeting people, to being around many people. Now my nerves simply will not stand it. I do not mean that I am not fond of each of you—you are all my students—or that I don't want you to feel free to come here. It is not that; never feel that. But it is all this unnecessary activity: passing in the hall, going to the bathroom, going to the kitchen, going back and forth, talking. I do not mean that you can't work on the magazine here. When you have reading to do or other work, certainly come here; but I will not have all this last-minute bustle going on. You will have to do it someplace else.

(He noticed the stark faces of the Berkeley devotees in the doorway.) Well, Sally, you should not hear all this. You are just starting out in life and you have to listen to an old man grumbling. (He folded his arms and leaned back in his chair and looked like an exceedingly young and healthy man.) I used to be able to enter into everything. Nothing was too much. Are you going to the *Durga Puja* [worship of the Divine Mother as the goddess Durga] in Berkeley?

Sally (determinedly): Yes. I will go.

Swami: You do not believe in it. But do you have to understand why air is necessary for life before you will breathe it? You go to the worship. Truth cannot hurt a man, and the untruth cannot hurt him—that is, if he himself is true and sincere.

One must go deep. You don't exist on the surface. If I touch you, I don't touch you but only your skin. You exist deep, deep down in the cavern of your being—deep, deep down. The *Katha*

Upanishad speaks of that. It is literally so. In a certain type of meditation, it is as though one enters into the cave of the heart, deep into the heart. A tunnel of light opens up. You have heard about the nerves that all lead to one nerve that leads to the heart. One literally sees that. It is as though one enters along that nerve to the depths of one's being, and there one comes into a realm of infinite light, infinite joy and festivity. All the world is filled with light. Trees, sky, the dust—everything seems to be bursting with honey. If you nudged the sky, heavy drops of honey would fall out.

October 31, 1953

Mara and I were talking to Swami in the hallway.
Swami (to Mara): Too much vacation and the mind becomes vacant. *(To me)* People who have no responsibility, nothing going on in the brain, have placid and serene faces, like your crazy friend, or like deaf people. They don't hear anything to disturb them; therefore, they are perfectly placid.
Mara: Sometimes it is an advantage to be deaf. Flossie [who was 100 years old] said it was wonderful. When she wants quiet, she just takes out the earphone.
Swami: In spiritual life everything can be turned to advantage. Every condition can be used to further one's progress. Of course, there is struggle, but there is joy in that kind of struggle because it is struggle for a purpose.
Me: What about pain, physical pain?
Swami: Yes. The spiritual person learns endurance through it. The mind learns to transcend it. One can turn pain to spiritual advantage. Hindus don't impose pain upon themselves as Christians do, but when it comes they use it; they learn to rise above it.

November 1, 1953

Kathleen, Mara, and Jeanette were sitting in the back office.
Swami (scolding Kathleen for an ill-advised remark): You have

the mentality of a dowager. All you need is a little more fat. You have become irresponsible like a dowager who thinks she can speak out anything and yet be respected.

(This went on for some time in scathing, lashing tones, after which the conversation resumed where it had left off.)

Swami (with eyes sparkling): Marie Louise, we have some new material about Swamiji that would make people sit up were it made known.

Me: Why don't we make it known?

Swami: All in good time. You found a lot of valuable things. I have other material. Some day we can put it together.

Josephine MacLeod [who devoted her life to Swami Vivekananda] always said that she was not a disciple of Swamiji, but a friend. However, she once said that Swamiji had told her to meditate on *Om*. When he asked her what result she had, she told him that she had seen light. Swamiji did not bother with formal initiation. She had probably heard of how people are ordinarily initiated—with ceremony and a mantra being whispered in the ear. But Swamiji did not have to bother with that rigmarole. Everyone he loved will attain to salvation. The Hale family, for instance, he loved very deeply, but they did as they pleased, thought as they pleased. They never became Vedantists. If Swamiji is true, then they need never worry about salvation. His love was enough.

November 2, 1953

Swami: Cheer up! Let the lion of Vedanta roar. Be happy. Make a hole in the world. This troublesome world is just a thin crust; poke a hole through it and the thick, sweet honey of Brahman will pour out.

Me: How can I make a hole?

Swami: Make your mind rest on Brahman. Dwell on Him. Know that in Him is all that the heart craves—all sweetness and love. All joy. Feel His presence. He is here.

November 6, 1953

Me: On Sundays in Los Gatos there are always guests.

Swami: Well, Marie Louise, see what you have given up—that life at Los Gatos with people, parties. You like people, don't you?

Me: No.

Swami: Yes. You like parties, acting silly, isn't it?

Me: Well, no. I used to hate them. But then I thought it was because I was maladjusted. So I learned to like them; for a while I became "the life of the party."

Swami (wryly): I thought so.

(I had been recently thinking about this phase of my life with some nostalgia, but I had not mentioned it. Swami knew. Those few words drove the whole thing from my mind.)

November 8, 1953

Me: I feel that there is some sort of stubborn creature inside of me that is putting up a terrible resistance.

Swami: What does it want to do?

Me: It doesn't want to do anything. That is just it; it wants to do nothing at all.

Swami: That is the negative side. What does it want to do on the positive side?

Me: Nothing. It refuses to do anything.

Swami: That is called spiritual struggle. Do you think there is anyone who hasn't had to struggle? You are not the only one. It is bound to happen. These periods of depression come because you are not fully enlightened. It is as though in climbing a high mountain you had reached a plateau. It is all level and beautiful there and you walk along without effort for a long time, enjoying the scenery, but you come to the end of it and have to start climbing again through a jungle—but it is all on the way up. Again you will come out onto a plateau on a higher level.

Me: I feel that I have gone back down into a jungle, not up into one.

Swami: Certainly. Jungle is jungle; they are similar in appearance. But you haven't gone back.
Me: I feel that to do anything at all is an unbearable effort, even to think about doing anything.
Swami: Take it easy for a few days. Don't take these moods too seriously; soothe it a little. I used to have a pain in my stomach, and I found that if I just stroked over it gently, it would disappear. (What a familiar gesture this was: Swami stroking his right side gently or—even more familiar—pressing his thumb into his side to relieve the pain.) It will pass; everything passes.

You must learn to regulate your life. Keep regular hours. That is very important. It doesn't matter if the work you do is good or bad, but do it regularly. Regularity in life is like the structure of a building. The hidden arches and supports of a building are the most important thing. A regular life, building up of good habits, is the foundation of spirituality. Keep regular hours.
Me: I can't.
Swami: Then there is no hope. (We stared at one another in silence.)

"I can't" (giving a perfect imitation of a weak little voice). If you were in a concentration camp under Hitler, you could do it . . . or if you were in the army. Men who have never gotten up early have been straightened around after a week or two in the army. If they don't get up, a tough sergeant will lash them until they do. When external pressure is brought to bear, you can do anything. As it is, your own mind has to lash you. Force yourself. Actually, you have no choice. You have to go on struggling for God. You are caught in a vice.

(He turned in his chair to get a book from the bookcase behind him, then back to me, speaking gently.) You will have happiness in life, Marie Louise, but not till later.
Me: In this life?
Swami: Certainly in this life.

(He yawned and leaned back, smiling.) Someday I will be lazy honorably. In three or four years, if I live that long, everything will be finished. Then I can be lazy with a good conscience.
Me: You could now; you have done so much.
Swami: No. If the work that has been started is not finished, all will have gone to waste. When the debts are paid off and the new temple and Sacramento are finished, and when Olema is well on its way—then I will be able to rest.
Me: To speak very selfishly, I hope those things will take a long time. They will keep you here.
Swami: Yes. If there were not those things, I wouldn't stay alive. There would be no purpose. Without a purpose, there is nothing to hold me here.

November 9, 1953

Swami: You have to face the fact that there is no other way. As long as the mind thinks there is another way, it will cause trouble. You will have to live a spiritual life sooner or later, but you may never get a better chance than now.

(Swami asked me if I had seen my friend Bobbie.)
Me: I will see her tonight. The last time I saw her I made the mistake of indulging in talk about the past. It had a bad effect on me.
Swami: Never do that! There is too much pressure on you. It would be different if you just came to lectures and thought a little more deeply than ordinarily. But you have put pressure on yourself. You never go to parties or entertainments or see any of the people you used to know. That is why the mind has such a violent reaction.

November 13, 1953

Swami (to me, on his way out): You have to lift yourself by yourself. In the Gita it says that. (He quoted the verse in Sanskrit, then repeated it in English.) "Let a man be lifted by his own self;

let him not lower himself; for he himself is his friend, and he himself is his enemy." You see, it is the truth. Sri Krishna has said that. It is not just talk or a nice idea. It is true.

November 14, 1953

Swami: Are you feeling better?
Me: Yes.
Swami: You see. If you push up, things get better.
Me: Yes.
Swami (sternly): Never push yourself deeper into a depression. That is indulgence. I have no sympathy with that. There are people who get a little sick and then take to bed and stay there. In that way they get what they want. Everyone waits on them and nothing is expected of them—at least, that is what they think. They avoid all responsibility. There is also a moral and spiritual invalidism.

Of course, one cannot avoid the original depression, just as one sometimes cannot avoid a slight illness. There is nothing wrong with that; it is bound to come as a reaction.
Me: A reaction to what?
Swami: You have been struggling, straining your nerves and mind, trying to mold them into a new pattern. The mind gets tired and wants to go back to its old ways. It wants to contract.
Me: Yes. It felt like that.
Swami: Never talk to worldly people about your problems. Do not even talk to devotees who are married or have children. They will sympathize with you and unsettle your mind. Ediben is different. She is a very exceptional person.

November 26, 1953

Swami: Feel His presence everywhere and that you are a part of it.
Me: Is that all that is necessary?

Swami: Patience, endurance, patience—no matter what the external circumstances, have patience. Do everything exactly right in speech and deed. Always act selflessly. Conduct is very important. Things look brown?
Me: Somewhat.
Swami: Not golden?
Me: As though they should be golden, but they are not.
Swami: That happens in the middle state. It is a difficult time. Mind is still divided. Be extremely careful. Contact with worldly life is extremely dangerous. The mind could turn.
Me: I don't want a worldly life.
Swami: You don't—the mind does. That is the nature of the mind. That is why you should not go to Los Gatos when crowds are there.
Me: The kind of crowd that is there nowadays doesn't appeal to me.
Swami (sternly): Nonetheless, some slight thing could turn the mind.
Me: I feel that something doesn't wake up inside of me.
Swami (smiling): It will wake up.
Me: As I was waking up the other morning, I was half dreaming of how my whole being was an offering to God. But then I saw this self that was the offering; I could feel my whole self through and through, and I was crazy about it. I did not see how I could ever give that up.
Swami: Yes, but the strength of that is also illusory. In Olema one year we used a spray to kill some weeds, but instead of dying, they grew to tremendous proportions, huge stalks. We tried to cut them down; I myself worked at it. Then it occurred to me that perhaps this violent growth was the way of destruction—they would just exhaust themselves, burn themselves out. Later we found, where we had not cut, there was a cleared space without a single trace of weed; not a shred was left. They had just

flared up to be completely destroyed. That is the way it is in spiritual life. Things flare up with tremendous strength before they become annihilated. Find fault with worldly life; deliberately pick it to pieces. Appreciate the value of spiritual life.

November 20, 1953

Swami: I am like a rubber band that has been stretched and stretched and stretched and has no more resilience. I used to come back, but now I stay stretched.

December 27, 1953

Sally Martin: I get confused with people saying the world is real, then saying it is unreal.

Swami: Well, if you want a partial answer to this question, I shall say yes, the world is real. It is real because I see it as spiritual substance. Western philosophers say it is impossible to separate form and substance. I don't care what they say, because I see clearly that form and substance are separate and there is one divine substance behind all this. Do you think I could joke with you, tease you, love you, and care for you if I saw you as form? No, it just would not work. I would become entangled. If you separate your own body from Spirit, you can see everyone as divine substance separate from form.

The original temple (later called the Old Temple) in San Francisco, Vedanta Society of Northern California

Swami Ashokananda in his office at the Old Temple

The house on Fillmore Street where the author lived in the top rear apartment from 1951 to 1969

Swami Shantaswarupananda, Edith Soulé, and Dr. Haridas Chaudhuri after the dedication of the American Academy of Asian Studies in San Francisco, 1952

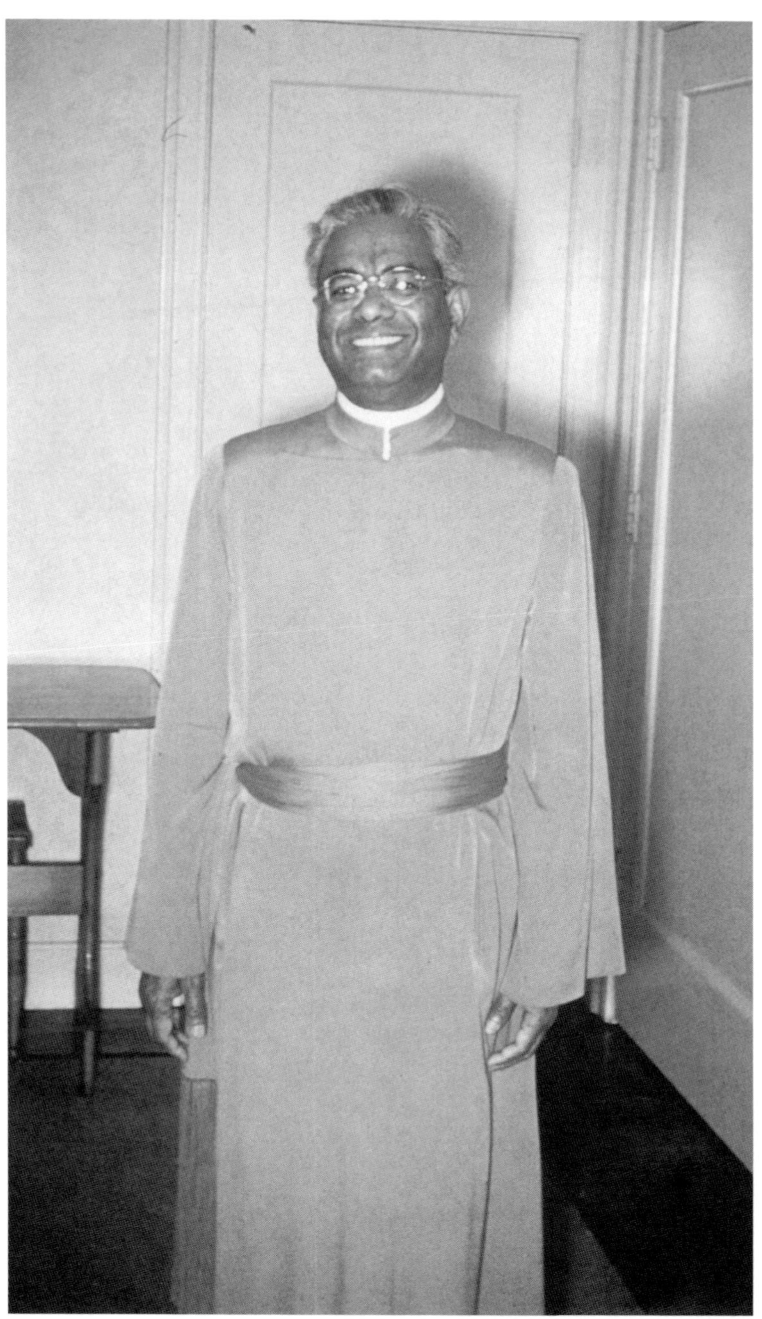

Swami Ashokananda after a lecture
at the Berkeley Temple, 1950s

Dorothy Madison, Swami Ashokananda, and Anna Webster
at the Vedanta Retreat at Olema, 1950

Workers at Olema, 1950.
Left to right: Jeanette Vollmer, Josephine Stanbury, Swami Ashokananda, Anna Webster, and Marion Langerman.

Virginia Varrentzoff *(left)* and Kathy Wyatt (now Pravrajika Vijnanaprana) at Olema, 1961

Dorothy Madison *(left)* and Mary Lou Williams at Olema, 1970

Marie Louise Burke at Mount Rose, 1956

Swami Ashokananda at Mount Rose, 1955

Picnic at Mount Rose, 1957.
Left to right: Helen Sutherland, Swami Ashokananda,
Marie Louise Burke, Marie Chenoweth, and Swami Akhilananda.

Swami Ashokananda in his cabin at Lake Tahoe, 1957

On the porch of Swami's cabin at Lake Tahoe, 1957.
In front, left to right: Marie Louise Burke, Marie Chenoweth, and Helen Sutherland. *Standing:* Swami Ashokananda, Swami Akhilananda, and Gladys Harvey.

Retreatants at Lake Tahoe, 1957.
Left to right: Dora Blaney, Marie Louise Burke, Edith Soulé, Carol Weston, Unknown, Edna Zulch, and Mara Lane.

Jo and Helen's cabin at Lake Tahoe.
Inset: Marie Louise Burke reading in the cabin, 1957.

5

DON'T WOBBLE!

1954

In 1954 my journal was left neglected. I was hard at work, at last, on writing day and night and doing research to boot. The magazine that had been restarted with trial issues in 1952 was a hungry dragon, demanding that articles and stories be delivered punctually. In addition, I was struggling to write about Swami Vivekananda while continuing to do research on his life in America. This last required the hateful task of writing innumerable letters to librarians throughout the United States (who were, as it happened, invariably gracious and helpful). For these reasons, my journal lay unopened on my desk for most of the year, except for sporadic entries that I found helpful on spiritual practice—a sampling of which follows.

March 3, 1954

Samples of rubber tile for the new temple were scattered on the floor in the hallway of the Old Temple. Swami sat on a chair and a group of devotees stood around him after the Wednesday night lecture. He was tired, but he talked with us from 10:30 to 11:45 p.m. Elna Olsen remarked upon the hour. Swami said, "Oh my—I have given two lectures."

The Sunday before he had also given "two lectures" when we stood about in his office until nearly six o'clock. On that occasion, when he realized how late it was, he said, "If one of the devotees [probably Jo] knew what you had been doing, she would have driven you out of here with a whip." He had had no food, or drink, or rest since early morning. "We are very selfish," I said. Swami said, "No, you are not selfish; you are inhuman. A selfish person has some decency left in regard to others. You are just inhuman."

Now we were being inhuman again, forcing questions upon him. His words flowed out in such a torrent that I can't remember them all.

Swami (to Sally): Did you like the lecture?

Sally: I found it very interesting. I enjoyed it very much.

Swami (laughing): My! She is becoming very aware of semantics.

Sally: I had hoped you wouldn't ask me.

Swami: Why—didn't you like it?

Sally: I like to hear about spiritual life.

Swami: What is spiritual life?

Sally: It is getting away from all the things you advocated in your lecture.

During his lecture, "The Coming of the Universal Man," Swami had spoken of the necessity in this age to become familiar with all cultures and ideas and had explained that this could be done only by referring all to the underlying, unifying Spirit.

Swami: There is a phase of spiritual life in which things of the world should be shunned, but later one takes a different view of them. One sees everything as Brahman. Sri Ramakrishna spoke of spiritual life as a ladder reaching to the roof. When you reach the roof you see that the stairs are made of the same material. Then you can go up and down.

If you want to realize God, the quickest way is to follow His manifestation in the age in which you live. Serve Him according to the spirit of the age. The spirit of this age is expansion and the service of man. There are, of course, many ways to think of service. Some do service to the glory of God or the glory of Christ; some for the purification of the mind, as Shankara taught. In Shankara's time, and also in Buddha's time, there was a great urge toward renunciation and contemplation. Hundreds of men and women wanted nothing but to realize God—to turn from the world entirely.

In this age, Swamiji taught service through the worship of Brahman in man. Some interpret this to mean the worship of the Divine dwelling in the heart of man, but Swamiji meant that man himself is actually Brahman—the whole man is Brahman Himself. Of course, one cannot do this kind of service without some meditation. But one cannot sit and meditate all the time; therefore, work with the consciousness that man is Brahman.

Miriam King: Swami, is intellectual knowledge a barrier to spiritual progress?

Swami: Sometimes it can be a barrier. It is a barrier unless spiritual knowledge is known to be the highest goal. It can also be a barrier if all one's best energies go into the pursuit of intellectual things.

(It was growing late. Someone had the sense to remind Swami again of the hour. He said, "Yes, all of you must go home now.")

March 1954

Swami: Do your best, every day your best. Don't torment yourself. I do not believe in that. What is the sense of making resolves and not keeping them? So much energy is lost in regret. Just do your best—that is all. You will be surprised how things will open up. Become a great scholar.

Me: All right. I won't despair even though it seems impossible that I should ever be a great scholar.

April 1, 1954

Swami: Devotion! Nothing can be accomplished without devotion. No real work can be done; there is no motive power without devotion.
Me: But devotion seems to be something spontaneous, not something one can acquire.
Swami: No, one can acquire it—through *japa,* through thinking of God. Of course, one must have the desire for devotion; one's intention must be to make devotion grow. A priest can go through all sorts of worship and ritual, but nothing will grow within him if he does not desire devotion to Christ. Some earnestly do their work for the sake of Christ, and then devotion grows in their hearts.

April 4, 1954

Me: Yesterday morning I woke up dreaming about the Ranch at Los Gatos. I woke up crying and I cried for a long time. It is not that I want to go there now—I don't. I was thinking about the way it was, something about the way of life there. The thought of it was just overwhelming.

(Swami smiled and nodded as though he had known this; I was so emotional about it, he must have sensed it.)

Swami: That is what the mind does. It picks out the good things from the past—the highlights.
Me: Yes, I tried to think that what I liked so much about it was really God Himself, and the thing to do is to find Him.
Swami: Yes.
Me: It was frightening. I thought that when I die, I will be thinking only about the Ranch and wanting that.
Swami (smiling): Then in your next life you will be born as a gopher in Los Gatos.

Me (continuing my thought): I was also afraid that it might take thousands of lives before those same happy circumstances could be duplicated. (I meant at the Ranch, but Swami understood me to mean the circumstances of my spiritual life—which was, of course, more to the point.)

Swami: You are absolutely right. It is said that it takes eight million lives before a person is ready to give up the world for God. Of course, it is a little different when a Divine Incarnation comes. If you get in the stream, it will sweep you on—providing you stay in it.

Be extremely cautious. Don't allow your mind to slip back. People cover the world with glamour. The glamour was all in your eyes. Actually there was a lot wrong with it; of course, there was good too or you wouldn't be thinking of it.

April 5, 1954

Swami (looking up from his book at me): Be strong. Don't wobble! Be strong—there is no substitute for strength.

July 16, 1954

Kathleen was in Swami's office. I went by, not intending to stop. Swami called me.

Swami: Hello! What is the matter? You seem subdued.

Me: I feel subdued.

Swami: Is something the matter?

Me: Internally, not externally.

Swami: What is it?

Me (with hesitation): Well, I feel that I am just skipping around on the surface. I feel I should go deep, but I don't know how.

Swami (kindly): That is a very good thought to have. Just by having it, you will go deeper. Please sit down.

(Others appeared in the doorway and the conversation became general.)

July 28, 1954

Swami asked me why I had returned so soon from Los Gatos. I had gone Monday and come back Tuesday. I told him. He spoke about living a spiritual life.

Me: I do not do all I should.

Swami: Why don't you?

Me: I don't know. I guess I haven't the willpower.

Swami: Develop willpower. Do you think it just falls from the sky?

Me: One has to have it in the first place in order to develop it.

Swami: You have enough to start with—build it up. *(After a few minutes)* To find happiness in God is a good sign. Sri Ramakrishna is like a flaming fire, a huge forest fire. Everything will burn in its path. You think you are too wet to catch fire?

Me: Yes.

Swami: No. You cannot be too wet. Everything will catch fire from that flame.

Me: Is it inevitable?

Swami: Yes, it is inevitable as long as you stay with him. Swamiji said that Sri Ramakrishna lifted not only this plane but the other *lokas* [spheres of existence]. Think of the power he had! Swamiji was the one who understood him. If he said that about him, it is true. Approach him.

Me: How can I know that I approach him?

Swami: Through me.

October 7, 1954

I came into the office to talk with Swami at 7:00 p.m. after I had meditated.

Swami: Please come in. Sit down. Is your meditation better?

Me: For a while it was; now it is no more.

Swami: If it was for a while, then it will be again.

Me (on the verge of tears): I think there is no hope.

Swami: Have you any alternative?

Me: No.

Swami: Then don't talk that way. Others have found it; why shouldn't you? Or are you going to be original and give up?

Me: No.

Swami: You know it is there.

Me: I don't know it is there.

Swami (forcefully): Forget all that. You are told to know it. You are not supposed to do original research. *(Smiling)* Don't give up in midstream. You will be all right and *(very sweetly)* you are not alone.

6

NEW DISCOVERIES

1955

When I look back on it, I realize that Swami had taken on a handful in me—as indeed he once said. He wanted me to write on command. I had written before; in fact, writing was what I had always wanted to do, but in my own way, at my own pace and for my own pleasure. I had no concept of working as though for a living—pounding out copy whether in the mood or not. Although I had made many resolves to work regularly and steadily, a persistent inertia had overcome my best intentions.

Now I faced not only a bimonthly magazine deadline but also the growing demands of my book about Swami Vivekananda that I had begun work on the previous year. The idea of writing about the greatest man who, I was sure, had ever walked on this earth—a man whom I could not possibly understand—did not inspire me; it paralyzed me. I had, it is true, what I considered to be a divine mandate to write about him, but I must admit that I was not enraptured by the commission, nor did I feel competent to fulfill it.

In the first two months of 1955, a deadline loomed for the next issue of *The Voice of India*, which we managed to meet at midnight on February 28. No sooner had we finished one typed copy and a carbon, and bound them separately in heavy, colored paper with contrasting tape for a spine, than Swami said, "Now, tomorrow, start work on the next issue." Exhausted, we did not obey to the letter.

March 2, 1955

Swami: Are you starting to work on the next magazine?
Me: No.
Swami: Get started. A good subject for you to write on would be "Is Man Hopeless?"
Me: Oh yes, I had thought of something like that. I was going to call it "Should Man Despair?"
Swami: Very good. The Catholic Church takes the line that man on his own is hopeless.
Me: Should I write the article from all different angles?
Swami: Certainly, make it comprehensive. Agitate the brain cells. Bring out all those cells that you have stored away in the gray matter. God alone knows what you are saving them for.
Me: I don't think I have any.
Swami: That is also a way of cheating. If someone comes to a man and asks for help and the man says, "I haven't got anything," what can anyone do? Learn to be a hack writer.

As for the book, Swami Ashokananda felt that a book about Swamiji based on the new research material should first come out as a series of articles for *Prabuddha Bharata* (one of the Order's English-language journals).

As far as I was concerned that was fine, but I could not get started. Days, if not weeks, went by; in the end, after refusing to listen to my protestations of inability, Swami had to dictate the first paragraph to me. "Put it in your own words," he said. After that I was on my own, but the first dam had been breached and the water started flowing—in fits and starts. I came up against many dams after that first blockade. "Push on!" Swami would say. "Write without fussing about style. Later you can go back and polish what you have done. Just write! You will find that the dam will break and things will flow." And, invariably, it would happen like that.

Sometimes, however, I embarked on some complicated theory about Swamiji or his mission and could not, no matter how laboriously I tried, make it work out. I could not write it. Then, after I had spent days of this frustrating effort, Swami would phone me.

"What are you doing?" he would ask.

"I am trying to write about . . . " And I would tell him my idea.

"Don't get into that!" he would say forcibly. "You will end up in a snarl."

My relief would be great, and I would throw out all the complicated snarls I was already in and get back to the main track of the story.

It was not only at such times that Swami would phone. Once, I decided to clean the kitchen stove, which from the time I had moved into the apartment badly needed a thorough scrubbing. I had probably hit a snag in the writing and the stove called out to me. I was deep in the cleaning process when the phone rang.

"What are you doing?" Swami demanded.

"I am cleaning the stove," I replied, feeling very virtuous to be finally doing such a messy and much needed piece of work.

He exploded. "What! Is that the way you write about Swamiji, by cleaning the stove?"

It was months before he got over this. "Do you know how she spends her time?" he would say to a roomful of devotees. "She cleans her stove!"

He would also phone when I was not cleaning the stove but

reading the *New Yorker* (in its halcyon days) or a book that I thought was relevant to my research—or, very likely, just a book. I would be admonished and sent back to my desk.

Sometimes he phoned when I had hit a large dam and was in despair. At those times he consoled me and encouraged me to go ahead.

Throughout the writing of the entire first book, *Swami Vivekananda in America: New Discoveries,* he kept his finger on every minute of it, and also on every word and comma. I would write several pages, perhaps ten or twelve, and show them to him. After he had read them, he would call me into his office. I would stand on his right, and he would go over the text sentence by sentence, pointing out my mistakes—anything from misplaced or omitted commas to errors of syntax, fact, or thought. In my days of "inspirational" writing, I had never paid much attention to things like commas. I was woefully ignorant, and those sessions with Swami were an education in the technique of writing. He would say with pride, "I am a good editor, isn't it?" And I would assure him (he who had become famous as the editor of *Prabuddha Bharata*) that indeed he was.

I also learned a great deal in this respect from Edna Zulch, one of the co-editors of *The Voice of India.* She told me patiently and with humor about such things as parallel constructions, the difference between relative and nonrelative clauses, and the unforgivable sin of dangling participles—all things that I never learned in high school but had somehow managed to get right, part of the time at least, by ear. In those days there were very few books (barring Fowler's *Modern English Usage*) on the subject of literary style. Strunk and White's *The Elements of Style* wasn't published in book form until 1957. Eric Partridge's *Usage and Abusage* first came out in America in the 1960s. In the very early 1950s I used to comb the bookstores for books on how to write—to no avail. Later in the 1950s they began to appear and I pored over them with delight, eagerly learning something that I had earlier overlooked, or forgotten, or never knew.

Swami Ashokananda, though, was my first teacher in the matter of writing. Always patient and always gentle, he never made me feel embarrassed by my mistakes. Sometimes he would simply return a marked-up manuscript to me. Except for an occasional large and baffling question mark in the left margin, his corrections were clear enough.

Once, early on, as he was going over my work with me, he wanted to see some research material. "I haven't got it with me," I said. "Where is it?" he demanded. I had to tell him that I didn't know, that perhaps it was at Jeanette's apartment, where I had been working on the magazine. That confession incited a long and intense admonishment, one sentence of which burned itself into my mind: "You will never be able to do this work if you are not organized!" I remember the torture of sorting out after that the welter of research material that I had accumulated. I would thenceforth always bring to my sessions with him a file box full of the material pertinent to the matter at hand; it was not neat, but it was all there. Years later he once said with a sort of parental pride, "Marie Louise is very well organized," and with a smile he added, "in her own way."

ONE BY ONE, the serial articles for *Prabuddha Bharata* were written and sent off to India. This process was still going on in August when, to my surprise, Swami asked me to go to the Society's retreat at Lake Tahoe in the summer or early fall of 1955. It would be the first of my many summers at the lake.

I thought something was up because of the car. Swami suddenly asked me if my car was in good shape. He told me to have it looked at, going into detail as to what I should have checked. I did all this. The next day he asked if I had had it done. "Yes,"

I said. "Did you have the radiator checked?" he asked. "No," I said. (He hadn't mentioned the radiator.) Swami sighed, "Marie Louise, you are becoming too dependent on me. I take care of you too much."

Something *was* up. I soon found out that I was to go to Lake Tahoe for a rest, and also to work—mainly to work. As Swami said, "It is not to be a pleasure trip. The altitude will clear your brain so that you can work better."

It was necessary for me to take someone with me, someone who could type as I wrote. Who? There seemed no one; then one day Ediben handed me a list of devotees. "Look through that," she said, "and pick someone." As I took the sheet of paper, I looked up into the rosy face of Virginia Varrentzoff, who was sitting in front of me. "How about that one?" I asked. Virginia beamed like the sun. Swami approved. "She has made a very good choice," he told Ediben.

Virginia and I were alone together in Ediben's cabin at Tahoe for nine days. I worked on the Detroit section of "New Discoveries." Virginia typed as I wrote. She also did the grocery shopping and cooking. The days were warm and still. We ate dinner on the porch and watched the shadow of night creep up the mountains across the lake.

Swami arrived at his cabin on Friday, August 26. He came over to see us around five-thirty. He sat on the porch, looking tired. He talked to Virginia and me. Jo told me later that Miriam King had left the convent for parts unknown and that Swami was terribly worried and hurt.

Meanwhile, Virginia felt that she should go back to San Francisco because Chela, her daughter, was unhappy at summer camp and wanted to come home. This caused Virginia much anguish. "Yes," Swami told her, "you should go." He no doubt knew that she felt sad, and so arranged to take us to Mount Rose [a mountainous area north of the lake] for a picnic on Saturday. Virginia was thrilled.

That summer Swami became absorbed in reading the letters of Swami Vivekananda in the light of "New Discoveries." He found many passages that he wanted me to insert in the manuscript, which meant tearing apart my painstakingly joined paragraphs in order to accommodate them. I must have been exhausted by then, having worked steadily for almost a year, both at the book and the magazine. Whenever I saw Swami approaching our cabin with volumes of *The Complete Works of Swami Vivekananda* in his hands, I would run to take a Miltown (one of the first tranquilizers on the market) to quiet my nerves. Somehow he knew.

"I am afraid to come here," he said to Ediben in my presence and with a twinkle deep in his eyes. "Whenever Marie Louise sees me coming, she runs to take a Miltown." I protested that it was in order to clear my brain so that I could understand him better. But he did not accept that reason, which actually was a true one.

THE *PRABUDDHA BHARATA* ARTICLES were published in 1955 in monthly issues from March through September. They were titled "New Discoveries Regarding Swami Vivekananda, by an American Devotee," and they dealt with whatever I had found that had not been known before about Swamiji's life and work in America from his arrival in Chicago in July of 1893 until he left Memphis, Tennessee, on January 22, 1894. The articles were well received in India. Swami Gambhirananda, then president of Advaita Ashrama, wanted to publish a book along the same lines that would cover Swamiji's entire visit in America. Meanwhile, I had been gathering more new material, about his stay in Detroit, for instance. So I soon found myself writing a full book instead of monthly articles.

I sometimes wonder if any other book was written and published in quite the same way as *Swami Vivekananda in America:*

New Discoveries. Generally, I think, a complete manuscript is received and accepted by the publishers before printing begins. It was not so in this case. As I wrote each chapter, we sent it to Advaita Ashrama in Calcutta and, as further writing was going on, we received page proofs.

Swami had insisted on seeing page proofs, not galleys, because the abundant inclusion of newspaper articles made the composition of pages extremely tricky. With his editor's eye and meticulous attention to detail, Swami demanded, for instance, that the headlines of the newspapers come on the same page as the body of the news article. The Calcutta compositors rarely, if ever, got this right, and Swami recomposed page after page. He was an expert at this, for his composition in 1930 of Romain Rolland's book, *Prophets of the New India,* with its voluminous footnotes, had given him good practice.

The *New Discoveries* copy was sometimes impossible to adjust. Often I would have to rewrite a paragraph or two, adding words or subtracting them, so that the usually extensive headlines would fall were they should. And, of course, this adjusting would affect the layout of the entire chapter. Nor would this be the end: the compositors in India did not always follow directions, and often a second batch of the same proofs would go back to Calcutta, again marked up, to be recomposed and sent back to San Francisco. This would give me more time to write the coming chapters, but eventually Advaita Ashrama caught up with me and at the end there was a rush.

I remember speeding to the main San Francisco post office with the latest installment ready to mail. Swami sent Miriam Kennedy, who was extremely efficient, with me to negotiate with the postal clerk and to register the manila envelope while I stood by, fuming. Could I not do this myself? It was a lesson in patience and humility. Miriam and I mailed each chapter twice—on different days, as Swami recommended, in case the first mailing went astray. Then page proofs of earlier chapters would arrive from India. And so it went, until the book was published.

Swami had put his heart into this book about his hero, Swami Vivekananda, from its very start to its completion. He was also editing me, and after a time I learned to write at will, whether I felt like it or not—I became a "hack writer." "Be prayerful when you write," Swami had said at the beginning; so gradually, over the next three years, I turned my resistance into prayer and finished the first book in early 1957.

That summer of 1955, Miriam King, who had secretly fled from the convent, was discovered in Hollywood. Swami insisted that she come to Lake Tahoe by bus to talk with him. She arrived on September 10. Miriam later told me that Swami said to her, "You could not have hurt me more if you had thrown a bucket of hot tar in my face." For the rest of the summer he gave her his full attention (except for reading Swamiji's letters) in an effort to win her back. He succeeded—temporarily.

That was a shattering summer for me. Without Swami's attention, I was an infant abandoned. I knew better, but knowing and feeling were two very different things and could by no means be brought in accord with one another. I hid my shameful heartbreak from Swami with apparent success, but there was no cure for it. I hid it also from Miriam; she and I got along very well, laughed together, liked each other. Back in San Francisco, Swami's attention was still riveted upon her; nevertheless, in a year or so she left for good without a word. She just left. Swami was, of course, pierced through.

In the fall of 1955 I developed a severe and, for a time, undiagnosed case of hyperthyroidism. My eyes burned and my pulse rate was habitually well over ninety. Because I was ill, Swami began to take me on drives through Golden Gate Park with Ediben at the wheel and me in the back seat. These afternoon outings took time away from Swami's rest, which he badly needed, but he would not listen to that side of it—not from anyone.

November 14, 1955

As Swami, Ediben, and I drove through the park, Swami gave me much needed words of encouragement.

Swami: Whenever one tries to work for Swami Vivekananda there are always obstructions. Don't think that Swamiji can't get hundreds of people to work for him. It is our great privilege to be allowed to work for him and for Sri Ramakrishna.

The book [*New Discoveries*] will help *many* people. Do you think that the world will like that? No—obstructions are put in the way of every good work. That is a fact. Push on! I am afraid you will not finish.

November 15, 1955

Swami went to the Olema retreat. Before going, he took Ediben, Jo, Anna Webster, and me to see the new temple (then in the final stages of construction) to decide about grills over the air vents in the auditorium.

Ediben (to me): Once you have felt jealousy in connection with your guru and conquer it, you will be rid of it forever.

Me: I conquer it only because Swami is so good to me.

Ediben: But of course he helps you—that is what the guru does.

November 26, 1955

Almost every day Swami, Ediben, and I drive around and around through Golden Gate Park. How beautiful the trees are—every shade of green and every shape and height, and now in the autumn, yellow and red, too.

Invariably we stop at the Japanese Tea Garden. I get out, and Swami says: "Buy two bags of fortune cookies, three bags of sesame cookies, four bags of melon candy." He gives me the money—a crisp five-dollar bill. I ask for change in clean, crisp one-dollar bills. The Japanese girl looks at me as though I were mad. Then we drive on. Swami opens a bag of fortune cookies and breaks one in half, giving half to Ediben, half to me. Then he eats one himself. The first time he did this, he read out the fortune: "'Your dearest wish will come true.' That is for you, Marie Louise," he said. "Before I opened it, I said to myself that whatever it would be would apply to you."

We ate all the cookies and candy, Swami giving one to me and one to Ediben for each one he ate. It couldn't have been worse for him with his diabetes, but as Ediben said, Swami was a law unto himself.

For Thanksgiving I went to my family's country home at Los Gatos. I wanted to see and smell the country, yet I dreaded to go because of the guests that would be there.

I came home a day later on Friday. As Ediben drove us through the Presidio, I told Swami about how upset I had become in Los Gatos. He said, "You were well served. I know you should not go to Los Gatos, but you people are all smarter than I am. Oh, yes! You cannot have spirituality and the world both. There is just no compromise between the two. Sri Ramakrishna said, 'If you don't want to eat fish, why go to the fish market?'"

November 29, 1955

Swami told me as I sat in his office, "No Christmas at home—you can spend Christmas here. Your family is here. Have Christmas with your new family, not your old family." There was no argument about it. I sat still and twisted my hands in my lap. I told him about a guest at the Ranch who had had a dream of Sri Ramakrishna when he was four or five years old. I asked Swami if it could have been true. He said, "Does he show any signs of renunciation? If it was Sri Ramakrishna, he would now be inclined towards renunciation."

I started to tell him about the man, but Swami suddenly got very severe. "Think of all men as rotting corpses. Of course, you shouldn't act towards anyone that way, but take that attitude. Do you think maya [cosmic delusion] will let you go so easily? No! Do you think the power that has created and sustained this whole universe will let you go without a struggle? All men to you are corpses—rotting corpses!"

Monday on our drive he asked me where I had had lunch. I had to admit that I had eaten in a restaurant on Lombard Street.
Swami: Do you think you can eat with anyone and everyone and not be affected? It is a wonder you people have any devotion at all. You think it does not matter where you eat, but it matters a great deal. People are animals when they eat. Do you think that vibration won't touch you? It will. That is why they read during meals in monasteries or try to think of God with every bite.

November 30, 1955

Following the Wednesday evening lecture, many devotees were standing in Swami's office and in the hall just outside his door.
Swami: You should not bow your head to anyone but God. Bow your head to God, not out of fear but because of a recognition of what He is. One feels like that. There are moods when one wants to bury oneself where His foot has fallen.

December 1, 1955

I went to the public library to look up the memoirs of Thomas Wentworth Higginson [a follower of transcendentalism who had befriended Swami Vivekananda] to see if he had mentioned Swamiji. He hadn't. Swami said, "They [the worldly people who met Swamiji] go right back to worldliness."

My doctor found that I hadn't improved. He said he would recommend surgery on my thyroid gland, but that I should get the opinion of a specialist first.

Last Tuesday, I rode in the back seat as Ediben drove Swami to I. Magnin to look at the store's pink marble floor. (Swami was looking at floors everywhere for the new temple.) From there, we went to the Golden Poppy on Polk Street. Swami gave me two crisp five-dollar bills and I bought candy for Ediben and myself. As we drove on to the Marina, Ediben reminded Swami that it was Miriam Kennedy's birthday.

"I am very glad that I didn't scold her this morning," Swami said.

"Yes," said Ediben. "You were very gentle with her. I thought you must know it was her birthday."

"No," Swami said, "I didn't know. It just happened that I didn't scold her. I am awfully glad."

We went back to the Golden Poppy to buy birthday candy for Miriam. Ediben got out to get it; she knows better than I what Miriam likes.

As soon as she was out of sight, Swami turned to me and, with the mischievous look of a little boy, said, "Come on, Marie Louise." He pointed. There was a nut store! We got out and looked in the window; but the nuts didn't look very good nor did the place look very clean, so he didn't buy anything. We got back in the car.

December 2, 1955

Again in search of floor tile for the new temple, Swami went with Jo to Old St. Mary's on Grant Avenue to look at the floor there. Afterward he said, "I strongly felt the vivid presence of Sri Ramakrishna and Holy Mother and the Madonna at St. Mary's."

Jo told me that he knelt down and made the sign of the cross for the sake of the people who were looking at him.

Disciple: How could they be there where Christ and the Madonna are worshiped?
Swami: I can't draw you a diagram of it; it can't be described. But there were the three, the three in one. They are they! Once a Hindu Christian came to Dakshineswar during Sri Ramakrishna's lifetime. He recognized Christ in Sri Ramakrishna. He told everyone: "You do not know what you have here!"

December 3, 1955

Today Swami and Ediben went to visit a devotee in St. Francis Hospital while I waited in the car. "She will not die," Swami said of the devotee. [Later she came so close to death that everyone, including her doctors, gave her up, but she did not die.] Then we drove to the Marina. There was a gray-silver sheen on the water. I saw a strange sea creature rear its black head, swim along, and then go under again. I pointed this out. It was not a porpoise or a shark—a mystery! I mentioned the dugong, the sea elephant, Eugenie, now at the aquarium.
Swami: Where do you get so much knowledge?
Me: You told me to read *Time*.
Swami: Work on Swamiji's book. That is enough knowledge. Concentrate on that. Worship takes great concentration. Then God is pleased. What you are doing is worship. Do it with concentration. Only then will it be good.

(We returned to the Temple. Swami seemed unbearably tired as he went upstairs.)

December 5, 1955

I was given all sorts of tests at Stanford Hospital for the activity of the thyroid. Later, Swami, Ediben, and I drove through Golden Gate Park in rain that was silvery.

Back at the Temple I learned that Jo (and no doubt others) thinks that I am putting on being sick so that I will get attention from Swami. Oh God! One thinks one has friends and then finds that they know nothing at all of what one is like, nor have they any real fondness. The knife comes out in a moment. The tongue is all too ready to say the mean thing, and the heart is all too ready to believe it.

I told Ediben this had hurt me through and through to the backbone, and I cried on her shoulder (figuratively). She said, "That is something you have to learn—that you have no real friends, and you have to learn to live with it," meaning, I think, that few friends understand what one is made of.

Well, who cares? This is more Jo's problem than mine. Let her fret over it. She said sanctimoniously that it was not fair to Swami for me to go on pretending to be sick.

"It is just that little thing—jealousy," Ediben explained. Of course. And that little thing twists the world all out of shape. Swami told me the mind is not to be trusted, that I must watch and watch and watch.

Let me never say that someone is malingering to get attention from Swami! How could anyone fool Swami in the first place?

But Jo did not mean any of this. It was momentary.

December 6, 1955

Me: Some people think that I am putting this on.

Swami: Who thinks that?

Me: Well, I heard that Jo said that, and others.

Swami: Never believe anything you hear secondhand. Only believe it if you hear it directly. People get things wrong.

Me: Yes, that is probably true. What upsets me is that I think people understand me and know me, but they don't at all.

Swami: Marie Louise, you expect people to be Godlike, 100 percent perfect. They are not. Some may be good but they have many faults also. Recognize that. Otherwise, life will be unbearable. Don't let it bother you. Face Jo with it.

I have the same thing said about me. Some swamis think that I'm not sick at all, just putting it on. In India, when I had an ulcer, I heard that someone had said that it was just in my mind. I faced him with it: "Do you think all these x-rays are just in my mind?" He was stopped. Face Jo with it. Ask her if she thinks what all the doctors say—your rapid pulse and all that—is not real. People are not good, but what can you do about it? The inside is God, but not the outside.

Me: Besides, it is only temporary.

Swami: Yes, it is just temporary. There are also some good people.

Me: God is the only real thing.

Swami: Yes.

December 9, 1955

The doctors decided that instead of surgery on the thyroid, I am to drink radioactive iodine, which will destroy the overactive gland in four to six weeks.

Swami: Work on Swamiji. That is like meditation. It will lift your mind. Your physical condition lowers your mind; idleness, unfortunately, doesn't lift it—it only lowers it further. You must work regularly, live regularly, with rhythm. The mind sags down otherwise.

Me: Has my mind sagged down far?

Swami: No, not very far. But work on Swamiji's book. That will lift your mind so that it will stay up permanently.

Swami gave me many questions to ask the doctor. I forgot to ask the most important ones, the very ones Swami invariably questioned me about when I returned. He became disgusted.

December 12, 1955

After looking at the new temple where a leak had been discovered, Swami said to Ediben while driving one day, "I wonder, is it more blessed to have everything fall into one's hands without an effort or to have to work and struggle for everything one wants to do? It has been a struggle for every inch of the new temple, and now it is leaking."

Ediben told Swami that it was more blessed to struggle, for that laid strong foundations, and anyhow she liked it that way because of her pioneer blood. Swami turned to me in the back seat and asked me which way I liked it. I said I liked the struggle too but added, "I'm sorry you have to have so much trouble." He answered, "Never mind me; that is neither here nor there."

Another time Swami said, "I hope I can stay here until everything is finished. I would hate to go, leaving everything unfinished, in a mess, a great burden of debt. People will say, 'What a rogue he was! No sense of responsibility.' When a man does big things and finishes them, he is well thought of; but if he does not finish them, he is considered worthless. Marie Louise, listening back there, will think that I am thinking only of myself and not of the students." I said I was thinking no such thing.

Jo brought me my dinner Saturday night. I had "faced her" with her remark.

December 13, 1955

Swami: Everything must be very realistic in spiritual life. Of course, it is a higher kind of realism, but realistic it must be.

That afternoon

We drove along the ocean and through Golden Gate Park. When we got back to the Temple, Swami found that he had lost his beads (rosary), which, evidently, he always carries in his pocket wherever he goes. He went upstairs to look for them, thinking he had not taken them; then he came down again. He and Ediben looked in the car, but they were not there. After he had gone upstairs again, I left with Ediben and saw Swami's beads lying in the gutter, just where the back wheel of Ediben's car would have run over them. They were the beads that Swami Shivananda [a direct disciple of Sri Ramakrishna] had given him. I handed them to Ediben and she went back into the Temple to phone Swami.

"Tell Marie Louise many thanks!" he said, but he was sorry that they had been in the street. Moreover (although Swami did not say this), both Ediben and I, who had been eating cookies and candy, had touched them. But, as Ediben said, "Ganges water will fix that." Anyhow, at least the car didn't run over them. How nice to have found Swami's beads for him!

December 1955

Swami: Be strong! Be strong mentally and physically. Look at Swamiji's pictures [referring to photographs he had just received from Almora—Swamiji with shaven head and a background of trees]. If you want to work for Swamiji, if you want to follow in his footsteps, you must be strong like that.

Me (smiling foolishly): I try.

Swami: Yes, you do very well; but you must do better.

7

BALANCING ON A RAIL

1956

Before I discovered Vedanta and came to know Swami Ashokananda and other swamis of the Ramakrishna Order, I had thirstily read books by authors such as Gerald Heard and John Burton and, even earlier, P.D. Ouspensky and G.I. Gurdjieff. I knew about the concepts of renunciation, selflessness, recollection, and so on. I knew people who helped their less fortunate fellow human beings, who lived frugally so that they could give more to others, and who gave thought to God. I knew many genuinely good people. If they did not exist, we humans would have long since gone back to the trees.

While I had heard and read about selflessness, purity, and goodness, and while I thought I knew people who exemplified those golden qualities, actually I had not the faintest idea of the true meaning of a life lived for others, without any allowance made for oneself. I do not mean a life of martyrdom or penance but one of overflowing love, where a thought of self, however small, is a desecration—is, in fact, impossible.

Only when I came to know Swami Ashokananda did I see the ocean of selflessness for the first time. My only thought was "Oh! That's it." I did not pinpoint characteristics such as generosity, charitableness, and kindness. There were no overlays, good or bad; there was just a being whose only need and desire was to help others. He was not merely unselfish—there was just no self, no ego to affirm or to efface. Out of that emptiness, that Buddhistic void, came a strength and a wisdom without shadows or doubts. This was true selflessness.

I do not want to sound partial or fanatical, but next to that ocean of revealed selflessness the goodly people of my former acquaintance seemed like dewdrops—however lovable, admirable, deserving of praise, and necessary to the ongoing dance of civilization. Even in thinking of his own eventual death, Swami Ashokananda's only concern was the effect it would have on his students.

January 8, 1956

Last week when I was sitting in Swami's office, he said, apropos of his not finishing the new temple, "I don't think I will die soon, but my health is so uncertain that I must think of that possibility."

Then he went on to say, "You must carry on. Perhaps you think that a new swami won't make a place for you. But don't worry about that. Sri Ramakrishna will make a place for you. This is his house. It does not belong to any one swami. Always remember that. Don't worry. The only reason people are left out is because they themselves become bothersome. They want to push themselves forward because of their own ego. Work for Sri Ramakrishna and Swamiji. Of course, sometimes a surreptitious ego enters that work also, but it is harmless. Work on; you will see that a place is made for you. Don't worry about that. Your work will go on."

I said that I didn't worry about that so much; I worried about not having him in my life.

"There will be greater swamis than me," he replied. "That is impossible," I said. Knowing he would object, I hurriedly added, "Even so, you are my guru." Swami agreed, "Yes, that is so, but Sri Ramakrishna will take care of that too."

Swami still takes me driving through Golden Gate Park almost every day. Ediben says she can practically feel and see the healing power he is pouring over me.

So many wonderful things I hear every day both on rides and at the Temple. I should have a miniature recording machine like Luke's, or else a good memory.

January 9, 1956

Swami took me to the Vedanta Retreat at Olema along with Ediben. I took a walk alone. It was misty and God seemed to be brooding over the whole 2,000 acres.

January 12, 1956

Today on a drive Swami said (speaking of one of the devotees), "A person who has been good all his life becomes fearless, not only because he has a sense that what he does is right, but because he has literally become in tune with the moral law—the cosmic law."

January 19, 1956

Swami went to Sacramento today. Before he left he called me into his office and spoke very severely about the fact that I am having dinner with Leila, my sister, tonight at Clay Street, the family home where Leila and her husband are living.

Swami (sternly): You are making a regular habit of that. Why are you doing that? You will get a liking for domesticity. You will want a home and a husband. It is one thing if you want a little religion and a domestic life; but if you want to make religion your whole life, you must exercise extreme caution. A little chink will come in the dam, then another little chink—you will think it is nothing, but the whole dam will be washed away.

(I made numerous excuses about how I had not had dinner at Clay Street last week, and about how Leila didn't like to eat alone.)

Swami: You are no longer your sister's guardian.

Me: You mean I want to be cozy.

Swami: Yes.

Me: I sometimes feel like that.

Swami: I know you do. (He strode from his office.)

January 21, 1956

Yesterday, a newel post was being placed in the balcony of the new temple. Swami wondered if it could be seen above the balcony rail from the auditorium. Ediben and Anna went to look. They came back and reported, "Yes, it can be seen about one-half inch from the very front of the auditorium." "How much can be seen from the platform?" Swami asked. Ediben and Anna had not gone up onto the platform.

I took note of this little story because of the fine anger it brought out in Swami, the glaring and the scolding and, finally, the striding off, like a wind rushing by and down the stairs to see for himself. That striding—erect, purposeful, and so fast! There is not room enough for it in the Old Temple.

Driving through the park later with Ediben at the wheel, Swami said, "Sometimes as we drive I have a small flash of memory, a feeling the same as when I was a student in India. I would take walks for hours and hours in a sort of ecstasy. A tiny spark of that comes back like a flash."

He turned to me in the back seat and said, "Would you believe it, Marie Louise? I was a poet in those days." I said I believed it, and that he was still a poet.

In February of 1956, Swami Ashokananda was anticipating the coming visit of Swami Madhavananda (the general secretary of the Ramakrishna Order) and his traveling companion, Swami Nirvanananda. He wondered what Swami Madhavananda would think of the changes that had been made since he had been here in 1929; he wondered how the weather would be, and if the swamis would be comfortable. He was anxious about their visit, as though Sri Ramakrishna and Swami Vivekananda themselves were coming to inspect the work.

There was, perhaps, good reason for Swami's apprehension. A journal entry of mine explained the situation. When the Sacramento temple became a branch of the Vedanta Society of Northern California in 1952, Swami Ashokananda wrote to Swami Vireswarananda, the president of the Order, to inform him about it. His letter mentioned that he was sure Sri Ramakrishna wanted the Sacramento temple. The president showed the letter to Swami Madhavananda, the general secretary, who became furious and sent a harsh letter back to Swami Ashokananda in which he wrote sarcastically of "esoteric reasons" (referring to Swami Ashokananda's allusion to Sri Ramakrishna's wish). In turn, Swami Ashokananda wrote a scathing reply to Swami Madhavananda. This heated correspondence continued back and forth for some time.

Probably because of this controversy (at least, this may have been one reason), Swami Madhavananda came to San Francisco in 1956 with a sour mind, determined not to like anything.

On Wednesday, February 29, Swami Madhavananda and Swami Nirvanananda flew directly to San Francisco from Los Angeles, where they had been the guests of Swami Prabhavananda at the Vedanta Society of Southern California. Brought from the airport to the Temple, they stood unsmiling in the downstairs hall. They wore dark gray Nehru jackets, and in the dim light their faces looked ashen, stonelike. Swami Ashokananda introduced me to them. I did not know enough to make *pranams* (to touch their feet)—and Swami did not tell me to. Perhaps, because they were accustomed to this Hindu gesture of respect everywhere they went, the lack of it offended them. I don't remember what I said or what they said, but it was clear to me that they had come full of criticism. I remember that I went home and cried.

The next week everything that could go wrong went wrong. The visiting swamis immediately declared that the food prepared for them was not right. When they were driven over the Golden Gate Bridge to see Olema, the car was stopped for speeding. Its registration card was made out to a business in San Jose, and the clear implication was that these dark-skinned people had stolen it. Somehow, Al Clifton, who was driving, placated the police officer and they drove on to Olema, which Swami Madhavananda found to be much too big—unnecessarily big. Sacramento was also an unnecessary expansion, he thought. Shanti Ashrama (a holy retreat in the San Antone Valley)—well, it was Swami Vivekananda's acquisition, but the day of the swamis' visit it was cold and rainy and altogether miserable. The temple under construction in San Francisco was far too substantial, as though built to last hundreds of years. ("It is not temples that are needed," the general secretary said with cold disapproval to Ediben. "It is devotees." And Ediben, barely hiding her fury, had replied, "But, sir, how can there be devotees without temples for them to come to?") In Swami Madhavananda's eyes, the Berkeley center was just as unnecessary as that of Sacramento. I don't remember whether or not the swamis were driven to Lake Tahoe; but if they were, they probably viewed the place with stony, unaccepting eyes. And all the while Swami Ashokananda's heart was breaking. Some said later that he acted like a little boy in the presence of stern, faultfinding mentors.

Early on two things happened that softened, if not changed, the whole picture. First, the day after the swamis arrived they were given a dinner in the commodious house which then served as a convent, and afterward there was a reception. Many devotees were present, all of them enthusiastic and eager. Questions about Holy Mother, Swami Brahmananda, Swami Shivananda, Swami Premananda, and other direct disciples of Sri Ramakrishna flowed out, obviously with great devotion. Swami Madhavananda's replies, at first stiff, then increasingly warm, were listened to with eagerness, and slowly his face visibly changed. It became smooth and rounded; he began to smile, and by the time the reception was over, he was a different man altogether. He seemed now like the gracious spiritual swami we had heard of—no longer was he an unyielding chunk of granite, from which no light had seemed to emanate. He even gave his blessings to the budding convent (an act that he would later forget).

The second event that wrought a change was a question-and-answer class the following evening, presided over by Swami Madhavananda in the auditorium of the Temple. The questions were written beforehand and presented earlier that day to the swamis. Suddenly, Swami Nirvanananda came running downstairs to the first floor, a bunch of papers in his hand. He rushed into Swami Ashokananda's office. "Look!" He cried, "These questions! So thoughtful! So brilliant! They show a real understanding of Vedanta. So many questions, all of them keen and intelligent!" I do not remember what Swami Ashokananda said in reply; perhaps he just smiled. In any case, the class that evening was a great success. Swami Madhavananda answered the questions with warmth and as though they were worth answering.

And so, having seen with their own eyes that the devotees in San Francisco were not only true devotees but brainy and knowledgeable, and that Al Clifton, as he said, was a true monk, Swami Madhavananda and Swami Nirvanananda completed their visit with a very different attitude than they had had when they arrived. Later, word got back to Swami Ashokananda that Swami Madhavananda had said in Seattle that real work on a deep level was being done in San Francisco, and that in India he had remarked, "There is no one who can take Swami Ashokananda's place." Later, in an unguarded moment on a visit to San Francisco, Swami Pavitrananda mentioned that Swami Madhavananda had said to him in New York, "Never again will I listen to anyone else's opinion; I will see for myself!" "Ah?" Swami Ashokananda inquired, "You mean to say that he listened to Swami Prabhavananda?" Swami Pavitrananda bit his tongue and was silent.

Swami Madhavananda's retrospective kind and understanding words went far to console Swami Ashokananda. Still, the stress of that visit had gone very deep. Swami Ashokananda was sick afterward and never fully regained his health. Though the work went on with the same vigor and confidence as before, never again did I hear him laugh with the same carefree wholeheartedness that had earlier echoed through the downstairs rooms of the Temple.

In April of 1956 we had sent the first installment of *New Discoveries* to the publication office of Advaita Ashrama for typesetting. On July 3, 1956, we sent the last installment—except for the epilogue and a long reflective essay for the close of chapter 4 that discussed, among other topics, Swami Vivekananda's reasons for coming to America. I started to work on the essay at Lake Tahoe in late July, and the first draft was huge. Swami Ashokananda had supplied me with a vast amount of new research material, which, so far as I could see, had no relation to the themes at hand.

I had arrived at Tahoe that summer in a state of exhaustion. Swami Akhilananda, who was visiting, pleaded with Swami Ashokananda to let me rest for at least one day; but Swami Ashokananda felt—rightly, I think—that if I lay down, the book would disintegrate beyond all restoration. So I wrote on in a more or less comatose state. The words, once so halting, now flowed in a mindless, turgid flood onto the pages. The result was not only voluminous; it was endlessly boring. "It needs condensing," Swami said. "Reduce eighty pages to twenty."

For the rest of the summer and fall I scrapped the eighty-odd pages and started over, trying to make sense in my own mind of the themes to be tackled and pounded into comprehensive shape. For the most part this mental battle was fought while I lay sprawled face down and balanced rather precariously on the top railing of Ediben's porch, much to her amusement. Once I had the squirming combatant limp in my hands, I would move to the kitchen table and pin him onto paper. Slowly, agonizingly, the reflective essay took shape throughout the rest of 1956 and the early part of 1957.

I WAS SO BUSY throughout 1956 writing the book that my journal contains very few entries recording the conversations that we had as a group with Swami Ashokananda about spiritual life. What follows are two of the best.

Durga Puja Festival, October 22, 1956

Swami: Do you feel inclined to work or to go to Berkeley [for the *puja*] this afternoon?

Me: I don't feel particularly inclined to work, but I don't feel inclined to go to Berkeley either.

Swami: Why not?

Me: I don't understand worship.

Swami: What do you feel like doing?

Me: I don't know—maybe rest.
Swami: Or are you thinking of Los Gatos?
Me: No. But last night I was looking at some family pictures with Jo [my dinner guest] because she wanted to see a photograph of my mother. There were also many of me in various stages of growth.
Swami: When the devotees get together, they ruin one another! Mother, father, sisters, brothers, husbands . . . I suppose Jo has told you about her husband. All worldly talk!
Me: Yes, she has told me a little about him.
Swami (disgusted): What hope is there for any of you?
Me: Looking at the pictures, I really didn't feel—
Swami (very cross and severe): Just listen to what I tell you. You are not my colleague! You can still learn something from me.

With this, Swami got up and went into the back office, leaving me unable to move for a while. Tears flowed. I pulled myself together and went into the back office where Swami was talking with the devotees.
Elna: I always like these *puja* days.
Swami: It is idolatry. When you find the externals very pleasant, you don't go within. That is what happens to a religion. You will always find that when a great deal of attention is given to externals, the religion is beginning to degenerate. Its inner strength is gone.
Elna: Still, there is something about the external worship that is very uplifting.
Swami: Then you know better than I. Very good.
Elna: I didn't mean to contradict you, Swami. I just wanted to get my thinking straight.
Swami: You heard what I said about it—but of course you can think as you like. If you think this kind of day has something special about it, that is because you don't want to make the ef-

fort to think of *every* day as God's day. Every day is special. God is everywhere—always.

October 27, 1956

I came this evening to Swami's office to show him what I have done on the book, but the conversation took an unexpected turn.

Me: Do you feel better, Swami?

Swami (making a wry face and shaking his head): No. I am an old man now. I am on the decline.

Me (not accepting this): Swami, there is something I don't understand. You are working for Sri Ramakrishna and Swamiji—why don't they keep you well?

Swami: Do you think they should guarantee that I stay healthy because I am doing their work?

Me: Well, they should.

Swami: You are being childish about it. God has His ways that can't be understood from an ordinary standpoint.

Me: They are odd ways.

Swami: For many years I have had the energy to do the work.

Me: But evidently Sri Ramakrishna wants you to do more. You should have the energy to do it. Otherwise, it is cruel.

Swami: Don't be childish! Besides, how do you know Sri Ramakrishna wants me to do more?

Me: You have said yourself that there is a lot to finish.

Swami: That doesn't mean Sri Ramakrishna wants *me* to finish it. Perhaps he wants someone else to do it. God has reasons for doing what He does.

Me: Do you understand them?

Swami: You see, there has to be a sort of transitional period. Through suffering, one turns away from the desire to do this and that. The soul seeks the Formless. One has to reach a higher state.

Me: For people like me, suffering is necessary—but why for you?

Swami: No, for me too. Even Swamiji had to go through a transition period; it was even more necessary for him. Don't you see, he was a world teacher; he wanted to help everyone, not just a few people. His desire to help was so strong! Think of the force of that desire—there *had* to be a period during which his mind turned away from the world. People needing his help began to seem unreal to him; his mind reached toward the Formless. Toward the end of his life, Swamiji used to recite a verse from the *Brihadaranyaka Upanishad* that Brahman alone is real.

Me: But he had *nirvikalpa samadhi* all along.

Swami: Yes, but his desire to help the world held him here. Before he left, he must have been assured that what he had done was enough for hundreds of years. I don't think Swamiji would have left this world if he hadn't known that.

Me: Did his mind turn away because his work was done, or because of suffering—or both?

Swami: Both.

8

WHEW!

In December or early January, the birthday of Sri Sarada Devi (Holy Mother) is celebrated annually with great devotion at Vedanta centers around the world. Sri Sarada Devi (1853–1920) was the wife of Sri Ramakrishna, his spiritual consort, of whom even the great Swami Vivekananda and other direct monastic disciples of Sri Ramakrishna were in supreme awe. Swami Ashokananda had paid his first visit to Holy Mother in 1913 when he was a college student.

January 6, 1957

Swami: When Holy Mother blessed a person, no obstacle in the whole universe could obstruct his progress. She herself said so.
Me: My! How lucky the people were who knew her.
Swami: Yes, but that power still exists. That love is always there. Only now one has to know how to find it. Holy Mother came to prove that there was such a protective power that one could call on.

January 7, 1957

Swami: Without real spiritual power, do you think religion will prevail against what is going on in the world? Bunk! This is the tragic part of it. The whole meaning of religion is understood differently in the West than in India.

My conclusion is that freedom of the practice of religion is full of snares. It should be based on a deep respect for all religions. The world is such that unless people become deeply spiritual, life will become hellfire. People will be forced to become spiritual. We don't have to do anything about it. If they want to be Christian, they will have to be *deeply* Christian.

January 8, 1957

Swami Gambhirananda wrote from Advaita Ashrama to Swami Ashokananda that the proposed length of *New Discoveries* had frightened him—"It must not be over 500 pages." Nor, he added, can they make the list of corrections that we had sent.

I drafted a letter of reply to Swami Gambhirananda and showed it to Swami Ashokananda.

Swami: Just imagine it! They are thinking only of the financial side. They are, of course, worried about paying their bills. They probably put aside $10,000 and now it looks as if this book will come to $15,000 or so.

Me: I understand their worry.

Swami: No. Everything we want to do is difficult. I had such a hard struggle, for instance, printing Romain Rolland's book.

January 9, 1957

Swami: No one can do good to the whole world. A little is all anyone can do; but a little, if it goes deep, does a lot of good. Yet in the mind there is infinite knowledge and infinite ability. If you rub it and rub it, it will all come out. Ponder over things and the answer will come.

January 11, 1957

Swami (laughing): Smokers will probably go to Smoke *Loka* [smokers' heaven], but it won't be what they think. God answers desires, but He always puts a sting in it. America has settled down to enjoy—everyone can drink and smoke and have a fine time. Perhaps there is a meaning in it; in their next lives, people will be jaded with all that, satiated, and will want to progress. At other times, though, pleasure-seeking seems meaningless. A river will take many turns, running here and there, then back upon itself, and all the time it is going to the ocean. It could just go just straight (shooting his arm out straight)—that is what spiritual life is. One learns to avoid all the unnecessary turns.

January 12, 1957

Swami is feeling depressed and seems hurt at the reaction in India to the length of the book. He had so hoped they would appreciate it. He told me to pray every day to Sri Ramakrishna that they will publish it.

January 13, 1957

I am working with Swami to polish the reflective essay on Swami Vivekananda for the fourth chapter of *New Discoveries* before its final typing.

Swami: You have worked so hard, but all this work will go for nothing. They [the publishers] will hack it up.

Me: In any case, it won't have gone for nothing [meaning I have gained much from doing it], but I think they will publish it. (We go on with the work.)

January 15, 1957

Swami: Self-doubt is the beginning of wisdom; cock-sureness is the beginning of downfall. (This was about my need to check and recheck the facts in the manuscript.)

January 17, 1957

Me: I have trouble with self-consciousness when I meditate.

Swami: Pray to Sri Ramakrishna. Willpower or effort won't

help. Pray to him during your meditation, without interrupting it too long, that you may have his vision.

January 19, 1957

A few days ago I realized that I had lost my fountain pen, the green pen that Swami had given to me and that was identical with the one he had at Lake Tahoe, which I had admired. When I discovered this loss I raised a hue and cry, searching everywhere and asking everyone. I even asked Swami if he had my pen. He laughed heartily.

Swami: You are careless with your things, and then you accuse people of stealing them.

Me: Not of stealing, of just taking by mistake.

Swami: Oh yes, you are too much of a lady to say anyone stole. Well, things are mortal; they come easily, go easily. (I searched further.)

Today, after having scolded me severely for not working with enough urgency, Swami asked me if I had found my pen. I said no, disconsolately. He reached into his pocket and drew out a pen. "Does this look like your pen?" he asked, smiling like an indulgent father.

Me: Oh, yes!

Swami (smiling more): Does it write like your pen?

I tried it. The cartridge was empty. I had another and Swami, with some trouble, put it in. I wrote with it. Was it his pen that he gave me to take the place of mine, or mine that he had found lying around and picked up to teach me a lesson? I don't know. I think it was his. In fact, I know it was his. The old cartridge that came out of it was his kind of ink. Of course it was his!

Me: It is better—for having been in your pocket.

Swami: Now take care of it; I don't trust you.

Me: Oh yes, I will take care of it.

January 29, 1957

A letter finally arrived from Swami Gambhirananda. It appears that he will print the entire manuscript after all.

January 30, 1957

Swami: Those who serve God are very, very fortunate. It is a great good luck to be allowed to serve Him. It is not a question of just wanting to do it. Many people cry their hearts out and yet they cannot serve Him.

February 1, 1957

At last, Miriam Kennedy and I airmailed the last pieces of the *New Discoveries* book to India—the essay for the end of chapter 4 and the epilogue. I have worked on the essay since late July, steadily and painfully. Whew!

When I put it in its envelope, Swami said to it lovingly, "Goodbye, goodbye. Have a good trip." And he touched it to his head. "Pray that they won't hack it to pieces."

Through our months of mailing manuscripts to India, Miriam Kennedy had not been able to learn from the post office officials the details of the mailing system. Not that she hadn't tried. Swami said to her, "A monument to your inefficiency," but to me he blamed the post office officials for their ineptness. Still, Miriam bore the brunt of his immovable, penetrating stare, his look of utter contempt, and his cold, sarcastic "yes" in reply to her every explanation.

February 3, 1957

Swami (speaking of Bobbie Day, the only non-Vedantic friend I have kept): She is not even on the fence. *(Laughing)* She is sitting on her side of the fence and talking over the other side—but she is a very good person. Every soul has periods of rest, periods in which everything suits them. It is as though a traveler had walked enough for one day. He finds a nice spot and rests in it. He is con-

tent so he doesn't feel any need to go on for that day. In the morning he becomes restless again and must walk on. It is just like that. After a while, conditions will no longer satisfy the soul; it becomes restless. People can reach a high state and rest there also.
Me: Once one has started on a spiritual life, how can one find rest again in the world?
Swami: This world has produced Buddhas and Sri Ramakrishnas. One can find the highest in it. A person can be spiritual, can have advanced in spiritual life, and can find everything wonderful. He doesn't feel like going on. He has a fine time. He likes everyone.
Me: Couldn't he slip back?
Swami: Yes, there is that danger. He can get caught again in the world. Then he is spurred on to greater effort. Through the early practice of *vairagya* [renunciation] one avoids that state. *Vairagya* pushes one on. That is why one should practice it from the beginning—to form a habit of mind, even though one does not seem ready for it. One cannot acquire it in that state of rest.

That evening

Jo, Dorothy Madison, Kathleen, and Mara were sitting in the back office. Dorothy said she was confused by the morning's lecture; she couldn't understand why one should worship God as man on the one hand, if, on the other hand, form did not exist.
Swami: When you worship God in man you must take the whole man. You don't analyze. Love never analyzes. You don't worship God and at the same time tear Him to pieces. To analyze is all right, but that is a different practice—*jnana* [knowledge]. The same person can practice both *bhakti* [devotion] and *jnana*, but not at the same time. Love does not question.

Swamiji was a *jnani,* but he was also a great *bhakta.* Swamiji and Buddha were both *jnanis,* but they both had infinite love and compassion. When Swamiji came down from the experience of unity it would seem to him as though Brahman were caught in a net. His heart would break. In that lower state there is a sense of individuality.

Such compassion can only be known after the knowledge of unity, after one has known what man really is. Sri Ramakrishna wanted to be kept in that [lower] state so he could serve man. Swamiji is still at Belur Math now. People have seen him. He lives there. Swami Shivananda confirmed it.

February 7, 1957

Swami (referring to me): She thinks life is a long vacation. When one doesn't work, one deteriorates. The sixteen or eighteen hours of waking life should be filled. One should go from one thing to another. Then the mind has no chance to dwell on wrong things. Those things become starved out; the mind becomes pure. One should not, on the other hand, have to drive oneself. If there must be rest—say at three o'clock—then rest. Do nothing but rest at that time.

Me: Well, I will go home to work.

Swami (laughing): You can stay a little longer.

February 8, 1957

After Swami's class today, Ediben was signing invitations to Sri Ramakrishna's birthday in the back office. Other devotees were discussing the possibility of using a rubber stamp for her signature. Swami came in after a while and sat in his chair. There was general conversation, in which Ediben joined, continuing to sign invitations.

Swami (suddenly turning on Ediben very vehemently): You are inviting devotees to Sri Ramakrishna's birthday. When you do that, give your whole heart and soul to it! If you want to talk, put them away.

(Ediben stopped signing the invitations.)

February 16, 1957

Devotee: Does one become free from karma when the level of the throat chakra is reached?

Swami: Yes. One pays a token karma—one cent on the dollar.

Me: Yet even in the beginning of spiritual life, when one has taken refuge in Sri Ramakrishna, as you said, then doesn't one become a little free from karma?

Swami: At first spiritual life is only sentiment, like a flower stuck in the ground. That is not enough. It must take root; then wonderful blooms come.

February 17, 1957

Swami (about my habitually forgetting to buy food): You will pay the consequences. Someone will come along and live with you to buy food for you. Do you want to fall into that trap?

One must have the creature comforts—good food, good clothes, a house, warmth. Otherwise, the mind will think this is no kind of life; it will turn to domesticity. That is why extreme austerity is not good. It can have the opposite effect. It can turn the mind back to the world.

February 18, 1957

Swami: Never think whether your meditation is good or bad. You would call a person morbid if he fussed about the weather all the time. Sometimes it's good, sometimes it's bad. Just go on. All the emotions that are considered romantic in worldly life have no place at all in spiritual life—despair, regret, repentance—that is all self-indulgence. Whatever the poets write about is all wrong. Those things are dissipation.

Me: I do not always become despairing over a poor meditation.

Swami: Once is enough to set you back. If a child sets fire to a house, will it do any good for him to say, "I don't always put a match to the house"? Never analyze your meditation; you only block it. Of course you can have good meditation! Of course you are pure! Swamiji said the life of a devotee is a "purity-drilling machine." You will be scraped clean.

April 4, 1957

Many devotees assembled in the back office were talking about the coming arrival of Swami Shraddhananda, who was on his way from India to be Swami Ashokananda's assistant. Luke said, "This place will be full of lions" (meaning three swamis, counting Swami Shantaswarupananda, then at the Berkeley center).

I was sitting next to Luke. I turned to her and said in a low voice, "One lion and two lion cubs." Swami heard, and I received the first full and unbuffered blast of my life.

Swami (fiercely): I will come to hate you for fanatical talk like that. Do you want me to associate you with fanaticism? I hate that kind of thing from the bottom of my soul. What do you expect to gain by that kind of talk? What good does it do you or me or anyone? Why must you make comparisons? Let me tell you that I sincerely feel that the two swamis here are superior to me. I appreciate your feeling for me. But you should keep it within. Why must you parade it publicly?

There was more, all delivered with such tremendous power and fury that it had me paralyzed. When it began, I had been sitting in a rather nonchalant position—legs crossed, my arm dangling over the back of the chair, turned sideways. I could not move out of that position. Naturally, I could not speak. Dorothy Madison broke the tension somewhat by saying, "But Swami, I don't understand what you are scolding her for." (Dorothy had not been around the San Francisco Temple for long.)

Swami: You don't have to understand. Am I scolding you?

Dorothy: No, thank God. *(Laughter.)*

Swami: She understands. (I understood all right.)

The rest of the evening I spent alternating between hot and cold and trying not to cry. Swami was nice to me afterward, but I continued to lick my wounds. At one point he said tenderly, "Don't feel bad," and then resumed the general conversation.

Swami: Swami Brahmananda said that the vision Swamiji had as a boy was of Shankara, but Swamiji himself said he felt it was of Buddha. I would be inclined to give more credit to what Swamiji felt about it.

Me (trying to act natural): On what grounds did Swami Brahmananda think it was Shankara?

Swami: What a question to ask!

Me (half laughing, half hurt): I guess I should go home.

Swami (more gently): Well, it is all right to ask that question. But do you think I inquired into it in those days? I wasn't writing a book. You have been writing a book. You want to check up on everything. Swami Brahmananda also said that when Swamiji died he had entered into *nirvikalpa samadhi* and couldn't return, yet there is evidence that Swamiji knew when he would die.

Dorothy Madison (suddenly changing the subject): Swami, is it true that in order to realize God, one has to sing?

Swami: Yes, that is true—sing to Him with your heart. Singing and worship are very necessary; the mind dwells on God.

Mara: If one offers incense, is that enough?

Swami: How long does it take to offer incense? What will you do with the rest of the time?

Me: What if one can't sing?

Swami: That is just an excuse. What you mean is that you don't want to sing. *(To others)* She is perfectly happy as she is. She is just content to float along.

(After I had gone home, Swami phoned me.)

Swami: Well, are you moping?

Me: No—well, a little bit. I have been thinking that you said I was complacent.

Swami: I ask you to sing. You make up all kinds of excuses.
Me: Do you *really* want me to sing?
Swami: Yes, surely you should sing—hum.
Me: I did not think you would ever hate me.
Swami: Did I say I will hate you?
Me: Yes.
Swami: No, I never will. I will hate your fanaticism.

April 5, 1957

Swami: Whatever I say to you, I say for your own good. You must just swallow it. I am your teacher. But you are not forced to do anything; you came here of your own accord. I will get so that I will be afraid to tell you anything. I don't want to hurt you, and I don't want to be put on the defensive. I don't have to explain everything I say. We are human here. Do you want to be one of those people I am afraid to say things to? There are some people like that. Years have gone by and I haven't told them anything; but I guess God will take care of them.

April 7, 1957

This evening, Jo, Kathleen, and Dorothy Madison were talking with Swami in the back office.
Dorothy: Jo had on such a beautiful hat this morning. (A night or so before, Dorothy had also spoken enthusiastically of Kathleen's skin, which was as smooth as a young girl's.)
Swami: That is new kind of talk here. That is the talk of a worldly person. Why must you give so much attention to superficial things like skin, clothes, and hair?
Dorothy: I can't help observing, Swami.
Swami: Learn to help it. One way of learning is not to give expression to what you observe.
Dorothy: Isn't there such as thing as aesthetic appreciation? When I was a girl, you used to get after me a lot for being so slop-

pily dressed. Once you said, "Think of the aesthetic side of it."
Swami: Yes, you dressed sloppily. That was *tamas*. Now go beyond that. Must everything I said to you twenty years ago apply to you now? If you can see the Divine Spirit in everyone, then you will see real beauty. Aesthetics! Worldly people run around to concerts and to art galleries. What benefit do they derive? Are they any better for it? Most aesthetic appreciation is sensuality. I admit that for spiritually minded people, music and art can be of value, but such people are in the minority.

Don't be conspicuous in any way. Don't attract attention either by being so badly dressed that people wonder or by making yourself so attractive that people notice you and admire you. The senses of people literally feed upon you. You will be consumed. That is what happens to public performers—actors and dancers. They end up by becoming empty shells. It is a fact.
Dorothy: How horrible! It sounds like something very strange is going on.
Swami: Don't be naive. You are too naive for such an intelligent girl. It is not strange. The senses are of the mind; they feed on the mind of another person.

April 17, 1957

I asked Swami about Fledermaus (my dachshund, whom I had left). She is old and in bad physical shape. The Williamsons, whom she had lived with and loved, have gone. She will have to live with strangers. The vet says she cannot live much longer—maybe days, maybe months.
Me: Would it be all right to put her away? (What an awful expression!)
Swami: Follow the custom of your own country, but let your sister make the decision. I cannot tell you what you should do. I am a Hindu and my ideas on the subject would be colored by the customs of my country. I can see merit in both ideas.

(I expressed sadness for the awfulness of life, particularly the life of old animals and old people.)
Swami: Don't think about those things—that is self-indulgence.

April 21, 1957

Fledermaus died tonight.

April 22, 1957

I mentioned to Swami that in the *Gospel of Sri Ramakrishna,* Sri Ramakrishna said again and again that karma yoga was not meant for this age.
Swami: By karma yoga he probably meant rituals, and so on.
Me: Not always. He also spoke of serving man as God as karma yoga, and he said it was too difficult for this age.
Swami: You have to remember that the conversations M [Mahendranath Gupta, the author of the *Gospel of Sri Ramakrishna*] recorded were given to householders. You must always take into consideration whom Sri Ramakrishna was talking to. He gave instruction that was right for the particular person. He didn't think he had a message—Sri Ramakrishna just said what he had to say to whomever was there. He left it to his disciples to formulate a rounded message. That was Swami Vivekananda's work.

One might say that Sri Ramakrishna always insisted upon the harmony of religions. Yes, one could say that that was his message. Also, he always insisted that everyone must seek God. He insisted on that, too. He said that householders must go for days or weeks into seclusion for spiritual practice; when they had found God, then they could live in the world.

April 24, 1957

Swami: Keep constantly occupied. Work! See how Sri Ramakrishna made Holy Mother work. She was always busy.

Me: I thought only people in a low state like me had to work all the time, so as not to degenerate.

Swami: Do you think knowers of God don't work? Have you got some idea that you will reach a point where you can just sit back and dream? That is your goal? No, you will always have to work. The spiritually enlightened feel that they are not working. They are the witness, but their bodies and minds are intensely active.

Me: That would be all right. I would like to reach that state.

Swami (firmly): You are going to reach it. You are going to reach it if it takes you twenty thousand years.

9

BONANZA

During the course of my research on Swami Vivekananda, I tried to learn something about Mrs. Ole (Sara) Bull, who had advanced his work in New York and New England, and whom he admired and trusted probably more than any other American woman he knew. I read a biography of her husband, Ole Bull, written by Mortimer Smith (the ex-husband of Mrs. Bull's granddaughter, Sylvea). Apart from information about Mrs. Bull, the book contained photographs that I wanted to reproduce.

I wrote to Mortimer Smith asking for his permission to copy the photos. In reply, he very kindly sent prints of them, granted me permission to reproduce them, and casually mentioned at the close of his letter that he had access to a collection of letters written to Sara Bull from several of Swami Vivekananda's other disciples. Would I be interested in seeing them, he asked, and if so, could I give him my credentials?

I at once bought some elegant stationary and spent many days composing and fine-tuning a letter so that every word would convince him of my probity, my sincerity, my good standing in the Vedanta community, and my panting, albeit scholarly, need for those letters.

I waited in suspense. A few months later I received a large, beat-up suit box. It was full of letters written to Mrs. Bull by J.J. Goodwin, Leon Landsberg, Ella Waldo, Miss Hamlin, and other disciples of Swami Vivekananda. There were also many letters from Swami Saradananda and, most precious of all, original letters from Swami Vivekananda himself. The letters were not arranged in any order, either by author or by date. My first job was to sort them out and make a list of them.

After writing to Mr. Smith to advise him of the letters' safe arrival and to thank him, my next task was to have photostatic copies made in batches of one hundred sheets, so no sheet would remain out of my hands overnight. In all, there were more than four hundred sheets, including envelopes. The process took at least one week. When it was completed, I sent the originals, all tied in orderly bunches, back to Mr. Smith, who, in turn, restored them to his ex-wife, Sylvea. (Sylvea later bequeathed these priceless documents to the Vedanta Society of Northern California.) Next, Swami Ashokananda asked a few devotees who were good typists to type out the photocopies.

Most of the letters pertained to a time that followed the period covered by the newly completed first *New Discoveries* book. It was as though Swami Vivekananda, pleased with my efforts so far, had pulled a string in the sky that released this flood of research material, allowing it to fall directly into my lap. (The letters would later become the main course, as well as the garnishing, of volumes 3 and 4 of *Swami Vivekananda in the West: New Discoveries*, published in the mid-1980s.)

In connection with my correspondence with Mortimer Smith, I had been tempted to write to him at length, entering into a literary correspondence. It was caught in time.

April 26, 1957

Me: It is good I wrote at *some* length, at least, because his reply was informative.

Swami: Yes, but be very reserved. Be extremely cautious. The mind is very tricky. Never trust it. Even Swamiji didn't trust his mind.

Me: Even Swamiji? I thought that after *nirvikalpa samadhi*—

Swami: The mind belongs to maya, even the pure mind. Of course, Swamiji's mind couldn't harm him. But see how it made him suffer. He said his heart kept him entangled here. The higher one aspires in spiritual life, the more cautious one must be. The mind becomes extremely subtle, extremely sensitive. From the start one must form the habit of caution. Later, that habit will stand by you and protect you. You won't have to reason about it.

Swami, who was invariably right, would prove to be so again in the case of Mortimer Smith. Several years later I saw a picture of Mr. Smith in *Time* magazine and found him to be very attractive. Just then, he happened to write me again out of the blue to say that he was coming to San Francisco and would like to have tea with me. On hearing this news Swami said, "Sometimes desires have a way of being realized. The mind draws things. You were at peace—now here comes Mortimer Smith." I told him it wouldn't upset me, to which he simply replied, "Hmm."

A few days later, I received a note from Mr. Smith that he was arriving in San Francisco and would phone. The thought of meeting him made me exceedingly shaky. Mr. Smith's voice on the telephone was very pleasant, although it was entirely unlike what I had expected. Since he had more materials for me, we had tea at the St. Francis Hotel, during which he also told me intriguing details about Mrs. Bull and her family. He was very helpful to my research, but he bore hardly any resemblance to his photograph in *Time*. My apprehension about finding him too attractive turned out to have no basis in reality.

Swami said about this shattered dream, "It is said that nobody knows what the mind of a woman will do—I was certainly worried." Then he went on to tease me, "In the eyes shining stars, but then in the heart mooning. One wakes from a many-splendored dream into the morning reality."

SWAMI ASHOKANANDA'S CONCERN for his disciples extended to every aspect of their lives, for there was nothing that did not bear upon their spiritual welfare. He kept his finger on our every thought and deed, as on the pulse of a feverish child. In his conversations, he gave the most ordinary things a spiritual turn.

April 29, 1957

I came from the dentist and stopped at Swami's door to salute him, Hindu style, with folded hands. Edna was in his office.

Swami (to me): Well, hello! Have you been working?

Me: No, I have been to the dentist.

Swami: That is work. *(To Edna)* She has a look about her as though she had been working, concentrating. *(To me)* You have been concentrating on your teeth?

Me: Yes, I certainly have. Then I decided to concentrate on the fact that I am not the body; I am the Self.

Swami (smiling): It hurt?

Me: Yes, terribly. I felt I was working out a lot of karma.

Swami: No, it is not that easy.

Me and Edna (surprised): It's not?

Swami: No. It is true that a person works out some karma through a severe illness. I have noticed that when people have been through a severe illness, they get a pure look. They look very innocent. *(Laughing)* But it doesn't last.

Me: Like going to bathe in the Ganges. The sins wait on the shore to jump back onto the bather.

Swami: Yes.

April 30, 1957

Swami (to Virginia Varrentzoff about me): She is a very methodical person. I never used to think so, but she has her own way of doing things.

May 3, 1957

Swami talked to a large group of devotees about a Walt Disney movie that he had seen years ago. He described the story of *Dumbo* in detail. "Such a beautiful picture of mother love I have never seen anywhere," he said. He had asked Miriam Kennedy, who was then a new student from Hollywood, to try to get still pictures from the movie, and she had managed to purchase three. "What trouble she went to," Swami said appreciatively, "and how much money she must have spent!"

May 13, 1957

Swami came into the back office briefly this afternoon before going upstairs. He seemed very tired today, and his blood pressure has been dangerously high. Virginia was telling him about a girl she knows who is a little interested in Vedanta but who is mostly interested in getting married.

Swami: That is the big trap. One gets married and has children. Life gets so complicated that it is not possible to undertake spiritual practice. A person is blessed when God makes life simple for him. When a person is close to God, he becomes very simple. Swamiji once said, "The greatest truths are the most simple." God is very simple. When He makes someone's life simple, it is a sign; he wants to liberate that soul.

May 15, 1957

Swami (to a group of devotees): Learn to take hard knocks from the world and remain soft. Don't fight back. Be understanding. Practice positive kindness. The world will let you go. Goodness will be free to come out from you. Fear won't block it.

We arrived in June for our annual summer retreat at Lake Tahoe. In addition to Swami Ashokananda's cabin, where visiting swamis also stayed, there were two cabins, one on either side, owned by devotees. Widely spaced, all three cabins stood on a forested hill overlooking the lake. Ediben Soulé's cabin, where I usually stayed, was full to overflowing the summer of 1957 with her husband, Doug, her daughter, Anne, and Janet Blodgett, one of Anne's young friends. Nor was there any room for me at Jo and Helen's cabin. So Swami asked Jo to search for a resort cabin that I could rent nearby. All she could find was a place about seven miles away.

The cabin Jo secured for me was a small, poorly lighted, flimsy one-room hut. When Swami admonished Jo for her poor choice, she assured him that it was the only place available for miles around. I moved in. There were no actual rats, snakes, spiders, or furry black moths, but the small derelict cottage gave the impression of harboring all these creatures. I did not much like it, but anything was better than not being at Tahoe with Swami.

June 11, 1957

Swami, Ediben, Jo, Helen, and I took a boat ride today to scatter Sarah Fox's ashes in the lake on the Nevada side, where it is legal. [Sarah Fox, a disciple of Swami Saradananda, was highly regarded by Swami Ashokananda].

Swami (seriously): Don't talk shop while we are doing this.

June 12, 1957

Swami (about Sri Ramakrishna): Light poured from him, from all over, in all directions. We [meaning himself and the swamis of his generation] are just little pinpricks through which light shines.

June 13, 1957

Ediben spent an hour or so at Swami's cabin this evening. Swami Akhilananda, the head of the Boston center, was there as Swami Ashokananda's guest. She told me that Swami Ashokananda had made faces of disgust at Swami Akhilananda when he spoke naively. At one such remark, Swami Ashokananda had exclaimed, "Bunk, brother!" They laughed over stories that Swami Akhilananda told, such as the one about Saint Theresa when she came down from heaven to see how things were going with her convents. Saint Peter had asked her to phone him. She phoned him from New York and Chicago, each time saying, "Saint Peter? This is Saint Theresa. I find things going very well." Then she phoned him from Hollywood and said, "Hi Pete, this is Tess." The swamis laughed uproariously.

June 14, 1957

There was a dinner party at Ediben's cabin. After the meal, Swami Akhilananda told Jo many complicated Indian recipes while Helen took notes. Then he told us the story of how he had been mistreated by Swami Paramananda when he first came to this country as his assistant in 1927. Later, Swami Akhilananda had started his own center in Providence, Rhode Island, with the help of two wealthy devotees, Mrs. Anna Worcester and Miss Helen Ruble. There had been many compensations for the initial period of suffering.

"I am amazed at it," he said, his face wreathed in smiles. "Such grace! I have no qualifications at all, and yet I am asked to speak everywhere; everyone loves me."

When Swami Ashokananda said, "I think we should go now," Swami Akhilananda said to him, "I can see how much these people love you, and I love you; so I want to do something for them."

Everyone: Now?

Swami Akhilananda (mysteriously): Yes, now. I want to do something.

Swami Akhilananda had relics of Sri Ramakrishna, Holy Mother, Swamiji, and Swami Brahmananda in a small pillbox, which he carries always in his vest pocket. We washed our hands and rinsed our mouths and went into Ediben's room, where her shrine is. There was a breathlessness. Swami Akhilananda handed Swami a small bottle of Ganges water, which he also carries with him. Swami sprinkled himself—tongue, head, and chest—and then sprinkled us on the head. Then Swami Akhilananda handed his box to Swami, who touched it to his head. Swami Akhilananda then held it on the top of Ediben's head, mine, Jo's, and Helen's, as we stood in a row.

June 16, 1957

As usual, we visited Swami's cabin after dinner. At the time, I was writing song lyrics for the dedication of the new temple, and I worked on this with Swami awhile, sitting on the floor by his chaise longue.

Swami phoned Sacramento and San Francisco on his newly installed phones—a yellow one in the bedroom, a gray-green one on a jack in the living room. "I selected the colors myself," Swami said. He loved these phones, testing the bells, tightening the mouth and earpieces. One would think he had never seen a phone before. All these years he has had to phone from a small, cold, smelly booth down the hill, standing for hours.

While he was phoning Mr. Clifton, we were sitting quietly—Swami Akhilananda, Jo, Helen, and I. I was sitting on the floor opposite Swami Akhilananda's chair, but at some distance, for

he had his feet up on the ottoman. I noticed that my shoes were dirty, and started to dust them with a piece of Kleenex.
Swami (suddenly and without covering the phone): Mrs. Burke (he pronounced it *Barke)*—what a place to clean your shoes, under the nose of the swami!
Me (abashed, to Swami Akhilananda): Excuse me, Swami.
Swami Akhilananda (in fits of laughter): No, no.
Swami: Apologize to the swami.
Me (again): Please excuse me.
Swami Akhilananda (still laughing): No, no . . .
Swami: Do it somewhere else. (I went behind a chair and finished the shoe cleaning.)

The mountainous area north of Lake Tahoe used to be called Mount Rose, a name derived specifically from the conical peak that reached 9,000 feet above sea level—the highest peak of the mountains surrounding the lake. The peak was rosy in color, and its upper reaches, rising above tree level, were as bare of greenery and the glint of water as is the planet Mars.

Swami wanted to buy a piece of this isolated, high-altitude desert, sparsely strewn with huge granite boulders, and to build a monastery there with the local stone. Ediben and Jo managed to dissuade him; although the air may have been pure and the glimpse of the blue lake lying far below enchanting, there was no electricity, water, or firewood, nor was there any means of emergency communication with the outside world during the long, snowbound winters that would inevitably grip the mountain in their frozen embrace.

Swami loved Mount Rose, but he had to be content with summer visits to those Himalayan-like areas. He always took his brother monks on picnic excursions up the mountain. Jo prepared the food and, with several holy passengers in her car, carefully maneuvered the winding road, braking hard on every curve. Those were festive days, and the bountiful picnics, spread out on plaid blankets, were a delight.

We usually picnicked at the foot of the peak in a small, hidden valley, a grove where a stream flowed and birch trees grew. It was very beautiful and protected, unlike the rest of the mountain. It came into view suddenly around a bend in a narrow dirt road off the highway. That summer would be one of our last to enjoy that leafy, shaded setting. Several years later, coming upon that little valley, we found to our horror not a sylvan dell, but total havoc. It was as though a giant hand had crushed it—devastation. The trees were uprooted. Branches lay strewn all over the ground. What a shock it was, a tragedy. Swami felt very bad about it. Thereafter we had our picnics beneath ancient, wind-twisted and gnarled juniper trees situated on an otherwise barren bluff overlooking the lake far below.

August 22, 1957

Jo phoned me around 2:30 p.m. to ask if I wanted to go to Mount Rose with her and Swami. I said sure. She said she did not know when they would come but asked me to be ready. I figured that they would be half an hour at least. I had just returned from a long, dusty walk, so I took a quick dip in the lake. Then I waited for the rest of the afternoon for them to pick me up. At 5:30 they stopped by on their way *back* from Mount Rose—they had missed me while I was swimming in the lake! I rushed into my cabin and cried bitterly. I had been miserable and lonely down here in my dingy cabin anyway.

August 24, 1957

I complained to Swami about where I live. I also complained about God.

Swami: Just wait at the Lord's door, even if it is closed. Wait like a cow. (He made a face like a cow waiting patiently at the master's door.) You have seen cows? You meditate a little and then throw your arms and legs around and tear out your hair because you don't see God. Don't do that.

(I said my case was hopeless.) That is a trick of the mind. Hundreds of people before you have said, "My case is hopeless, so I might as well return to the world." *(Sternly)* If you return to the world, every hair will be pulled from your head.

Me: I haven't that alternative.

Swami: Very good. I am glad to hear it. If you don't like where you live, why don't you spend more time at Ediben's?

Me: It is clear that she doesn't want me.

Swami: She does—she has shown you so much affection, and now you begin to doubt. Assume that you are wanted.

August 25, 1957

To our delight, Swamis Vividishananda and Pavitrananda, heads of the Seattle and New York Vedanta Societies, respectively, have arrived as Swami Ashokananda's new guests.

Swami (to Swami Vividishananda): Do you like Mrs. Burke?

Swami Vividishananda (smiling): What a question!

Swami: Answer it. Do you like her?

Swami Vividishananda: I do not want to embarrass her by praising her. She is the very personification of gentleness.

Me: Oh, no. There is another side.

Swami: Yes, she is gentle, but sometimes she protests.

Me: Oh, I have changed completely overnight. I am a completely different person today.

Swami Vividishananda: In what way are you different?

Me: I feel as if something has fallen off.

Swami: It is good to feel that way, but one must be cautious not to allow the other to come back. One can become careless.

Me: You have also said that one should put a damper on elation, or there will be a reaction. How does one do that?
Swami: By doing it. Once a young man asked me how he could have willpower. I told him, "By having it." He did not like that answer. One cannot tell another how to do things like that.
Me: Yes. One must feel it out for oneself.

We went to Mount Rose for a picnic—the three swamis, Ediben, Jo, Mara, Dorothy Peters, Nancy Jackman, and myself. I rode in Jo's car with Swami Pavitrananda, Dorothy, and Nancy, the last of whom we picked up on the way.

August 26, 1957

Mara is also living at a place by the lake. Swami asked me to take her for a drive. On the way, we stopped at King's Beach for tacos. We were parked at right angles to the curb, happily eating tacos. I was sitting sprawled, with one arm hanging out the car window with a cigarette in my hand. In my other hand was a bottle of Coca-Cola.

Up beside the car drove Ediben and Swami. I turned to encounter Swami's huge and furious face, close up to mine.
Swami (with disgust): Couldn't you find a worse place to debauch? Where will you go next? (He told Ediben to back out and drive on. They were on their way to Mount Rose.)

Later, having taken Mara back to her own place, I was walking along the road when Ediben and Swami, on their way back from Mount Rose, drove up alongside me.
Swami (very sternly, his eyes cold): You can do what you want. From one point of view, it is an innocent pleasure to eat tacos and drink Coca-Cola. But if you expect your mind to settle down at the same time, you are mistaken. Besides, I told you not

to eat out. (Ediben, seeing my chin quivering, made mothering sounds; Swami scolded her for interfering and they drove on.)

Notwithstanding my humble quarters and occasional tribulations, it was a blissfully long summer at Lake Tahoe in 1957. When Douglas and Anne Soulé left for San Francisco in early September, I moved into Ediben's cabin with a sigh of relief.

Swami Ashokananda's high blood pressure, dangerously high at 220/110 when we arrived, had fallen into the normal range before we left the retreat in late October. Back in San Francisco, Swami would resume his crushing schedule of lectures and appointments, along with the supervision of the three Vedanta centers in and around San Francisco as well as the Olema retreat, which he had built up.

An emergency greeted his return.

October 28, 1957

Yesterday, Virginia and John Varrentzoff ate poisonous mushrooms. They were rushed to a hospital. John had a fifty-fifty chance of surviving. Virginia was in better shape. The doctors worked over John all night. In the morning, Anna Webster took over. I did not hear about it until this morning. Swami was in his office, looking worse than I have ever seen him. He was wearing his clerical suit and had been out somewhere. Now he was waiting for Anna to phone to tell him how John was. It was around one o'clock. Swami was planning to go to see John, but said he did not think he could go out anywhere. "If only I knew how he is . . ." He sat in his chair, leaned back, and fell asleep waiting for the phone. Evidently he had had no sleep at all the night before, worrying about John and, I think, working for him as hard as the doctors had. Anna finally phoned. John was all right. Swami went upstairs.

November 2, 1957

Swami (to Marilyn Pearce): Define life.
Marilyn: Oh, Swami.
Swami: What is "Oh, Swami"?
Marilyn: I can't define life.
Swami: Life is the force which makes one look for the concrete, isn't it? Life makes the senses want to see, touch, hear the concrete. It makes one have a concrete body. That is very simple. I can't understand why you couldn't define it.

November 22, 1957

Swami: Progress—back and forth, back and forth. One must expect this. It is like crossing a rapid stream. Sometimes the current is too swift. One must go with it until one finds a place to cross. One should not expect spiritual life to be joyous all the time. Joy is not a measure of success. But there comes a time when there is a sense of great joy in battling the mind. One knows that one will triumph. That is a very advanced state. It is the kind of joy a hunter feels tracking down his quarry, or a fisherman fighting a big fish. He knows he will win.

November 24, 1957

I was telling Swami about my having a dim, wispy sense of being independent of body and mind.
Swami: Always be obedient to the guru. In that way you won't become egotistical.
Me: Whenever I feel that inner joy, it is not long before I am knocked down. I see the purpose now.
Swami: There is a rhythm. But also there is a purpose.

10

FIASCO

April 1958

Swami was telling us that one cannot escape all evil in this world—even Swami Vivekananda had fallen prey to crooks. "If one lives in San Francisco," he added, "one must take the foggy days with the sunny days; there is no escaping it. The thing is to transcend both, not to succumb."

Me: You have said that God looks out for His devotees.

Swami: Yes, he looks out for His devotees, but not in the sense of making life easy for them. He makes His devotees strong by giving hard blows if necessary. He makes them ready to receive His grace—one must be strong to sustain that experience—but He never lets go His hand, like a mother who holds her child with one arm and spanks it at the same time. God will never let His child fall. (Swami went through the gestures of holding a child lovingly and firmly in one arm and spanking it with the other hand—one could almost see a mother adoring the child while disciplining it.)

Sally: Why should God single out His devotees?

Swami: Didn't your parents give special care to you? Or did they buy food and clothes for every child on the block?

Sally: I don't like to think that God is like my parents—so partial.
Swami: There is no equality in the relative world, not even in respect to God. It is only when you have transcended the relative that you will find God is equally in everyone. *(To me)* Have devotion. Devotion is essential in every path, whether one is a devotee or a *jnani.* Devotion is intense yearning to realize the ideal.

May 1958

Me: I have not meditated well for the past two days.
Swami: Don't pay any attention to that. Sometimes meditation is good; sometimes it is not good—just go on. Be like a steamroller: when a steamroller comes to a depression, it doesn't stop and worry about it; it just pushes on and levels out everything. Just push on. After a time, an evenness will come.

Besides, when have you got time to worry? I thought you had a lot of work to do. "Work in itself is a means to salvation," Swamiji said. Do everything as though it were the only means to salvation, as though your salvation depended upon it. Work will help your meditation. It will keep your mind on a high level.

May 1958

On being asked how it happened that a certain highly advanced person had flaws in character, Swami explained that those tendencies must be worked out deliberately and separately. "Look at S—— for instance," he said. "She is such a good person with so many good qualities, and she is a real devotee; yet she has a side that is bad. She once looked at me with such poisonous hatred in her eyes that I was stunned. I could not look at her for months."

May 4, 1958

Today was the first Sunday that Swami was too sick to lecture. He went, nevertheless, late in the afternoon to the new temple and stayed until seven o'clock. When he returned to the Old Temple, exhausted, he talked with Luke, Kathleen, Mara, and me in the back office about the ancient methods of Indian medicine and of how he had been cured of malaria. This led him to talk of his days in school. So rarely does he talk of his own life! He talked to us until it grew dark. After eight o'clock when he started to stand up, he seemed to be in pain too great to move. It did not show on his face, but we all held our breath during the long interval between his first move to rise and his final standing.

May 16, 1958

Swami came downstairs this afternoon for about half an hour, after having been given strict orders by his doctor to take complete bed rest for two months and also to drink half-and-half every two hours for his duodenal ulcers. But he wanted to talk to Anna Webster about the base for Sri Ramakrishna's statue for the new temple's altar. Nancy, Ediben, and I were asked to participate in the discussion.

Swami looked so much better—his skin clearer and lighter and his eyes luminous—but he was thin and had a delicate, weak look. Sitting in the library, he asked me a question, which I did not answer exactly correctly. He called me "scatterbrained" and said, "Throw her out of the room." I tried to explain. He said to me, "Shut up," and to others he commanded, "Throw her out; she will give me acidity." "I will go," I said and walked out stiffly. In a few minutes he called me back, and we proceeded from where we had left off.

"One should have reverence for everything one does, even if it is an extraneous thing," Swami told us. Then, quoting Swami Vivekananda, he continued, "As Swamiji said, 'Do everything as though it were the means to salvation.'" He also praised a recent article of reminiscences about Swami Vivekananda in *Udbodhan* [the Bengali-language magazine of the Order] that described how Swamiji, toward the end of his life, had not just a few pets but a whole menagerie and how, when he fed them, an indescribably beautiful expression came over his face. The article also mentioned that Swamiji never grew angry.

"What about the blasts he gave his brother monks?" I asked.

"He blasted them, but never in anger," Swami replied.

"Yes, I understand," I said—for have I not again and again seen Swami Ashokananda himself scolding people with terrible and prolonged blasts that can turn one inside out, and yet never in anger?

May 20, 1958

I went to dinner at my sister Leila's house. My brother-in-law, Holloway, asked how it could be that Swami had ulcers, since ulcers are the result of worry and nervousness. How could a spiritual man have ulcers? I explained that Swami had taken on an immense responsibility. He could have lived in a cave in perfect serenity, but he had not chosen that path. Moreover, it wasn't that he worried but that his body had worn out. I added that Swami Vivekananda himself had worked so hard that his body had worn out.

Leila (a Christian Scientist) looked very skeptical, and neither did Holloway seem to understand. The horror of their insistence that a spiritual man must remain physically healthy while laying down his life for others—the ingratitude and smugness of it—filled me with grief. I could have cried, but I said no more. They have no conception of what Swami Ashokananda accomplishes, the enormous load he carries for others.

May 21, 1958

I reported this conversation to Swami. He smiled.

Swami: I see I have to make excuses for myself. Tell your brother-in-law that, in the first place, it is not medically correct to say that worry is the only cause of ulcers; that hasn't been proven. And tell him that if a man who was not spiritual—a worldly man—did as much as I have done, he would long ago have had a hundred ulcers. In fact, he would long ago have been dead.

And it is not true that I worry—I don't worry; it is the pressure. Every day there is so much to attend to, both big things and small things, and they are unavoidable. The body cannot stand that, but it is only the body; my mind has not broken, has it? Each day is too full. It is like pumping more into the body than it can hold. The pressure is too much for my body but not for my mind.

(Swami then asked me if I had had a good dinner at my sister's and, when I replied "Yes," asked what I had eaten. I recited the menu.) There will come a time when you will have to give up all meat.

Me: Can I do that now?

Swami: No, not yet. Your body needs some meat. A time comes in spiritual life when the body doesn't need much food.

May 27, 1958

An unbound volume of *New Discoveries* has arrived from India. I have asked Mrs. Roundtree, a devotee, to bind the loose pages into a book for Swami as a surprise. I think he guessed it long ago, though I have kept it a secret.

As soon as the package came, I phoned Mrs. Roundtree, but her line was busy and remained busy. In a frenzy of impatience, I drove to her house with the loose folios but she was not home. I finally reached her, after repeated calls, at six o'clock. She invited me to dinner, and we talked about bookbinding.

When we looked through the book carefully to be sure all was clean and in order, we discovered a terrible error: the text specified Isabelle McKindley as the recipient of a letter from Swami Vivekananda written to "Dear Sister" on March 17,

1894, but the photocopy of the envelope for this letter that appeared in the book was addressed to Harriet McKindley. Because of this discrepancy, should those pages be torn out? No, because some, perhaps many, books had already been distributed in India. Should I tell Swami? No, because then he would know that the unbound book has arrived and that will spoil his surprise gift.

May 29, 1958

Swami went to the doctor today. His ulcers were better and he will graduate soon from half-and-half to regular food (I learned this from Ediben), though he has been overdoing, not resting as he should. He had much on his mind, including, it appeared, the delay in receipt of *New Discoveries*.

Swami: Now you must write to India right away and find out why the book hasn't come. I got an invoice saying they had sent it.

Me: What book? The book for me, or the other, or both?

Swami: That unbound copy you wanted. The invoice is for that.

Me (realizing that I had to tell him): It came.

Swami (looking astonished, but smiling): You mean it came, and you didn't say anything?

Me: Yes.

Swami: When did it come?

Me: Oh, a day or two ago.

Swami: My, my, Marie Louise, you are clever.

Me: Well, now that you know, I can tell you that there is a terrible mistake in it. (I told him about the photocopy of the envelope.)

Swami: Oh, my! But I am sure Swamiji wrote that letter to Isabelle. It somehow got in the wrong envelope. Well, there is nothing we can do about it now. (He asked where the book was, and I said in an offhand way that I had it. His eyes twinkled and he asked no more. He knew, of course, exactly what I was up to.)

June 3, 1958

Swami Gambhirananda has now sent me a bound copy of *New Discoveries* from India. I told Swami Ashokananda it had arrived at the airport and he asked me to get it.

I drove via Mrs. Roundtree's house to first pick up her hand-bound copy for Swami Ashokananda, but I had forgotten that it was her day to go to Olema. I picked up the package at the airport and on the way home I again stopped at Mrs. Roundtree's. She was still out—so now there would be no chance to present Swami with his own copy of the book before he sees my bound copy from Swami Gambhirananda.

I did not open my package until Swami returned from Sausalito. I then asked him, "Don't you want to wait until tomorrow?"

"Why?" he asked.

"There is a book for you. I thought you should have it first."

"A book for me?" His eyes shone. But he told me to open the package, so I did.

There was great excitement. Swami looked at the book lovingly and with absorption. He seemed so relaxed and happy. Others came into his office to see. Everyone was happy and delighted.

June 4, 1958

I again drove to Mrs. Roundtree's to pick up the bound copy for Swami, which she had finished after much travail. She had sweated over it with me breathing down her neck every inch of the way. I took it home, stopping on the way to buy some candy. After I got home, Swami phoned.

"What have you been doing all morning?"

"I bought some candy."

"Is that all you have done the whole morning?"

"Well, something else. I will tell you later."

He said he would be back from the doctor around three.

When I arrived in his office, Nancy Jackman was also sitting there. I was so excited—too excited. I had written an inscription in the book after fretting all day over its wording. My heart was pounding, hands sweating and shaking. Impatient and sort of wild, I burst into Swami's office to give him the book. He stopped me. "Just wait a little while," he said. It was like a blow on the head.

I went into the library and said to Edna and Elna, "He doesn't want it yet." I felt roasting, my face and my brain bursting with blood, my heart racing, and I wanted to sob. I forced myself to work on my perpetual letter of reply to Swami Madhavananda (that I had been working on since last summer) and thus slowly calmed down.

Then Swami called me. I picked up his copy of the book and again dashed in. Nancy was still there! Swami said, "Will you show your book to Nancy?" He meant the copy from Swami Gambhirananda. I said, "Yes, but I want to give you this." He said, "Just wait. Get your copy so Nancy can see it." My reaction at being put off a second time was not so violent—the edge was gone, though I was still upset.

Finally, Ediben took Nancy home (as a kindness to me) and Swami again called me into his office. This time I walked in without the book, as though not caring about it.

Swami: Where is the book? Don't you want to give it to me?

Me: Yes, I want to give it to you. (I got his copy and handed it to him. It was wrapped in tissue paper. He took it, his face beaming and eyes shining.)

Swami: I had no idea you were doing this. It didn't occur to me until a few days ago. So this is what you have been up to! It really didn't occur to me that this is what you wanted the unbound copy for.

Me: I thought you must have known. What else could I have wanted it for?

Swami (beaming): I thought you wanted to edit it.
Me: My, you are innocent!

It sounded fresh, too familiar. I had meant to say "unsuspecting" or something like that. The smile faded a little from Swami's face. He let the remark go, but I could sense—I knew—it had been wrong. Everything was wrong again.

He undid the tissue paper and looked at the book.
Swami: Why didn't you put your name on the cover? (Whether or not to put my name as the author had been one of those terrible things I could not decide, asking everyone.)
Me: I thought I should leave it off your copy.
Swami (without enthusiasm): Very good, thank you. (Then he read the inscription, which expressed the book's debt to him, and smiled wanly.) It is very sweet of you to have written that, Marie Louise; but it is not true.
Me (exclaiming, but sick at heart because everything had gone wrong): Oh, it is absolutely true!
Swami: Who did you have bind it?
Me: Mrs. Roundtree.
Swami: Why did you ask her to do it? You shouldn't bother people like that. She has been sick only recently. She has gotten very thin.
Me: She took every care with it.
Swami: I have no doubt of that. But you shouldn't have put her to that trouble. Why didn't you have a professional do it?
Me: I thought it would be better to have a devotee do it. (He shook his head.) But she was overjoyed to do it!
Swami: I don't doubt that. But you shouldn't bother people.

Then he said that my copy from Swami Gambhirananda had a better binding. I pointed out that this wasn't true because it did not have real leather on the back and was not sewn as well. He was surprised about it not being real leather, but still he was not convinced in the slightest that Mrs. Roundtree's binding was better. (Never must she know this—what pains she took and with what devotion—and it *is* well bound.)

I told Swami that he could not keep the newly bound book because it still had to be kept under pressure. I asked him if he would keep something on top of it when he was not looking at it. He said, "No." Now I would have to take it back—a fiasco from start to finish! I asked him if I could tell Mrs. Roundtree that he liked the book. He said, "Yes, surely tell her. Say it is very good." With relief, I told her.

June 5, 1958

Swami was talking to me on the phone about my letter to Swami Madhavananda. I said as he was about to hang up, "Swami, would you like me to have my name stamped on the cover of your copy of the book? It can be done."

He was suddenly cross. "Just forget that!" he said, and then he added, "You should have had it bound by a professional. Who advised you to have Mrs. Roundtree do it?" I was silent.

Swami (demanding an answer): Who told you that?

Me: Anna Webster.

Swami: Who?

Me: Anna Webster.

Swami: How did she know about it?

Me: She was going to do it herself. In fact, it was her idea—a long time ago.

Swami (after a long pause): Always have things like that done by professionals, not by these amateurs. I don't say that only about the book but as a method of work.

Me: All right, Swami. (It was all I could manage to get out.)

I have kept the book at home under pressure. It does not seem so terrible. I don't like the way the title is stamped on the spine, but that was entirely my fault. A professional could have given better advice, I guess. I am so sad that the book was not just exactly right, sad that Swami was not happy with it. It seems like some terrible and irrevocable mistake. I plan to have one copy rebound for him by a professional when the shipment of books arrives from India.

In mid-June, Swami began wondering what the reaction of the swamis in India would be to *New Discoveries,* then being distributed by Advaita Ashrama. "They probably won't even bother to read it," he said. "They no longer care about Swamiji. They have gone back to the old way—meditation and worship. I have noticed that the new swami here has that attitude. All he thinks is important are the Upanishads, Shankara, and the Gita—finished."

Swami began to get feedback from India almost immediately. Some of the big-shot swamis there, whom I did not know but of whom I was in awe, wrote to him glowingly of the book. Now and then Swami would read me excerpts from their letters, and invariably the next day he would find occasion to pounce upon me lest my head had swollen. I used to brace myself for the scolding that was bound to come after lavish praise from India had been relayed to me.

The response to the book was not all good. There was talk about prohibiting a second edition because one swami had vociferously felt that the book was disparaging of his revered guru Swami Brahmananda—a criticism that stunned me.

Hearing of this, Swami told me to prepare a second edition and to change not a single word of the first edition. But that was more than I was capable of. Reading over the first edition during 1959, I found many sentences that needed changing. It was impossible for me not to correct faulty grammar and clumsy wording. And so I made some changes, thinking no harm could be done. When I showed the manuscript to Swami, he scolded me severely. "I told you not to make any changes. I have never known such an ego. Do you think this is *your* book?" And so it went for quite some time. Then, more softly, he added, "Don't you see, Marie Louise, if you change anything, they will ask why you cannot change what has been objected to?"—that is, a sentence or two implying that Swami Vivekananda had scolded his brother disciple Swami Brahmananda.

Swami eventually let me retain most of my corrections, and the manuscript for the second edition went to Advaita Ashrama in 1965. The first printing of the second edition read that the book was by "Marie *Lousie* Burke" (italics mine), which I hoped was not Swami Vivekananda's judgment upon me. In any case, the cover and title page had to be redone. The revised second edition of *Swami Vivekananda in America: New Discoveries* was finally published in 1966 by the Ramakrishna Order.

11

MILTOWN

In May of 1958 the Society's books were removed from the library of the Old Temple. As I drove with boxes of books in my car to the new temple up the hill, I knew that it was the beginning of the end of an era at the Vedanta Society of Northern California. A door had not been slammed but had been loosened from the wall and was swinging shut. It would be more than a year before the latch clicked and a new era began.

Meanwhile, books or no books, things went on more or less as before in the Old Temple. Sitting in his small office at the center of the Society's activities, Swami, despite his ill health, kept his guiding hand on everything, including his disciples with all their quirks (pronounced *quarks*), moods, and balky egos. He was like a blacksmith firing and hammering out what he hoped would be shining swords. No one escaped this forging.

The new temple, four blocks away, was nearly finished. There remained the construction of the altar and the sculpting of the figures that were to be installed on it. The sculptor, Mr. Robert Shinn, lived and had his studio in Sausalito, a town across the Golden Gate Bridge. Swami went to the studio almost every day to supervise the modeling of the statues before they were cast into bronze. Generally, I was Swami's chauffeur to and from Sausalito.

My journal for the last half of 1958 included snatches of the conversations that took place during those drives and elsewhere.

July 1958

Now that Ediben has gone to Lake Tahoe, I am driving Swami, and often Dorothy Peters, to Mr. Shinn's studio in Sausalito at least every other day to look at the statues in progress for the altar of the new temple.

On our way back from Sausalito the other day, Swami was speaking of how delicate it is to get artists to accept criticism from him while working on the statue of Swamiji. I said, "You are so gentle and patient. You can't just tell them what to do." Swami looked at me, his eyes shining with amusement. "I seem to remember," he said, "someone who resorted to a great deal of Miltown." To Dorothy, he explained, "She resisted me when she was writing *New Discoveries*. I would say, 'Put this about Swamiji in here; put that in there.' It got so that whenever she saw me coming along the path to Ediben's cabin at Tahoe, she would run for the Miltown."

July 10, 1958

Swami asked me to bring the copy of the book that Mrs. Roundtree had bound for him. I told him it should stay under pressure longer. He said it had been long enough—he wanted to let the monks read it. I took it to him. Looking fondly at the inscription, he said he would have to take it out.

Me (trying to be casual): That page can be cut out; you didn't like it anyhow.

Swami: You can write what you want. You are a poet and a prose writer. (His eyes sparkled, and he looked so kind and indulgent.) I admit I nagged you. It is my privilege to nag you.

Me: It is my privilege to be nagged—if that is what you call it.
Swami (to Dorothy Peters): She used to run for the Miltown every time she saw me coming. I was really frightened for a while.
Me: I will never get across to anyone the right interpretation of that story.

July 12, 1958

I feel sad. I feel that today everything I say is wrong. Dorothy Peters gasps every time I speak.
Swami: Are you feeling gloomy and melancholy?
Me: Yes. That is, I was . . .
Swami: What is the cause of it?
Me: I don't know exactly.
Swami: The removal of the bookcases to the new temple?
Me: I guess that is part of it.
Swami (seriously): You mustn't let things like that affect your mind. Circumstances are bound to change. Life itself is change. Never let it drag your mind down. Be cautious about it.
Me: I guess it was subconscious.
Swami: That is why you must be especially careful and watchful.

July 15, 1958

Swami: When you can feel free of the body, nothing can hurt you; things can no longer affect you. Birth, death, and suffering—none of those things have any meaning.
Me: What about the suffering of others?
Swami: People think that if one becomes detached, one becomes hard-hearted. Actually, one becomes extremely kindhearted. But there is a different feeling than before; there is a different meaning in it. One sees that man is Spirit, but one also sees that he is caught in maya. One feels a great tenderness. The suffering of others has a different meaning altogether.

July 16, 1958

Due to his prolonged illness, Swami has not lectured at the Temple since May 4.

Swami: Next Sunday I will lecture. I do not know what will happen. I have forgotten how to lecture. I don't know why people like my lectures. I just ramble on and on—no organization, nothing. And they are so long; people have to sit for two hours.

Me: Your lectures are entertaining.

Swami (with mock horror, explosively): What?

Kathleen: You lift people.

Me: Yes, that too, but people are vastly entertained—not on a superficial level. They like your brilliance.

Swami (smiling): I don't know what I will say about Buddha. (Kathleen brought out a children's book on Buddha from the Sunday school closet and said, laughing, that he might like to read it; Swami was seriously grateful and interested.)

July 18, 1958

Swami: Do you offer all your work to Sri Ramakrishna?

Me (hesitantly): Yes—generally.

Swami: Be sure to do it. After you have finished working, offer it. Become more and more conscious that you are working for Sri Ramakrishna. Otherwise, your work won't be a spiritual practice.

October 28, 1958

Me: Swami . . .

Swami (looking up from his reading): Yes?

Me: Swamiji says that *no one* can help anyone. One must do everything for oneself. But what about the guru?

Swami: Yes, the guru helps, but the disciple must do the main part. The willingness of the disciple to change, to be ready to learn, is the important thing. And later, when the disciple is ad-

vanced, he must stand on his own feet. There is a tremendous struggle. He must go through it himself.
Me: But the guru does give the initial help.
Swami: Yes. Swamiji spoke in a general sense. How often does a Divine Incarnation come? A Divine Incarnation and his disciples, of course, help. They can even, if they want, remove someone's unwillingness and transform him. But when it comes to the ordinary guru, the disciple must help himself.
Me: In the advanced struggle, doesn't the guru also help?
Swami: Yes, somewhat, but the disciple must do most of it. It is said that one must have the grace of four things: God, one's *Ishta,* and the devotees. The fourth thing is the grace of one's own mind. Without that, the first three are nullified.

All spiritual life is not as you have it here—security, happiness, serenity. (Swami lifted his hands, palms upward, and tilted his head up with a look of vapid bliss in imitation of my state.) There comes a period of intense struggle. It is said that God will do everything. But even there, it is the devotee who must surrender to God. That only comes with struggle.

November 4, 1958

Mrs. Fahey (a professional bookbinder—the best) came to my apartment this morning to discuss the binding of the book. At the end of a long, detailed discussion, I asked the price. It was $125, probably very little. I told her it was too much for me to afford. When I asked Swami if I could have it done, he said, "No, you may not."

November 9, 1958

After his Sunday lecture this morning, Swami came into the back office and talked to us. Then he waited until 3:40 for a young man who hadn't arrived for his 2:30 appointment. Swami seemed so tired, hardly able to talk. "If he forgets his appointments," I said, because he had done so before, "is he worth giving them to?" Swami glared at me. Finally he went upstairs.

That night

We celebrated Anna Webster's seventieth birthday with ice cream and cake in the back office.

Swami (at the close of the evening): Many, many happy returns!

Anna: Oh, not too many, please.

Swami (smiling): If you are happy, what difference does it make how many? You people think so strangely. You do not know what will happen to you after death, but you assume it will be better than what you have. You know what you have here, and yet you want to exchange it for the unknown.

Anna: Swami, from all you have said, I thought I didn't have to have any fear of death at all.

Swami: You don't know what will happen.

Me: At least death will be a rest.

Swami: Who told you that?

Me: You did—in your lecture this morning.

Swami: You are certainly a fool! Do you think in a public lecture I would tell about the bad side of it? There are hells that souls go to also. The Buddhists have pictured hells that make the Christian hells seem like child's play.

Me: People go also to those seven worlds below?

Swami: Souls, not people. Well, Sri Ramakrishna promised he would appear to his devotees at the time of their death.

Devotee: What is the definition of a devotee?

Swami: When the great masters say something, no one asks them exactly what they mean. After they are gone, people begin wondering.

Devotee: The commentaries that will be written!

Anna (hotly): If one knows what it means to love, one knows what it means to be a devotee.

Swami: Why bother about all these hazy statements? Just do your best. What have you achieved?
Anna: I haven't achieved anything.
Swami: Do your best. Keep on.

When Swami was on his way upstairs, he said regretfully, "I am afraid that I upset Mrs. Webster by that talk about death."
Me: She recovered.
Swami (shaking his head): No, she felt dampened.

November 1958

Swami was reading the newspaper in his office.
Swami: Someone suddenly dies. It makes me remember that someday my name will be in the paper as having died. The very thought of my death fills me with ecstasy.
Me: It doesn't fill me with ecstasy.
Swami: Think of going on and on. It is unbearable.
Me: Yes, for you it is unbearable. But it is unbearable for me to think of going on and on without you here.
Swami: You will find something better within. You won't even want to look at me.
Me: If I really saw you now, I guess it wouldn't matter if you were in your body or not.
Swami: See Sri Ramakrishna.
Me: If I really saw you, I would see Sri Ramakrishna.
Swami: See *him.*

November 13, 1958

I have been expressing my opinion lately too vociferously. It sounds egotistical. No doubt, it is egotistical. The other night Mara mentioned that Swami Shantaswarupananda [an assistant swami] used the expression "clumsy-minded." She said she didn't like it. I said to her, "Oh, I like it!" Swami heard and pounced up me fiercely. "Who gives *a whale of a bean* whether you like it or not?"

November 16, 1958

Swami was speaking to a few devotees about the philosophy of Ramanuja [the great South Indian saint who founded the school of Vedanta called qualified nondualism].

Swami: Read these things! In three or four generations you will be a sect of idiots—"the swami did this; that swami flew through the air; the other swami did such and such"—there will be no similarity between you people and true Vedantists. Study philosophy, but it is good to have devotion; no matter what path you follow, you have to have devotion. Devotion is a movement in the heart, a cry of the heart. Otherwise, it is like trying to start a car without any gasoline, isn't it?

One can have devotion without thinking of oneself as a miserable sinner. Doesn't the prince love his father, the king, more than a beggar can love him? Actually, the true devotee forgets himself in the love of God. He feels insignificant; he cannot think of himself at all. But ordinary devotees take the language of devotion literally—miserable sinner, and so on.

November 20, 1958

I went to the Temple about 1:15 p.m. Swami asked me to come into his office and sit down. He asked what I had been doing all morning. I said, "Writing in a diary that I keep off and on—a sort of journal about you." He was delighted that I keep such a diary and said I should write in it every day.

He was reading an Indian newspaper. I interrupted from time to time to ask about various small matters. Then he finished with his newspaper and looked at me, asking me to say anything that was on my mind. Generally, when he asks this, ready to talk to me, I have nothing to say. This time, I asked, "Is it because the mind is part of maya that the objective world seems to be reasonable?" Swami seemed to be pleased with this question. His eyes shone and his face was bright. I felt happy inside, glowing and excited.

Swami: Reasonable or not, it is because of the dual aspects of maya—the mental or subjective aspect, and the world or objective aspect—that the mind finds the world chummy.

Me: So, because the mind is itself maya, the outer world of maya seems to make sense?

Swami: Yes.

Me: But *actually* there is no rhyme or reason to the world of maya, as Swamiji said.

Swami: That is right. From the point of view of the Absolute, one cannot say at all what the universe is like; it is different from what we think.

Me: I shouldn't think one would see the world at all from that point of view.

Swami: One catches glimpses. When one comes down from the Absolute, one sees the world and sees that things happen without any reason. That is what is meant by the *lila* of God—the divine play—no meaning at all.

Me: Then how can the study of philosophy lead anywhere?

Swami: Through studying philosophy one becomes convinced of the unreality of the world. The mind looks deeper and deeper for the Real.

November 1958

After the Sunday lecture, Swami sat in his chair in the back office and talked to a roomful of devotees. In the course of the talk, he discovered that a book of instruction about the elaborate worship of Sri Ramakrishna was being sold in the Berkeley Temple. He scolded Mrs. Harvey, the secretary of the Berkeley Vedanta Society. "You people will form a cult. You go in for mystery mongering: 'Ring, bing, rah, ping' [imitating ritualistic worship]. Don't do all that. It is enough to have devotion. Practice what Swamiji taught; that is a higher practice—the worship of God in man."

Someone asked if the worship of Sri Ramakrishna was not performed daily at Belur Math. Swami said, "What has that to do with you? Why should you know what is done at Belur? Besides, it is done correctly there, with great devotion. The Hindus understand those things. But you will be like the Christian missionaries in India if you try to introduce Indian customs in America—eat Hindu food, dress like Hindus, take Sanskrit names—you will become fifth-rate Hindus. What is there in that?"

Later the crowd thinned out. "You had all better go now," Swami had said many times, though he remained in his chair. Someone reminded him that it was nearly four o'clock and that he had had no rest or lunch. "Yes, in a moment," he said. "I have to come down a little. Lecturing stirs me up. If I had learned the art of lecturing, it wouldn't affect me.

"One cannot have both. If one wants many people to come to Vedanta, one will have to make compromises in the religion. People want candy; if you give them quinine, they run away."

December 1, 1958

Saturday night in the back office I kept saying rather stupid things, for which Swami scolded me. This is not unusual, but this time I felt hurt, crushed, my pride wounded. This may have been because of the presence of a certain very critical devotee (that is, because of my reaction to this particular devotee). In any case, I felt that my brain was indeed getting soft, as Swami said.

So to recoup my forces, and also with some idea of standing aloof and on my dignity, I did not go to the back office after the Sunday lecture yesterday to meet Swami and the devotees, nor did I go last night. Swami phoned around nine-thirty to ask if I was coming or not. I said I was not. He asked if I was well. I said, yes, I was well, thank you. That was all.

This morning I went to the Temple, still dignified. Swami was not downstairs, so I phoned him in regard to some work.

Swami: Why didn't you come yesterday? You did not come after the lecture or at night. Are you in a mood?

Me (hesitating): No.

Swami: Then what was the matter? Did my lecture make you moody?

Me: Oh, no. It was a wonderful lecture. It made me unmoody.

Swami: So then, there was a mood before the lecture?

Me: Yes. Sort of, and I returned to it.

Swami: Why? What was the mood about?

Me: I feel I am so stupid that I shouldn't come around.

Swami: Well, be stupid, but come around. Don't let yourself get in a mood. To be in a mood is egotism.

Me: I know.

Swami: One never knows what the mind will do when it gets moody. You will say, "Oh, I don't like Vedanta anyhow."

Me: I would never say that. I would say, "I am not good enough for Vedanta."

Swami: No. Moodiness itself is egotism. So the egotistical mind would say, "Vedanta is no good." Isn't it?

Me: Well, I guess so.

Swami: Yes. That is it. Be very careful.

December 2, 1958

I drove Swami and Dorothy Peters to Mr. Shinn's. He is now working on the statue of Swami Vivekananda. Dorothy goes along to photograph the statues and then she and Swami study the photographs at length. It is the same painstaking process that went on with the statues of Sri Ramakrishna and Holy

Mother. By now, though, Mr. Shinn does not fight Swami every inch of the way.

Back at the Temple, Swami talked to Dorothy for a minute or two in his office. I waited in the hall to say good-bye to him before he went upstairs. When he and Dorothy came out of his office, he said, "What are you doing out here?" I answered somberly and perhaps in a sepulchral voice, "I am waiting to say good-bye to you." Swami looked genuinely startled. "My," he said, "you sound so ominous."

Me: I mean good-bye for a few minutes or hours, not forever.

Swami (to Dorothy and me): Florence Wenner did like that. She came one morning and said, "Good-bye, Swami." I did not think anything of it. I said, "You are going home?" She said, "No. I am leaving. I am going to get a Ph.D. at Berkeley. After that I will come back."

Me: I didn't know she had intended to come back.

Swami: Oh, yes, but she was a poet and one never can believe poets. What they say is true only for the mood they happen to be in. Frivolous! In America women are supposed to have that right, aren't they? They can say, "What I said was true then, but it is not true now. My mood has changed." They are supposed to have that right?

Me: Yes. It is a woman's privilege to change her mind.

Swami: Florence got the idea into her head that I had stopped the magazine because I wanted to make someone else editor. She had the impression that I thought she couldn't write good English. The idea was firmly rooted; she wrote a great many sonnets about it and gave them to me, but I didn't read them. If I had read them, I would have known what was on her mind. Now, whenever someone gives me a poem, I feel I have to read it.

Me: She probably thought you had read them and didn't respond properly.

Swami: Yes, she probably thought that. (Swami sat down, looking tired.) Who knows what was the real reason behind it? Desires are like water—they will find a way. When one sees water dripping from a ceiling, the real leak is rarely directly above the drip but has come from a long way, deviously. Water always finds its own way; no one can say how it got where it did.

December 3, 1958

Swami: Once one has fallen from spiritual life, very seldom can one get back in that lifetime.

Dorothy Peters: Why is that, Swami?

Swami: It is like falling from the heights of a mountain. One is crushed by it and hasn't the strength to climb back.

There was once a monk who used to have very deep meditation. One day he got up to answer the call of nature, and he was in such a hurry to get back that he didn't bother to clean himself. Because of that, he couldn't concentrate well again. He said he saw a semicircle of little green people in front of him jumping up and down and clapping their hands in glee. It took him years to get back.

Me: I don't understand. (I did not understand why the monk couldn't concentrate again, but Swami thought I meant about the little green people.)

Swami: Don't you think that there are many people who would be delighted if you would give up your religion? They would start inviting you to cocktail parties right away. You would not have to announce anything. They would know instinctively. Maya seeks any foothold. Just a small mood can be enough.

Wild elephants used to enter a village in India and trample the crops. The villagers dug a deep pit and filled it with mud. One of the elephants fell in and struggled all night to get out, but he couldn't get any foothold in the mud. The next morning, one of the villagers started teasing him by poking him with a stick. The elephant wrapped his trunk around the stick and pulled the man in, then stepped on his body to climb out, and went on to ravage the poor villagers' crops—the man's body had given him the foothold. That is maya; just the smallest thing can be enough to wreak havoc. In spiritual life one cannot afford to have moods.

Swami (referring to me): She was in a mood the other day. She didn't come here.

Me: That is why he has told us these stories.

Dorothy: Oh, not to entertain us?

Swami (to me): You had better go now. Don't you have shopping to do? You had better have your cap cleaned. (It had fallen in the dust in Sausalito.)

December 4, 1958

On the drive to Sausalito today, I realized that I had on my reading glasses and started fishing in my bag for the right ones.

Swami (very cross): Why is it that all women have to get things out of their pocketbooks when they are driving? It is sloppy. If you need other glasses, why didn't you put them on before you started? Sloppy! Dis-*gust*-ing! Driving with one hand and exploring a pocketbook with the other—it is just disgusting. (This was delivered with such vehemence that I could not remove the grin from my face.)

Coming back from Sausalito, before crossing the bridge, Swami asked me if I had change for the toll ready or if I had to fish in my purse. I said proudly that I had it.

Swami: My, Marie Louise, you are learning.

Me (laughing): It is a touch-and-go business.

Swami: Old habits never die. Like old soldiers. One thinks one has killed them, but they reassert themselves. Sister Nivedita [a fearless disciple of Swami Vivekananda] wrote that she taught the children in India to cross out their mistakes with a bold stroke. That is the way—not a feeble, indecisive line.

That evening

Returning home, I found a package from Mortimer Smith, which contained the enshrined portrait of Swami Vivekananda that Mr. Smith had promised to send me. I took it to the Temple. Swami did not come down to his office until nearly ten o'clock. I told him I had received a package in the mail. His eyes lit up as he realized what it must be. I had put it on a chair in his office. I got it and handed it to him unopened. I said I wanted him to open it. I helped with scissors while he carefully unwrapped it. Jo, Mara, Kathleen, and I looked on, excited. There was a great deal of excelsior and tissue paper, and then the wooden shrine and in it the portrait painted on porcelain from the photograph—a wonderful likeness of Swamiji in meditation posture.

Swami: Well now, that is something. Mr. Shinn should see this. It would open his eyes. You see, there are not the shadows that are in the photographs. Would you mind if I took it to show Mr. Shinn?

Me: Of course not.

Swami: But I shouldn't leave it with him.

Me: Oh, no! If you want to, of course (I added hurriedly)—whatever you want to do.

Swami (admiring it): It would be too much of a risk. It shows the eyes very well and the cheeks. (He touched it to his head.)

December 5, 1958

I told Swami that I had taken a book to Nancy Jackman, who is recovering from an operation.

Swami: Was she happy to see you?

Me: I don't know. She said she was happy.

Swami: Why do you say that? Do you think she wasn't really happy?

Me: I don't know. I guess she was.

Swami: Don't bother about how other people react to you. You do the right thing. Make a conscious effort not to think of what others are thinking about you. Remember.

December 7, 1958

Toward the end of the lecture this morning—"How to Find God"—Swami spoke movingly about true love of God, of how the soul longs for Him. For the first time since I have attended his lectures, Swami seemed so deeply moved by what he was saying that his voice sounded for a few minutes as though he was going to cry. Later, I mentioned it to him.

Me: You seemed overcome by what you were saying.

Swami: Where were you sitting?

Me: In the back row.

Swami (smiling): How could you notice all that from so far away?

Me: It is not that far. The auditorium isn't so big that the last row is far, far away.

December 1958

Swami: Divine grace, if it does not at once bring the vision of God, takes the form of great longing to see Him and great effort. It makes you strong. Grace goes with renunciation and effort.

Swamiji wanted to create a new kind of man—one who would combine "the heroic virtues of the West with the calm virtues of the Hindus." Be strong. Undertake difficult accomplishments. Don't water down the teachings of Vedanta. Follow the teachings of monistic Vedanta and look the whole world in the eye.

December 1958

Swami was speaking about the possibility of Richard Nixon running for president in the next election.

Kathleen (passionately): How terrible it would be if we had him for president!

Swami (fixing her with a questioning smile): Why should you care so much?
Kathleen: That's right. I am the witness. I neither like nor dislike him.
Swami: No. If you had no likes or dislikes, you would be dead. Without them, you would be a blank. Have likes and dislikes, but don't become entangled in them. Even great souls have likes and dislikes, but there is no glue in them; they don't get stuck. Look at Sri Ramakrishna—when he met a devotee, his heart went out; he could not contain himself. But he disliked impure people; to them he was very harsh.

December 14, 1958

Swami: My lectures have become simple. That is why people like them better; there is not so much in them. There used to be so many ideas, now just a few. It is like a tree: when there are only a few leaves, one can see the structure of the trunk and the branches; but when they are full of leaves, one can't see it.

As a lecturer, one must say the same thing again and again. Suddenly it strikes home. Repetition wears away the outer crust; then something deep responds.
Me: One must have tremendous patience for that.
Swami: You have patience because your nature is eternal. To be impatient is to be the child of death. Patience is eternity; do you know that?
Me: I meant that the teacher must have patience.
Swami: Oh, the teacher—that is what teachers are for, that is their job. What would they talk about if not about God and spiritual things again and again?

December 15, 1958

Me: Am I a householder?
Swami: Do you feel you are a householder?
Me: No.

Swami: What do you feel you are?
Me: A monastic.
Swami: No. Monastics live a very regulated, austere life. Your life is in between. But in my opinion, that in-between life is the best for people in this country—particularly for women. And through it one can reach the very highest. It is my experience that an enormous amount of energy is wasted when women try to live together. There is too much tension, so much conflict. That is bound to be so. It is no reflection on the women themselves. Women have sensitive natures; that is their weakness and also their strength. They feel every little thing keenly. Men are more matter-of-fact.

Then Swami spoke of how hard monastic life is—how one can have no preferences and must live according to a strict routine; how one must respect the others with whom one lives and have no ego. The rough edges are all worn off.
Me: Do the advantages outweigh the disadvantages?
Swami: If one can stand it, yes. But generally speaking, women are much better off alone.
Me: Living alone, one *can* do better and better, can't one?
Swami: Surely. There is no limit to it. As I said, that kind of life can lead to the very highest.

That evening

Swami was reading the newspaper. Jo, Mara, Kathleen, and Edna were quietly sitting in his office.
Swami: People do not want to go deep into religion. Religion is supposed to make one healthy, well-adjusted, and cheerful; to enable one to keep on friendly terms with everyone, raise a family, and so forth.
Me: Give peace of mind?
Swami: No, not peace of mind. I think that one must kill the

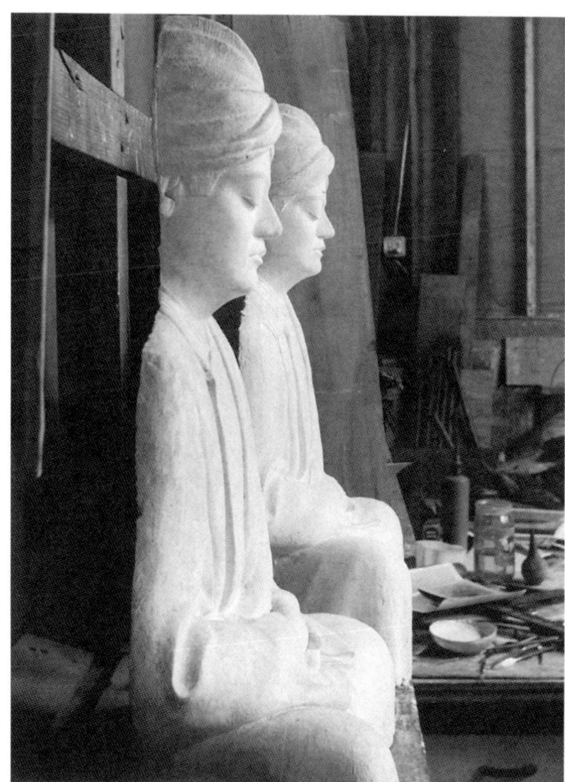

Plaster cast of Swami Vivekananda's statue for the altar of the New Temple

At the construction site of the New Temple, 1955. *Left to right:* Jean Boorman, Swami Ashokananda, Sally Martin, Jim Jackman, Marilyn Pearce, Nancy Jackman, and Anna Webster.

The New Temple in San Francisco

The entrance to the New Temple

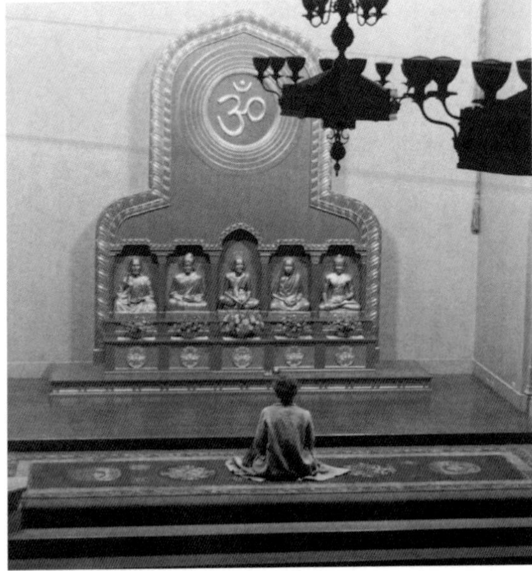

The New Temple shortly after its dedication, 1959. (The author is seated before the altar.)

The first nuns to take formal vows at the San Francisco convent, 1961. *Left to right:* Dorothy Peters, Miriam Kennedy, Eve Bunch, and Marilyn Pearce.

Dorothy Murdock in the garden of the New Temple, 1965

Kathleen Davis in her room in the convent building, 1975

Marie Louise Burke
(self-portrait), 1972

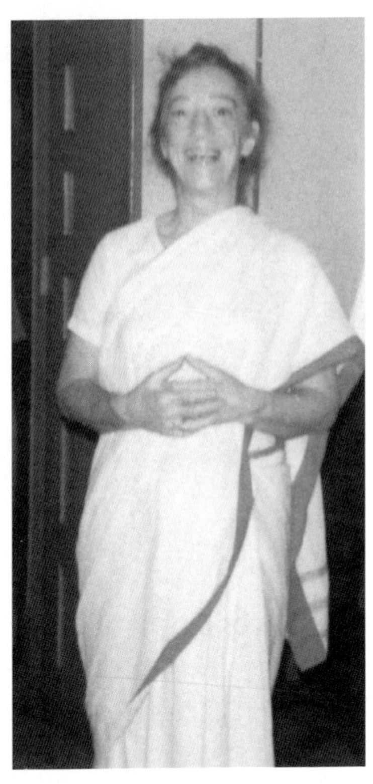

Right: The author (now Sister Gargi) at the Belur Math guesthouse, 1975

Sister Gargi with Bharat Maharaj at Belur Math, early 1980s

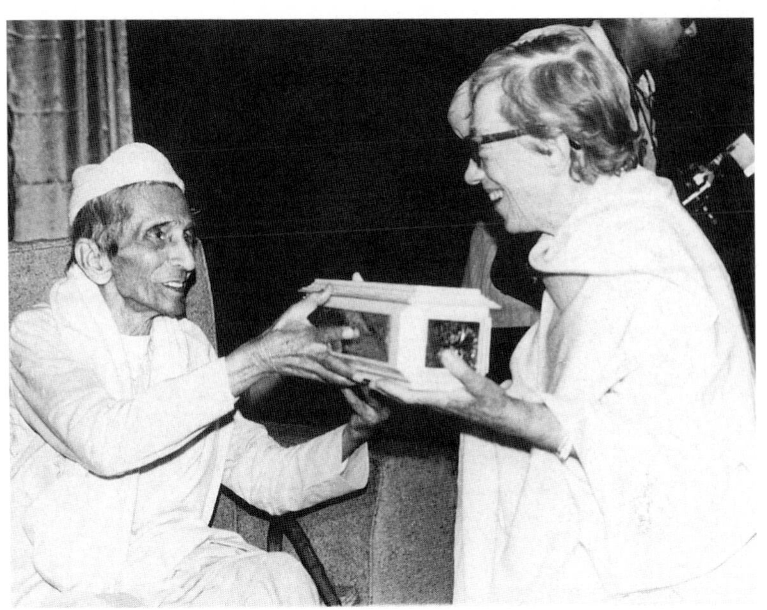

Sister Gargi receiving the Vivekananda Award from Swami Vireswarananda at the Ramakrishna Mission Institute of Culture, January 1983

Sister Gargi lecturing at the Vedanta Convention in Ganges, Michigan, August 1987

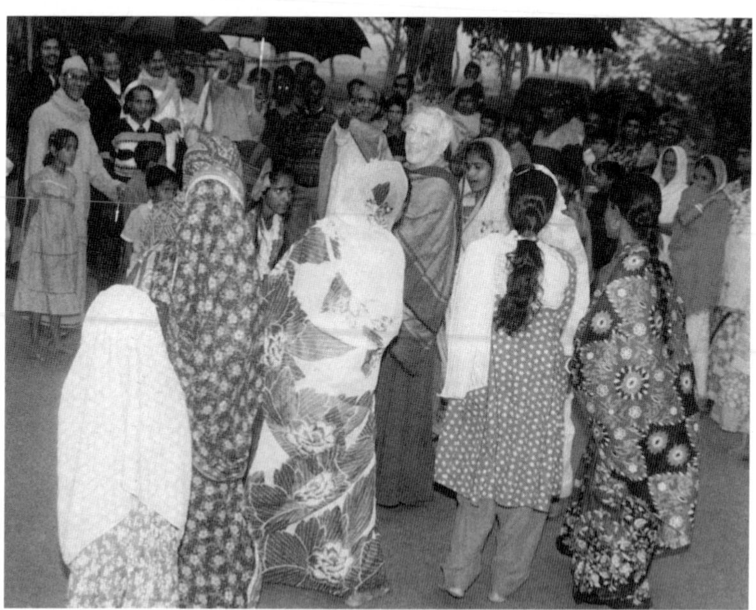

Sister Gargi dancing with the village women
at Durgapur, Bangladesh, 1994

Sister Gargi working at her desk in the Belur Math guesthouse, December 1992

Sister Gargi at Belur Math (in *gerua*), February 2002

Sister Gargi at Camp Taylor, California, June 2002

"Good-bye now"—Marie Louise Burke at age two

mind in order to find satisfaction in a life like that. The deeper instincts must be silenced. It is on the dead body of the deeper instincts that one can build up a happy worldly life. Unless the deeper instincts are dead, how can one be satisfied with the superficial? Those things have no real meaning.

December 30, 1958

At last I sent off my letter to Swami Madhavananda, explaining the things in *New Discoveries* to which he had objected in his letter to Swami Ashokananda last summer. It occurred to me that I had no personal feeling at all about Swami Madhavananda's objections. In my reply, I was playing a role. In the absence of any personal feeling, and without being told by Swami, how could I have known what tone to take?

Me: Swami, if one does not react, how does one know *how* to react?

Swami: Not to react is to be calm. You are learning not to react.

Me: But regarding this letter, for instance, Swami Madhavananda seems unreal to me. I could have replied to him in any way you told me to; I could have been abject, or bold, or—

Swami: Never be abject to anyone! Always remember that! In India they expect you to be abject, to take the dust of their feet, no matter what. Don't ever do it! Swamiji did not want that. Stand up for what you know is right—but be polite about it.

New Year's Eve, December 31, 1958

Swami meditated with us at midnight in the auditorium and then stayed downstairs until 1:00 a.m. Someone wished that the new year would be happy for him.

Swami: I can no longer think of being happy. It has been so long since I have been happy; it does not enter my mind. I don't think about it at all. I just take what comes. I have suffered so much in this life—too much suffering, too much.

I have never before heard Swami speak like this of his suffering, and yet I could not grasp how deep and prolonged his suffering has been for his face was shining as he spoke. The suffering of a worldly man shatters his face; Swami's face, his very being, doesn't seem even nicked. Yet sometimes—and increasingly so as the years go by—even he looks tired to the breaking point, and one does not know how he can go on.

A drama of sacrifice is at the very heart of creation. It is a mystery to me. Is it the sacrifice of the Formless to form, or of form to the Formless—of God to God? Living in the company of Swami Ashokananda year after year, day in and day out, one sees enacted before one's eyes the sacrifice of the self to the Self. It is magnificent and it is heartbreaking, and also it is ennobling and uplifting. One sees the sacrifice and one also sees the transcendence of suffering. There is something here of such great proportions that the tragedies and dramas of the world, of life, seem paltry. Yet it unfolds so simply, so quietly, and so luminously. The days shine, just as Swami's face shines.

12

BE LIONS!

Swami Ashokananda's worships were always simple, consisting primarily of meditation. He did not break the mood with an English translation of the Sanskrit scriptures he chanted; it was enough to hear his chanting voice, sonorous like the unbroken flow of water in a mountain stream. One was caught up in that flow and was carried along by it into some inner cave of one's being. Whether his worship was meant only for a few close devotees—whoever chose to come—or on a larger scale for the general public, it created an atmosphere of profound, yet vibrant, peace in the Temple auditorium.

In deference to Holy Mother's innate modesty, and with deep reverence for the purity and sanctity of her nature, the swamis in charge of the Vedanta Society in San Francisco did not celebrate her birthday with public worship in the Old Temple. From the Society's beginning in 1900, they had shielded her. Swami Ashokananda followed this tradition in San Francisco; but after 1939, he or his assistant, Swami Shantaswarupananda, performed her worship at the Berkeley Temple on her birthday. The public was invited and consumed bounteous helpings of *prasad* [consecrated food] after the *puja* was over.

Holy Mother's Birthday, January 1, 1959

Swami Ashokananda performed a private worship at the San Francisco Temple in the morning. After the worship, he talked with Mara and me in the back office while we waited for Kathleen. What did he say? I remember only how sweet it was, how happy, as though Holy Mother was present. Then I drove with Mara and Kathleen to the Berkeley Temple to see Swami Shantaswarupananda's public worship in the afternoon.

That evening

As Swami talked with a number of devotees in the back office, the conversation somehow got onto the subject of how the Hindus eat with their hands. Swami upheld the rightness of this method, saying it was natural and that we in the West were afraid to acknowledge that we eat. We pretend we don't eat; otherwise, we would eat savagely. He mimicked a dinner party, talking graciously to one side and the other while surreptitiously sneaking a morsel of food into the mouth.

Swami: When there is real inner restraint, everything becomes graceful—whether one eats with one's hands or with utensils. Every expression, every movement becomes unconsciously rhythmical and graceful. An artificial grace, prim and self-conscious, is not the same thing at all. Inner restraint results in beauty. A flower is beautiful because of its inner restraint. The petals grow just so; they do not spread all over. You in the West have restraint, but it is too outgoing, lacking in inwardness. You are too intellectualized. You do not know how to intuit your being as a whole and manipulate it. You do not even know that you should do this.

January 2, 1959

Swami asked me in the library if I would drive Dorothy Peters to Mr. Shinn's so that she could take more photographs of Swamiji's statue. I said very sweetly and docilely that of course I would, but inwardly I was furiously rebelling.

Swami: You are a good, obedient disciple.

Me: I am not obedient in all things. (For instance, Swami had told me to write another book—but how could I write a book with so many interruptions?)

Swami (going into his office): Don't lecture so much. Don't talk so much. (I followed him and sat down, the tears streaming down my face.) Why are you crying? Don't you feel well?

Me: I feel fine—but I spend my entire life driving Dorothy Peters to Mr. Shinn's. I can never do any writing.

Swami (smiling): It is because of Dorothy. You don't object to driving me to Mr. Shinn's.

Me: That is true.

Swami: Now, Marie Louise, in this stage of the work one must be ready to do anything one is asked to do and keep on also with one's main work. We have so few people. You know you are not doing it for Dorothy or for me, but for Sri Ramakrishna.

Me: I know.

Swami: Then why are you crying?

Me (still sobbing): It's just that *(sob)* I haven't been able to do *(sob)* anything for months and months. Of course, I know I waste a lot of time.

Swami (smiling at me sweetly and tenderly): Be a good girl. Life is hard for you; these are hard times.

Me: But life is not hard for me at all.

Swami: You wouldn't be crying if it weren't hard.

Me: I don't want you to change anything, Swami. It's just that I want you to know that driving Dorothy takes a lot of time. As long as you know, it is all right.

During this speech Swami cocked his head to one side, pretending that he was listening to profound and amazing statements (many people kept coming in and out during this whole scene). "Hmmm," he said. Then I drove Dorothy to Mr. Shinn's.

In the evening Swami phoned to see how I was. I said I was all right and was sorry I had made a fuss. He said, "Uh huh." Then I went to the Temple and joined the others in the back office.

January 4, 1959

Swami was still downstairs after his Sunday morning lecture when I returned to the Temple after lunch with Bobbie at my place. He asked me to come into his office and sit down. "You may have to drive me to Mr. Shinn's this afternoon and also tomorrow," he said. I said, "That is good." He looked surprised (or pretended to). I said, "I feel bad about what I said. I hope you will forgive me." He didn't answer, but I think maybe I am forgiven. "I didn't mean it," I said, sitting down. Still no answer. He said he was going to the new temple at 3:00 p.m. and asked me to go along.

At the new temple, a long and concentrated discussion took place about the border for the altar, which Swami said must look structural and not just decorative. He added, "So much fuss over everything, but one cannot do the Lord's work without a big to-do. We are making a joyous noise." Later, he continued, "Our heart's blood has gone into every inch of this temple. In India there used to be an idea that a palace was not auspicious unless several of the workmen were buried alive in its walls. That has happened here. Our hearts have been buried in the walls."

January 16, 1959

Swami told me that I must buy a warm coat. I said I already had many coats, some of which could be relined for warmth—and besides, my clothes budget could not carry a new coat. Swami said that I must have a really warm coat for cold days so that I won't suffer. "Don't record it in your budget," he said.

So I went downtown and bought a coat at Saks. This I brought back and modeled for Swami. He thought it looked too small over a suit. "You should have a heavy winter suit and the coat should fit over it."

I took the coat to Edna for her opinion ("not too small"), but I asked her to go with me tomorrow for a more intensive study of the subject.

January 17, 1959

In the morning with Edna, I returned yesterday's coat to Saks and tried on a leather coat, which Edna at once admired. We returned to the Temple with the leather coat. Swami laughed. "My, Marie Louise, you are certainly surprising!"

Jo did not like the coat. Later, Swami said, "I really don't think it is dignified enough. It is the style now, but in a few years ladies won't wear leather coats. But keep it if you like it. You can buy another one a little later."

This was in the back office. Miriam Kennedy was there. She may have jumped slightly. Swami turned to her.

Swami (referring to me): It is all right for her to spend money on clothes when she needs them. She has made so many sacrifices.

Miriam: Yes, I know. I didn't think it wasn't all right.

Swami: She can do that.

(I decided to return the leather coat.)

February 1, 1959

Devotee (about another devotee): She is idealistic.

Swami: It is a destructive idealism. Idealism consists not only of condemning everything that is not idealistic enough but also of finding something to which you can give your life.

February 2, 1959

It was nearly 10:00 p.m. when I went to the Temple. Swami was sitting in the library. With him were Mara, Kathleen, Jo, and Dorothy Peters. Everyone looked very sleepy and I, too, could hardly keep my eyes open. Swami was reading the newspaper.

In a little while Dorothy Madison came in from the auditorium, where she had been meditating. Swami began to explain that people who were trying to live a spiritual life and whose minds had become sensitive could not afford to work among worldly people.

Swami (to Dorothy Madison): If I should send you to serve among the poor, say on Third and Howard Streets [then a Skid Row district], you would become a drunkard in three months. You people cannot stand a worldly atmosphere. You are serving here. It is a higher kind of service. In order that the swamis can give lectures and interviews, many workers are needed.

Dorothy: You mean dusting and scrubbing?

Swami: Yes, all kinds of work are needed—cleaning, running the Society, keeping books, and then there is the magazine. We don't have enough workers. You should also serve one another. When one of you gets sick, the others should take care of her, and not just among your own coterie.

One should serve, yes. But there are so many things to be thought of in connection with it. People hear a lecture about service, which has to be general, and then go off and start practicing on their own. They are too egotistical to come for individual spiritual instruction. They will bow down to a doctor, "Yes, sir; yes, sir." They will give their whole lives into the hands of a psychiatrist; but when it comes to the practice of religion, they want to do it their own way.

Swami then talked about serving man as God and related many incidents from his life. As he talked, it grew very late, but his face glowed and he suddenly seemed vital and strong.

February 5, 1959

On the drive over to Mr. Shinn's tonight, Swami spoke of his experiences with the English people in India.

Swami: When I was a young boy in my home village, I saw some Englishmen. There was a sort of main street, not very wide. An Englishman with a woman on each arm strolled along, taking up almost the entire road. No one could pass, but they were oblivious. They were not even arrogant—to be arrogant, one must make a sort of comparison between oneself and others—but they were unaware that anyone else existed. I remember how white the women's faces were. They wore tall hats with all sorts of feathers and fruit piled on top, long skirts that swept the ground, and pinched-in waists.

Another time, after I had become a monk, I saw this same attitude. There used to be a ferry that went from Calcutta up the Ganges. Once there was a young English couple on the boat. The girl lay with her head in the boy's lap and caressed his face; she was completely lost in him. They went on that way during the whole trip with dozens of people watching them. It occurred to me that they didn't consider that they were among human beings at all; it was as though they were alone in a field with some cattle. They were well dressed, well bred—it was just that to them Hindus were not people, so they acted as they pleased.

February 6, 1959

Swami told us that Swami Vivekananda wants big things from us. Swamiji's statue has to be a big affair. He wants his price. Everything has to have its price.

After scolding Dorothy Peters for a mistake in regard to Swamiji's statue, Swami remarked that qualified workers should be given freedom to work. Then he added, "But I haven't been able to do it yet."

Swami: First a worker must learn how to work without an egotistical motive. In the course of this training, he might lose self-confidence. But if the teacher can take the worker through that training period, then he can give him freedom in his work.

The main point about work is that the students should grow spiritually. You can guide a student through the training in a gentle way or in a scolding way. You people have the misfortune of having an irritable swami. Now Swami Akhilananda is very gentle and patient. He never blames anyone for a mistake, just brushes it aside.

Devotee: Can people learn that way?

Swami: Yes, surely, gentleness has a great effect.

Devotee: But can much work be done?

Swami: Perhaps not. That may be a difficulty.

February 13, 1959

Swami talked about how one could, through building up habits, train one's mind so it would be unaffected by bodily conditions: "Infinite patience is Eternity. When you become infinitely patient, you begin to taste Eternity. Outer circumstances do not faze you and the mind begins to unfold."

March 18, 1959

At the end of the annual meeting of the Vedanta Society this evening, Swami said that the lack of enthusiasm about the new temple frightened him. He then proceeded to lash into everyone, saying that we were becoming just "religious"—expecting blessings but taking no responsibility—and that to launch the work of a Divine Incarnation was a profound responsibility. "Be lions! Take this responsibility and work even if for no reward. If you can do this, you will be lions."

Swami's closing remarks as he scolded the members were recorded on tape and are given below with minimal editing.

> I am telling you all these things because when the new temple is open and innumerable problems arise before us, you will have to conquer them, and you will need courage. If you are frightened you will not do anything, and I have a kind of fear in my heart that you are all becoming complacent religious people. You go in for all kinds of su-

perstitions—the grace of God and things like that. But you never go in for the central teaching of Swami Vivekananda and of Vedanta—that the Atman is the All, and in It reposes infinite power and energy and resourcefulness. If you want to do the Lord's work and if you want to behave like human beings, as Vedanta looks upon a human being, then you have to call out the power that is within you and stand upon the ground of that power. Are you willing to do that, or do you want just a comfortable religion now?

This is the thing that has really impressed me this evening: all of you have quieted down a little. In this crucial year, instead of seeing great enthusiasm bubbling up in your hearts, which would make you ask a thousand questions, I see that you are becoming very peaceful Vedantins. That is a disappointing thing. Tall talk and piousness have no place in Vedanta. You have to think big things, to see large visions, and to call out powers to support those visions and make them real in your life. That is what I want to impress upon your mind. And if you do not come up to this, then all these new temples and other things that are being done are a big joke—and sometimes I am afraid that big joke will be played upon us to the hilt.

This was met by a stunned silence.

Later, in the back office, I said, "That was a rousing talk you gave." "It was not a talk—I meant it," Swami replied, "and I will see to it that something is done."

March 20, 1959

Swami expressed regret today over what he had said at the annual meeting.

Swami: I am afraid I made everyone feel bad and downhearted. They meet together like that only once a year. It should be joyous.
Me: I think you stirred people up. And if what you said—that enthusiasm has fallen off—is true, then it was good to stir it up.
Swami: Yes, I think it has fallen off. The attendance at Sunday lectures has dropped. It is not just that fewer strangers come; the members don't come.

March 22, 1959

Sally Martin suddenly returned after a harrowing escape from a primitive tribe in the Philippines, the headman of which—an all-powerful ruler—had decided to make her his eleventh wife. Sally's anthropological studies were abruptly broken off at this point. (This, at any rate, is the story she told.)

March 24, 1959

Swami spoke of many things but mainly about the *Durga Puja* that will take place at the dedication of the new temple—an elaborate worship requiring many ingredients, such as unhusked rice and wheat, oats, various seeds, blades of Bermuda grass (which will be grown for the purpose), and water from many different sources—ocean, river, well, lake, rain, dew, and so on.

When the Berkeley Temple had been dedicated in 1939, the worship was for members only. "We were afraid of the neighbors," Swami said. "There was no telling what they might do if they thought something strange was going on. They might have called the police. During the lives of the direct disciples, the worship of Sri Ramakrishna was extremely simple. He was offered things as though he were there. The next generation started making it extremely elaborate. That is how it goes."

That evening

Kathleen objected to the rush and inconvenience that she anticipated in going every night for *arati* [evening vespers] at the new temple, which Swami said we must attend after the temple is opened.

Swami (to Kathleen, after a severe tongue-lashing): You will grow more and more round; you will ease your fat body into a soft chair and just flap your fins. That is what you have planned for yourself.

March 25, 1959

Swami was reading the newspaper in the back office while Kathleen, Jeanette, and I were talking nonsense. Suddenly Swami looked up from his paper.

Swami (half joking, to me): What profound truths are you uttering?

Me (shamelessly): I asked Kathleen if Charlotte had given a big dinner party for Mara and her nephew or just—

Swami (becoming serious): That is what I thought, something like that. I consider it an insult to me that you people sit here in my presence and talk rubbish. I will banish you from here. You can go to your own homes and do your gossiping there.

I had kept saying, "Yes, yes," for the dreadfulness of taking such slop in the Temple in Swami's presence seemed appalling. He went back to reading his newspaper and we sat silent and ashamed. Our evenings with him in the back office are numbered—only seven months more before the move to the new temple.

I REALLY DIDN'T KNOW everything that was on Swami Ashokananda's mind in the early spring of 1959, but the inauguration of the new temple, scheduled for October, required attention to endless details. Needless to say, the move from the familiar and beloved Old Temple would be an upheaval for the Vedanta community in San Francisco, and the responsibility for the New Temple's success rested entirely on Swami's shoulders.

March 27, 1959

Swami told me that lately he can no longer sleep at night because of the worries and tensions of the day. It takes him hours to relax. If he sleeps it is only fitful, for some worry will awaken him. Then he gets up, I think, at four o'clock to meditate (although he only hinted at this).

Swami: It is only after the sun comes up that I get a real sleep. That is my best sleep, between about five and nine.

What kind of a Swami am I? Where can you see spirituality in me? I should be meditative, serene. I should just sit and talk about God to people, give people God realization at a touch. People should be able to come here and find peace and joy. As it is, I just think about buildings, statues, and going here and there.

Me: I wish you didn't have to do all that—wrestling with Mr. Shinn, for instance; that is terrible.

Swami: No, no, it is not that I shouldn't have to do it. I like to do it; it is my nature to be active. But where is there any spirituality in it?

Me: As I see it, it is a great sacrifice. Swami Vivekananda said that work is as good as meditation. The way you work, one can see that it is true. It is what you preach from the platform, and you prove it by your life.

Swami: None of the devotees would believe you if you said that. No swamis would believe you.

Me: Perhaps the swamis wouldn't, but the devotees would.

Swami: That is what you say.

Me: Swami, I think you could give anyone God-consciousness with a touch, if you wanted to. The trouble is no one is worthy. They would explode.

Swami (looking at me incredulously): You have written a book about Swamiji. Why is it you have no sense of proportion?
Me: I think I have a very good sense of proportion. Anyhow, I am fishing.
Swami: You are fishing in a dry riverbed.

March 30, 1959

Swami stayed in Mr. Shinn's studio for well over an hour this morning while I took a walk and read in the car. Driving back, I asked him if the statue of Swamiji was improving.
Swami: No, not at all. There are fundamental mistakes that have to be corrected or it will never come to life. The face is too small. Actually Swamiji's face was larger than Holy Mother's and also larger than Sri Ramakrishna's, but in the statue it looks smaller than both. Something is fundamentally wrong, but I can't tell Mr. Shinn that outright. I just have to ask him to change it little by little or he would resist. He has lost his initiative. He knows that whatever he does on his own we won't like, so he waits to be told. In a sense that is good, but it has its bad side. And then he is, of course, tired. He has worked on these figures for so long he has grown stale.

That evening

Swami had been working in the front room with Dorothy Peters on the photographs of Swamiji's statue, so he did not come into the back office to talk to us until after 11 p.m. Jo, Mara, and I were there. He asked what I had eaten for dinner. Then I suddenly remembered that I had started to cook some lentils and had left them on the stove with the gas burning.
Swami: Go home now and turn it off. Go right now!
Me: I think it will be all right. The flame was very low.
Jo: Lentils burn easily.
Swami: It will explode. Do you want a fire?
Me: No, but I don't want to go home now.

Swami (with a stern glare that meant "GO and do as you are told"): You sound like Sally Martin.
Me (in a temper): Oh, all right! Good-bye, Swami. (With control, I did not slam the front door.)

I walked as fast as possible to my apartment. The place smelled strongly of lentils. I rushed into the kitchen and turned off the gas. Nothing was burning yet. I walked rapidly back to the Temple. As I turned onto Webster Street, I saw Jo and Mara leave. Swami waited on the corner, watching them get into Jo's car.

I rushed up to him. Swami greeted me with "Ah! I thought so," meaning, I think, that he knew I would come back. He smiled very sweetly. "You know," he said, "fire is a very strange thing. One cannot trust it. One never knows what it will do." Jo and Mara drove off and Swami kept talking to me as I followed him back into the Temple. It was very late so I said, "I think I had better go home, Swami," but he asked me to sit down for a minute in his office. Then he told me the story of how a young monk in San Francisco, many years ago, had left an iron burning on the third floor of the Temple. The monk went to hear his lecture and afterward drove with Swami through Golden Gate Park. When they got home, they found that the iron had burned cleanly through the ironing board and through the floor into the space between floors, where it was burning the beams. The monk fished it out and poured water on the smoldering beams. "At any moment the Temple could have burst into flames!" Swami concluded. "It was just the grace of God that it didn't."

His point was taken. I said that I probably shouldn't try to cook things that take a long time because I invariably forget them. I left and he went outside with me and watched me walk all the way up the street. At the corner I turned and saw him still standing there.

March 31, 1959

Around one-thirty I was sitting in Swami's office. Ediben came in to tell Swami that a woman had come to the front door wanting to know if she could "rent" a book. The subject arose of the need for a reading room. Ediben, who had been a Christian Scientist before she came to Vedanta, contended that we must have a reading room in the new temple in order to draw young people. The whole matter infuriated Swami.

Swami: Your ideas are fantastic. You don't think anything through. Where to have it?

Ediben: Why, on the landing overlooking the garden. And on nice days people could sit on the balcony off the landing. We could put an awning up.

Swami (becoming more and more annoyed): In the first place, people would not be drawn by a reading room. Many people go to the Christian Science reading rooms because they think Christian Science will help them materially. They don't want what we have to offer—dry intellectualism and renunciation. Second, we don't want "young people." Young people are volatile. There is no sense wasting time on them. What we need are new recruits who have a few more years of work in them.

Ediben: Well, a reading room will draw new recruits.

Swami: Get the money. We can't have a reading room in the new temple where the offices will be. I won't have the place cluttered up.

Ediben (pausing in the doorway): Then let us have no more talk about young people being attracted to the Hollywood center!

Swami (mildly, to my surprise): I never said anything like that.

Ediben (in exasperation): Oh, Swami . . .

I enjoyed all this immensely. I took Swami's side throughout, for it seemed absurd to think that a reading room would draw people. Later, Ediben said she would cut my throat.

Ediben: You haven't thought it out.
Me: I haven't thought about it at all, but what Swami said seemed right.
Ediben: He hasn't thought about it either. I am thinking of when he won't be with us any more. Then how will people be drawn to the new temple? Certainly the other swamis won't be able to draw anyone.
Me: Neither will a reading room.
Ediben (insisting): It will!
Me: Then we can build a separate one next door.
Ediben: What with?

(Swami had been out of the room during this exchange. Now he was ready for me to drive him to Sausalito. Before we left, behind his back, I stuck my tongue out at Ediben, and she at me.)

That night

Kathleen, Mara, Jeanette, Dorothy Madison, Dorothy Peters, and Luke (Mary Lou Williams) were in the library. I came in rather late. Swami was reading the newspaper and there was silence. Kathleen was trying to decide whether or not to go home. "Why go?" I asked her quietly. "Swami did not greet me with much warmth," she said, aggrieved. But she stayed and it was fortunate, for finally Swami talked for a long time.

Dorothy Madison, who always had questions that start a conversation, asked why the devotees who had talked to M [Mahendranath Gupta, the author of *The Gospel of Sri Ramakrishna*] did not get a description of Sri Ramakrishna from him.
Swami: Why should he tell them? He would probably say, "Meditate and you will see for yourself."
Dorothy: That seems lazy.
Kathleen: Lazy?
Dorothy: I mean lazy of M not to bother to describe Sri Ramakrishna.
Swami: Why should he? Great souls don't like to talk about

those things. Most devotees aren't ready to hear about them; they just like to ask questions. Do you think those great souls [like M] are at the beck and call of everyone who asks them questions? They want to dwell in God; they don't want to talk.

Dorothy: Swami, you said you had a friend—I don't know if it was really a friend or yourself—who said that after he had seen God, he had a tremendous urge to share the experience with everyone.

Swami: Yes, some people do feel that way, but it does not necessarily follow. There is the idea that God Himself will do everything to enlighten souls. He created this world and He has not just left His creation to fend for itself. He Himself will bring souls to Him when they are ready.

Mara: Isn't that the same as just waiting for nature to take its course?

Swami: No, it is not the same; it comes directly from God.

Then the question came up as to how Holy Mother could see other forms of the Divine Mother, if she herself was the Divine Mother.

Swami: There is no end to that world [of divine forms]. One can get lost in it as in a maze. Always lean toward the Impersonal.

Dorothy Madison: If one's *Ishta* is Sri Ramakrishna, can one love Swamiji and Holy Mother also? That is, can one love all three equally?

Swami: No, love them because they are connected with Sri Ramakrishna. Have great love and reverence for them, but not the same as for Sri Ramakrishna. In India discussions often take place as to whether Holy Mother and Swamiji are the same as Sri Ramakrishna, or parts of him, and so on. I have never asked these questions; why should I bother about those things? One can go on spinning theories, but what is the use of it? Go straight. Always lean toward the Impersonal; the Personal God is the Impersonal.

Devotee: Can one love God without seeing Him?
Swami: Yes; you see Him all the time. You don't pay attention. It is as though a man were to come to your door every morning, but you don't look at him. Then one day you see him and ask, "Where have you been?" He answers, "I have been coming every morning but you never looked at me." Literally fall in love with God.

April 1, 1959

Swami: Are you getting ahead in your writing?
Me: No.
Swami: Why not? Don't you feel well?
Me: I feel all right. I have been trying to write a diary of sorts. It takes a lot of time.
Swami: What do you put in that diary?
Me: I try to write down what you say and do.
Swami: Oh, why bother to write about a trivial person?
Me: I think nothing is trivial if it is about someone who is not trivial. Besides, it is just for my own pleasure. In my old age I will read it.
Swami: So that is what you plan for your old age!
Me: When I am not thinking of God, I will think about you—that will be the same as thinking of God.
Swami: No. Your mind should be directly in God all the time. I thought you were writing about the past. Are you waiting until you have forgotten everything?
Me: I have forgotten so much!
Swami (disgustedly): Then just forget the whole thing.
Me: What I am writing now in my journal will someday be about the past, and that is how I will remember it.

That evening

There had been an earthquake a day or two earlier. Several devotees in the back office were talking about it as an inexorable force over which we have no control.

Swami: When even the earth gives way, there is nothing one can do.

Me: Earthquakes don't convince me. I have never been in a bad one. I am always sure they will stop, and they always have.

Luke: Swami, isn't any tremendous display of energy terrifying? Arjuna [the hero of the Bhagavad Gita], for instance, could not stand the vision of the Universal Form, it was so tremendous. There was fear and awe.

Swami: No. It is not fear one feels—awe, yes—but that vision, tremendous as it is, is not foreign to oneself. One doesn't feel fear exactly.

If one feels oneself separate from the body, these things [such as earthquakes] don't matter at all. One feels no fear. Even if twenty hydrogen bombs should burst over one's head it would not matter. What happens to the world is not important. People will sometimes be good and sometimes bad; sometimes they will be happy and sometimes they will suffer. It will always be like that. If Swamiji were here he would rebuke me for saying that—he had such feeling for the sufferings of others. But Swamiji also said the world is like a dog's curly tail [intractable].

The conversation somehow got around to a discussion of how this world is the only place in which spiritual progress can be made. With the exception of *Brahmaloka* [the highest divine realm], from which one can attain the Absolute, the other worlds are for enjoyment only.

Me: Devotees are supposed to see Sri Ramakrishna at the moment of death. Isn't that the same as the vision of God, and wouldn't it bring liberation?

Swami: Yes, it is the vision of God, to the extent that Sri Ramakrishna wants it to be. He comes to lead the soul to *Ramakrishnaloka* [a realm of joy and meditation], not necessarily to liberate the soul.

Me (deflated): Oh. *(Laughter.)*

Swami (sternly): Why talk about liberation? If God wanted to give it to you, you would run away in horror. "No! No!"
Me: Won't people get caught by the attractiveness of the higher *lokas* and forget all about wanting to be liberated?
Swami: Do you know everyone's mind?
Me: How do you mean?
Swami: Do you know how everyone feels about liberation? The desire for liberation in some people is so great that the *lokas* do not interest them at all; they seem unreal.

May 5, 1959

A great deal of discussion went on at the new temple about the base of the altar, but nothing was decided. Of one model I said loudly, flatly, and without being asked: "I think it is absolutely terrible." Swami gave me a prolonged glare. There was also some discussion about the chair for Swami on the platform. Helen had had a sample chair made, but Ediben said its legs looked too feminine. Helen, very cross over this, retorted with her most damning expletive, "You are a hasty pudding!"

Later that day

Speaking of a Divine Incarnation, Swami said, "The whole world can become that Divinity—in which there is no limitation; you can drown yourself in it." He went on to say, "I have never seen any contradiction between *jnana* and devotion. Only Spirit can truly love Spirit. Pour out your love without seeking anything in return. As long as you seek things for yourself, there will be reserve. There is so much wisdom, love, and joy in the soul, and so little of it has come out."
Devotee: It is a pity.
Swami: It is a catastrophe, too. It is as though you had sent a very intelligent boy to school and he got C's and D's.

Power is the thing. Power must come out from the soul. Then

nothing seems too great to accomplish. People who go to fake yogis, swamis, spiritualists, and so on are ruined for Vedanta. Their mind goes off in all directions. It is like erosion; nothing can stop it once it gets started—nothing.

Sri Ramakrishna has promised that he will come for his devotees at death. That doesn't necessarily mean liberation, but one's next life will probably be better.

Me (laughing): Probably? My, there is no guarantee anywhere.

Swami (looking at me sternly and then relenting): I can tell you this: You will have at the utmost two or three more lives. Isn't that better than having thousands more? Isn't that guarantee enough?

Me: Yes, that is certainly enough. That is wonderful.

Nancy: Is that absolutely certain?

Swami: Yes, certain. Those who have taken refuge in Sri Ramakrishna will have at the most two or three more lives. Moreover, I feel sure—it is my conviction—that those who have been devotees in this life will be born much further ahead in their next life, *much* further ahead.

May 6, 1959

When I write of the stories that Swami tells us about the great disciples of Sri Ramakrishna, little incidents, it does not sound like much. When he tells the story, though, the whole atmosphere of it comes alive, and we can feel the tremendous power of those direct disciples and their intense humanness. "They are proof of the existence of God," Swami has said. "Such infinite love and infinite kindness in a human being is proof that God exists."

Today Swami enchanted us with stories of his days of training under Swami Brahmananda at the monastery in Madras. Swami Brahmananda's attendant, Swami Nirvanananda, cooked for him at Madras, unleavened bread and vegetables. Waiting for his dinner, Swami Brahmananda would get hungry and come to watch the food being prepared. Once Swami Nirvanananda allowed something extraneous, like a matchstick, to fall in the vegetables. Swami Brahmananda was angry at this carelessness and told him, "Don't cook for me anymore!" So for several days Swami Nirvanananda sat very quietly while someone else did the cooking. He just sat silently without resentment or fuss. "We watched this going on with great amusement," Swami Ashokananda said. "We knew that Swami Brahmananda would relent." In a moment, he added, "Ah ha ha! Those days have gone forever."

13

RICHES

May 7, 1959

For many months Swami has talked to us every night in the back office, sometimes until after midnight. All kinds of subjects are discussed. If I could remember one-tenth of what he says I would be well off, for I haven't read or heard these things anywhere else. Once in a while I jot down notes. A few jottings represent an entire evening's conversation in which there are riches galore. Those riches sink into me and into everyone present, but I feel they should be captured on paper. I am restless and ill at ease—as though something were happening that has never happened before, something that will be lost if it is not written down.

One morning a week or so ago when I drove Swami to Mr. Shinn's studio, Swami told me to meditate while I waited in the car. He said he would probably be gone about an hour if Mr. Shinn was in a good mood and he could work with him; but if Mr. Shinn was in a bad mood, Swami would not stay long. I meditated for half an hour or so, feeling sure that I would hear Swami when he returned and opened the car door.

It was not a very intense or deep meditation, but there was an undercurrent of peace and light about it. Suddenly I heard a gentle, almost inaudible, knocking on the car door. I looked up and there, about twenty feet away from the car on the side of the road, was Swami. He could not have knocked. He was standing very straight and still, the picture of patience. I had no idea how long he had been there, just waiting for me to finish meditating. If I had not opened my eyes for another hour, I think he still would not have disturbed me.

"But, Swami," I said after he was in the car, "my meditation isn't worth that; it can be interrupted any time."

"Never mind," Swami said.

May 8, 1959

As we drove home from the daily visit to Mr. Shinn's, Swami suddenly turned to me.

Swami: Marie Louise, are you growing tired of me?

Me: Of course not, Swami—how could you think such a thing? *(After a pause)* But last night I felt for the first time that I was tired of Vedanta.

Swami: What made you feel that?

Me: It was during the lecture. I looked around and everybody seemed so wan. I wondered what they thought they were doing. I have never felt like that before. It was as though some light had faded.

Swami (smiling): You are being poetic about it, but in spiritual life there are periods like that when one must be very cautious. The mind can suddenly turn to the world. Not only will the mind be drawn to the world, but also Vedanta will seem all wrong. Then loyalty is the only thing that can save one.

Me: But if one should feel that Vedanta is all wrong, then loyalty to it would also seem wrong.

Swami: "Better death than to betray one's word."

To illustrate this saying, Swami told me the story from the

Ramayana. Queen Kaikeyi had nursed her husband, King Dasaratha, back to life after he had been wounded in battle, so he granted her two boons. Kaikeyi (his second wife) asked him for the extraordinary boon to make her son, Bharata, the heir apparent to the throne and to banish the king's firstborn son and natural heir, Rama. The king was thunderstruck, but he had given his word. Rama, too, insisted that the king keep his word and prepared to go into exile. The people of the kingdom were grief stricken at the loss of Rama, and King Dasaratha died brokenhearted. When Bharata himself offered Rama the throne, Rama insisted that Bharata keep his father's word and run the kingdom, while he, Rama, went into exile.

I drove slowly down Filbert Street as Swami told me this story. He made it vivid and gave many details. We arrived at the Temple and I parked at the corner. Swami went on to tell me how Bharata, rather than rule himself, had installed Rama's slippers on the throne and worshipped them. As Swami was saying this he suddenly stopped in midsentence. He was unable to speak. I didn't know what was the matter. Then, again, he started to tell about the slippers—and again he stopped as tears came into his eyes. In a moment he went on as if nothing had happened. I have never known him to do anything like that before. Was it because he was moved by Bharata's devotion to Rama? Then he went on to say that one's word must be kept and loyalty did not know reason; it was blind. "Loyalty to the guru is the saving thing." He got out of the car in a little while with all his usual vigor, and I put the car away.

In his office Swami was looking at the pictures of Holy Mother's statue and nothing seemed wrong. He told me about a student who had remained with Swami Bodhananda at the Vedanta Society of New York after almost everyone else had followed Swami Nikhilananda to a new center in Manhattan. She remained faithful to Swami Bodhananda throughout his lifetime and even remained faithful to Swami Bodhananda's successor, Swami Pavitrananda—faithful to that Vedanta Society until she died.

Me: Will I have to go through a period in which Vedanta means nothing?

Swami: There is no reason why you should, but there is always that possibility. A river isn't always in full flood; sometimes it is just a trickle. One must watch the mind. I have noticed lately that if I don't do just what you want, you flare up. That is not good.

Me (embarrassed): It is only momentary, when I am tired.

Swami: Yes, I know, but the mind makes use of the slightest thing.

July 7, 1959

Swami asked me to come to the new temple. Dorothy Peters and Anna Webster were working on the plaster cast of Swamiji—adding plaster to the cheeks to fill them out, widening the face, then smoothing the plaster, scraping it off and adding more. Swami was also working on the plaster cast, to the horror of Dorothy and Anna, though Swami himself looked vastly pleased and amused. He smoothed the wet plaster with his fingers. Someone handed him a tool. "You people," he said, "always have to use tools for everything instead of your hands. You have to eat with tools. If you did not have knives and forks, you would use the ferrule of your umbrella."

As Swami went on he became more and more expert. Absorbed in his work—scraping, leaning back to look, taking off a little here, showing where more should be added there—he was enjoying himself with complete confidence and self-assurance. "I feel very bold," he said. "Can you imagine how bold we are? Mr. Shinn [then in Washington, D.C.] must be squirming."

The next day, and for several days following, he was back

working for hours on Swamiji's statue with Dorothy and Anna, but only on the cheeks and chin, not on the more delicate and tricky features, such as eyes, lips, and nose; nonetheless it was a terrifying business. As I watched I felt the statue was becoming more like Swamiji, more manly and mature. It would have taken Swami at least four months to persuade Mr. Shinn to make these changes. I myself had always wished Swami would just take a tool in hand and go ahead, and here he is doing it. Swami's sculpting, of course must remain a deep and dark secret.

Swami Nikhilananda was here on his way to Honolulu to attend the East-West Philosophers' Conference. He knew from my name that I had written about Swami Vivekananda and he said a few complimentary things, but he did not seem to remember that I had been in New York.

One night Swami Ashokananda pried out from Sally Martin that Swami Nikhilananda had criticized him to her while she was in India, and he made her tell him what Swami Nikhilananda had said. It was largely to the effect that Swami Ashokananda, a promising writer, had failed to write any books.

"Why should that upset you so much?" Swami asked Sally. "There are worse things than that. And why should I have worked intellectually? What is there in that? You should have said to him, 'Swami, I do not remember having read in the Vedantic scriptures that one can realize God through the intellect.' My work here has been to build up the Society, so I have done that; I have done whatever the work called for. Actually, I did not write very much when I was in India, but whatever I wrote was because of my work there."

Later that day

Swami: We are never given the choice of avoiding suffering. Never. Neither God, nor life, nor our own selves will permit it. Good people turn suffering to advantage; bad people get caught in it so that it leads to more suffering. That is the only difference.

July 8, 1959

The bronze statue of Sri Ramakrishna arrived at the new temple from the Brooklyn foundry toward the end of June. I first saw it the night of June 28 and was bowled over. It seemed to me that Sri Ramakrishna himself was sitting there, and the tears started to flow down my cheeks. The statue was so lifelike and had such an effect on me that I could not look at it critically, observing what was right or wrong, as Swami wanted us to do.

July 9, 1959

Swami talked with us in the back office, as usual, until late. In the auditorium the choir was rehearsing for the dedication ceremony. Swami enjoyed their singing so we opened the door of the back office to hear the music, which sounded like Gregorian chant. After the rehearsal, some of the singers stood in the doorway as Swami talked of Swami Premananda [a direct disciple of Sri Ramakrishna] and of how extraordinary he was—so full of love that one felt one could tell him anything and that he would understand; he would never forsake one, no matter what one had done.

"It is only when Divine Incarnations come that such great souls come to earth—that is our chance to see what they are like," Swami said. "How else could one know what human beings can be, what heights they can reach? One cannot imagine it without seeing them."

A kind of breathless wonder comes into the room whenever Swami talks about the great disciples; one catches something of Swami's own wonder and love as he recalls them.

July 10, 1959

Swami (to a devotee): They say there are one hundred nerves that converge upon the heart. One of these nerves leads to Brahman. One must find that nerve and travel along it. I do not know about the one hundred nerves, but I know that there is that one nerve. A friend of mine [probably Swami himself] told me that every time he sat for meditation, his mind would at once go deep, within thirty seconds. It was as though he were entering a tunnel of light. The light seemed to be coming from the end of the tunnel; it was like looking through a long tunnel toward the sun. He would travel along that tunnel that led to Brahman. You must find that tunnel, that nerve. One cannot force the experience; it just happens.

July 12, 1959

Swami was recalling his high school and college days. He told us how he pushed his mind to see Brahman everywhere every minute of his waking hours, breaking all his old patterns of thought. After several years that way of thinking became a natural state with him; he no longer had to force his mind. He actually saw Brahman everywhere.

Swami: One cannot retain that state and work at the same time. One cannot build temples and all that. That is why there is the tradition in India that monks should not work.

Devotee: Yet the path of karma yoga [selfless work] is supposed to lead to the highest.

Swami: Yes, that is true, but there are different types of karma yoga. In advanced states one should do a different kind of work. Just as there are different stages of bhakti yoga [path of devotion], so there are different stages of karma yoga. It is still work, but it is not building temples and attending to all such kinds of things.

August 7, 1959

In the back office, Swami was speaking of the Divine Mother and of how the whole universe was really She.

Swami: I once saw the whole universe as the tremendous, tumultuous play of living energy. That is the way things really are—everything is the tumultuous and joyous play of living energy, both good and evil.

Me: Why is it that it is more pleasant not to work than to work?

Swami: It is the nature of man to be self-indulgent. One must force oneself to work. Only those who are highly advanced spiritually can afford to act according to their preferences; for others the mind must be kept alert or it will create trouble for itself. Responsibility keeps the mind alert. I don't think you people have any idea what dangers there are in the spiritual path. One must be extremely cautious and extremely alert.

Me: What kind of dangers?

Swami: Are you really unintelligent?

Me: You mean the mind can turn?

Swami: Of course.

Mr. Shinn has now completed work on the revised plaster cast of Swamiji. He brought it to the new temple in order to see the effect of the light. To spare Mr. Shinn's feelings, Swami did not tell him how he, Anna, and Dorothy Peters worked on the plaster cast in Mr. Shinn's absence—only that it had been damaged and that this was his (Swami's) fault.

Swami: When one is working with people one cannot always tell the truth, for telling the truth can sometimes cause untold trouble and create all kinds of unnecessary difficulty.

Me: One must need a great sense of responsibility in order to be able not to tell the truth sometimes.
Swami: Yes. It is a dangerous kind of thing.

August 13, 1959

As soon as choir rehearsal was over this evening, Dora Blaney, the music director, and the singers crowded into the doorway of the back office. Swami spoke about the main worship that would take place at the dedication.
Swami: It will be terribly complicated. One cannot worship only Sri Ramakrishna; it involves the worship of all sorts of gods and goddesses. There are swamis in India who are past masters at this kind of thing—like singers who have mastered all the technique and can perform effortlessly. It is wonderful to watch them.
Dora: Everyone is working very hard.
Swami: Yes, everyone is. Sri Ramakrishna is very pleased.
Dora (incredulous): Is he really pleased?
Swami (very emphatically): Absolutely! I will tell you a story. It is about another center. The swami-in-charge had been working very hard and went into the shrine. Sri Ramakrishna came right out of the photograph on the altar and came toward the swami with the speed of an arrow. Like an arrow, Sri Ramakrishna pierced him in the chest and entered into his heart. The swami felt great joy and he knew that Sri Ramakrishna was very pleased that so much work was being done for him—very pleased.

Telling this story, Swami looked glowing, and he showed just exactly how Sri Ramakrishna had pierced the chest: "He hit the swami just here." I do not think there is any doubt that this had happened to Swami himself and had happened quite recently—probably at Sacramento, when the altar of the temporary chapel was installed.

August 17, 1959

Hard labor has gone into creating a garden behind the new temple. The workers have also been digging new plots along the front and side of the temple. Swami has supervised all these activities.

At one time Swami did not want the women to wear blue jeans while working in the garden, but when skirts proved impractical, he consented. He still insisted, though, that we wear skirts in the temple auditorium or out on the street. For such occasions, Dorothy Peters wore a voluminous denim jumper with woolen stockings—a strange-looking getup. Yesterday, when Swami asked her while she was in blue jeans to come out on the sidewalk so he could tell her about some work to be done there, she said, "I will change into a skirt in a jiffy." Swami said, "What is it that you wear? Some sort of Mother Hubbard? What you have on is better than that. Why do you get yourself up in a Mother Hubbard?" So Dorothy was allowed out on the street in her jeans.

August 19, 1959

Swami said that he would write his talk for the dedication and read it from the lectern. The devotees objected to this because it was Swami's custom to speak extemporaneously. Swami answered that in this way he would not lose control of himself and talk too long. There were further objections.

Devotee: Swami, do you remember what the subject of your Sunday lecture is going to be before you read the title on the lectern?

Swami: Oh, yes, I know.

Devotee: Have you thought about what you are going to say beforehand?

Swami: No, except when I am going to give a biographical lecture; then I look up dates so I will get them right. And when I speak on Christian subjects, I read some Christian commentaries. But usually I don't think about what I am going to say until Sunday morning. In the morning my mind becomes very intense. I don't like to be disturbed. Thoughts are coming up and gathering together. There is also a little nervousness, but not so much any more—my nerves have grown slack, sagged down.

It is better not to prepare lectures, I think. I knew a professor who used to speak wonderfully in conversation. He would answer questions very clearly and logically, but when he lectured he would become stiff and formal. I feel that people come to my lectures with questions in their minds—I just answer them. Thoughts used to come like lightning into my mind, and all ordered, but I always returned to the main theme without any trouble at all after a long digression. Now I sometimes forget what I have been saying.

When I was in Madras I used to go to the beach at noon to bathe. Later, I learned that the undertow was very dangerous so I stopped going in the water. Once, as I stood on the beach, suddenly my mind opened up and ideas began to come like lightning. They were ideas I had never had before, had never read anywhere—completely new and original ideas. They were of another order than the ideas one usually has, an entirely different order. I thought I would write them down but I had no paper or pencil with me, and later I forgot. They were not related to anything on this plane of thought. It made me think that there is a vast thought world and that our minds are only on the fringe of it.

It is a wonderful experience to lecture. When my thoughts are coming fast, I feel a great silence. The audience becomes absorbed and all other thoughts are quiet. There is deep silence.

When I lectured at the Century Club [in San Francisco], I realized that I had a habit of repeating the same idea in a slightly different way; I would say one sentence and then repeat it a little differently. I also noticed that I used too many words to say something that could be said in a few words. I determined to correct those faults. At first it was difficult because the mind wanted to repeat the old habits, but after a lecture or two it became natural.

August 24, 1959

This afternoon, in a snit, I went for a long walk and ended up in a Catholic church, seeking comfort.

Swami (quoting a Bengali verse to me): "Never revile or worship another *Ishta*. Never take food that has been offered to another *Ishta*." That is what Sri Chaitanya said—never partake of offerings to another form of God.

Me: I didn't partake of offerings.

Swami: Never mind that. Just swallow what I say. Swallow it without salt.

Sri Ramakrishna will accept all the work you do for Him. That is all you have to think about. Whether others like it or not, he accepts it. Just know that you have done your best. You will have to put up with all sorts of things in this work. When you have to cooperate with others, there will be all kinds of things to put up with; but never be upset by it. You must learn that. Some criticism will be valuable and some will be worthless—take what is of value and reject the rest.

Me: When you are not here to judge, I do not know what I will do. I can't fight with people.

Swami: No, don't fight. If you think what you have done is right, say so and let it go at that.

(After a pause) Marie Louise, I don't try to make you suffer; that is not my life's work. If your heart breaks so often, I don't know how you will live. You have come to Sri Ramakrishna. Remember that nothing bad can ever happen to you here. That knowledge will be your armor. But if you think that anything

bad can happen to you—then there is already a chink in your armor.

Late morning

Mr. Shinn was working in the new temple on the statue of Holy Mother. Dorothy Peters was there to take pictures.
Swami (to Dorothy): If you have nothing to do, just sit quietly.
Dorothy (jumping up a few minutes later): I will be right back.
Swami: Where are you going?
Dorothy: I want to tell them that I won't be there for lunch.
Swami: Sit down. Couldn't you have told them that before?
Dorothy: Yes, Swami.
Swami: One of the skills of work is to do everything at the right time and then sit calmly and peacefully—furious activity and then repose. Sri Ramakrishna had a brahmin cook who used to come in the morning. In the night Sri Ramakrishna would get everything ready for him—everything. When someone asked why he did that, he answered: "Because when he comes I will be meditating and he won't have to ask me for anything."
Dorothy: My, he taught us everything!
Swami: Yes. Get everything done at once—and then rest in perfect peace. Swami Akhilananda is like that. He works furiously and then, when he has done everything, he sits with complete peace. I am not a good example to you.
Dorothy: Oh, yes, Swami you are.
Swami: You are deluded.

The inauguration in San Francisco of the new temple (now dedicated and referred to hereafter as the New Temple) was celebrated with five days of morning and afternoon worship during

Durga Puja in October of 1959. Many of the devotees played a part, either in connection with the *puja* itself or with serving *prasad* after the ceremony to the huge audience that overflowed the auditorium into the lobby. Everything took place without a hitch: the choir's music was sublime, the altar and chancel looked beautiful with flowers and candles, and all seemed steeped in an unearthly glow that one could only call *sattvic*—possessing the quality of light and purity. I understood for the first time the reason for ceremonial cleanliness in the service of the Deity—no impurity, not even of thought, must touch the altar or the articles of worship. During the five days of this flawless worship, the New Temple seemed transported to a different, purer, world.

My own part in the dedication was the only sour note; it was a disaster from start to finish. I had been assigned to drive the visiting swamis on sightseeing trips and wherever else they wanted to go. The job was a great honor (and a great terror) to me. I prided myself on being a good and experienced driver, without any accidents or serious violations on my record; but to chauffeur all those senior monks—Swamis Akhilananda, Nikhilananda, Pavitrananda, Satprakashananda, and Vividishananda, none of whom I knew well enough to feel at ease with—was daunting.

My nervousness bore almost immediate fruit. On the first excursion, when I drove Swami Pavitrananda and Swami Vividishananda to Sausalito, I somehow managed to engage the front bumper of my big Cadillac with the wire fence outside Mr. Shinn's studio. It was an almost inextricable tangle from which I could move neither forward nor backward without destroying the fence. During my maneuvers the swamis looked on, and from time to time Swami Vividishananda said consolingly, "It is very *deef*-fee-cult to drive."

An outing or two later, I drove all five of the swamis across the Bay Bridge to the Berkeley Temple, where they had been invited to dinner. Swami Akhilananda had an appointment to visit one of his old students at her Berkeley home half an hour before the dinner engagement. He had not seen her for many years and she was, of course, eagerly awaiting his arrival. I was just as anxious to get him there on time; but, unnerved by a carload of swamis and unsure of the way to the bridge, I sailed through a stoplight in downtown traffic. The sickening sound of a police siren stopped me cold, and the business of receiving a ticket and getting a stern reprimand from the police officer not only humiliated me but also delayed our progress long enough for us to get caught in stalled traffic on the approach to the bridge itself.

The car was facing west, straight into the setting sun. Its hot rays shone mercilessly through the windshield onto all the swamis, from which there was no escape. "It is very *deef*-fee-cult to drive," Swami Vividishananda repeated. All the swamis were very gracious about their discomfort, assuring me that it was of no consequence; but we were stuck facing the sun for at least half an hour. Finally, the traffic moved and we arrived at the student's house in time for Swami Akhilananda to have a short five-minute visit before we went on to the Berkeley Temple. I drove home alone. After their dinner, the swamis were driven back to San Francisco by a monastic probationer, no doubt without incident.

The next day the swamis were scheduled to go sightseeing. I arrived on time to pick them up and they all assembled on the sidewalk in front of the Old Temple, including Swami Ashokananda, who was there to see them off—or was it to deal with me? In either case, the latter is what he did, right there in the open street.

"So," he said, and continued in a voice loud enough to bring all the neighboring housewives to their windows, "you have now become a famous writer who doesn't have to pay attention to traffic signs!" He went on at length about how I had inconvenienced the swamis, had caused them great discomfort, and was altogether unworthy to drive them anywhere. During this reprimand, Swami Akhilananda stood behind Swami Ashokananda's right shoulder, shaking his head at me and mouthing, "No, no"—as though to say, "Pay no attention; none of it is true." Swami Nikhilananda walked away in embarrassment and Swami Vividishananda softly repeated, "It is very *deef*-fee-cult to drive."

Finally, Swami Ashokananda finished scolding me. His brother monks got in the car and I, choking back tears, drove them off on a sightseeing tour that none of them really cared about. That was the part I played in the dedication of the New Temple. Notwithstanding these antics in the wings, the Vedanta Society of Northern California entered a new era with a clear and joyful noise.

14

A GOOD BOOK

Throughout the 1960s my journal lay not only unopened on my desk but also hidden deep under stacks of shifting research material for the second book of *New Discoveries* and other precariously piled works in progress. Now and then, however, Swami Ashokananda would let fall a gem of spiritual wisdom or advice that I felt needed to be preserved. From that sparse collection, I have selected entries that strike me as being of use to spiritual aspirants of all ages and persuasions.

October 15, 1960

Me: Does God really exist, or is it just a matter of speaking?
Swami: God really exists! The One wants to become the many—at that point there is the Personal God. He is the same as the Absolute, but He has a relationship with souls.
Me: In what sense does Sri Ramakrishna exist differently now than he existed before he was incarnated on earth?
Swami: He exists now in a subtle body. That is different from his eternal form. There is one opinion that the subtle body of Divine Incarnations lasts till the end of the cosmic cycle. Others say that they go after a time and that probably their power lessens.

October 1960

We were gathered around Swami this evening at the Old Temple.

Ann Myren: The Absolute must have form, since it would not be complete otherwise.

Swami: You want the joy that order gives. The sense of order, reason, and beauty comes from the Absolute, but there is no order in the Absolute—order implies relations, and there can be no relations in the Absolute. There is only One.

October 1960

A group of devotees gathered in the foyer after the Sunday lecture in the New Temple, waiting for Swami to talk with them—often it would be four o'clock before they left after this "second" lecture. A debilitating disease of some kind was being discussed.

Swami: Prepare for illness. Rise above it in youth.

Devotee: But in youth one is healthy. How can one prepare then for illness?

Swami: Rise above health. Don't glory in it. Train the mind to rise above the body.

Devotee: It takes a long time to train the mind.

Swami: Have patience. What is the hurry? Look at the positive side of things. Think how wonderful it is that every day you have thought of God. Don't emphasize the struggle.

November 3, 1960

When I came to the Old Temple this morning, Swami was in the front room, waiting for me. After a minute or two he looked at me and asked, "Yes? Do you want to say something? What is it?"

Me: Nothing.

Swami: You look as though you expected some answer.

Me (laughing): I always expect some answer from you.

Swami: What answer?

Me: Sudden illumination.
Swami: Why do you want that? It would spoil things for you. You would no longer be able to find pleasure in smoking, or in sleeping, or in serving the Lord, or in being with me.
Me: If I were illumined, I would not need those things. I would have them—or the pleasure they give me—even more.
Swami: You are not ready yet to ask for illumination. If you got it, you wouldn't be able to contain it.
Me: Well, in that case, I would like just a little more than I have.
Swami: Be content with whatever you have. In spiritual life one should never be discontent. That spoils everything.
Me: Yes. What I have is more than I deserve.

Swami continued to talk to me as we went out the door and walked to his car, parked around the corner.
Swami: Be content, but be earnest. Many devotees get into a state of discontent and spoil everything for themselves. They read about saints who are always demanding more and who are longing for illumination. They think that is the way to be and they try to imitate it. Yes, there is a stage when there comes a great discontent, when one wants to probe deeper and deeper into reality—but that is a very high state. Discontent is right at that time. Before that state is reached, though, one makes progress more through contentment than through discontentment.

December 3, 1961

Several devotees were sitting in the front room of the Old Temple. Swami sat on the couch, as always. On Sunday evenings his mind is still soaring high from his morning lecture. He likes to talk to us at that time. I came in rather late and the conversation was already going on.
Dorothy Madison: Sri Ramakrishna says in the *Gospel [Gospel of Sri Ramakrishna]* that love for God should be as strong as three kinds of love combined—the love of a mother for her

child, a husband for a chaste wife, and a miser for his gold. Did he mean that one should love God in all those ways or that one should have the combined strength of all those loves?

Swami: I would say he was speaking of the quantity rather than the quality—one should have the power of those loves combined. Love for God has a quality of its own. It is not just like any worldly loves.

Dorothy: But how can one possibly have that much love?

Swami: You have an obsession. You are thinking of your love for your mother. Do you think that is the be-all and end-all of love?

Dorothy: I can't imagine a stronger love than that.

Swami: Why do you judge everything by your own experience? When one feels real love for God, it is a tremendous thing. One's whole being becomes charged with love.

Me: Swami, I have an obsession too. It seems to me that unless God is real to a person—that is, really real, not just a strong idea or conviction—unless He is real, then one cannot have such intense love for Him. I can see that if He does seem real, then one could not help but have such love. But unless He is known as real, one cannot have that kind of love; and without that kind of love, one cannot know Him as real. That seems quite a dilemma.

Swami (smiling): You have said a mouthful. But your supposition is wrong. One can have love for God before realizing Him, because He *is* real. He is real for you all the time. It is just your ignorance that hides that fact from you.

Swami went on to speak of the great Bengali saint Sri Chaitanya, who was mad with love for God. Chaitanya once flung himself into the ocean. A fisherman found him several days later floating about, still in an ecstatic trance. The fisherman brought him in to shore; but having touched Chaitanya when he was in that exalted spiritual state, the fisherman was himself out of his mind with divine ecstasy, dancing around, singing, and weeping.

The people asked Chaitanya to bring the fisherman back to his senses. Chaitanya told them to get some food from a very worldly house and make him eat it. They did so, and the fisherman's mind at once came down to normal.

Swami: Things happen like that. One who is not ready for spiritual experience may have it by accident, but it cannot be retained.

Once a man was brought to Sri Ramakrishna. He had been at a *kirtan* [devotional songfest] and had gone into ecstasy, such that he could not speak. Sri Ramakrishna told the man's family not to worry; he wouldn't be able to retain that state and his mind would soon come down. Actually it did; in a few days the man was back to normal.

Anna Webster: Isn't it good to have that happen—even if one isn't up to it? I mean, when a person isn't ready for an experience like that, isn't it good just the same?

Swami: No, it can be very harmful.

Anna: Harmful?

Swami: When the body and mind aren't prepared, it can be a terrible thing. The body can be shattered. One could have a stroke.

Anna: What of it?

Swami: Do you want to spend the rest of your life paralyzed?

Anna: I wouldn't mind—what difference would it make if one's inner state were good? I mean—

Swami: The mental state would not remain up. It could become worse that it had been before. The reaction could be very severe. It is much better to prepare one's body and mind so that they can retain spiritual experience. One should progress along all lines simultaneously.

September 21, 1962

We were at our annual Lake Tahoe retreat. Swami began talking to us about the work at Sacramento and the struggle involved in changing the soil for the gardens, and so forth.

Swami: To work for the Lord is never easy; there is always struggle. Always! There is no other way. It is good to have the spirit of struggle. Out of that, growth comes.

If spiritual life is made devoid of struggle, there is a danger in it. The danger is twofold: first, there is the danger that the work will gradually peter out, and second, that it will draw third-rate people who are seeking comfort and enjoyment. Those who have a little substance in them will find themselves in the minority and will go away. Those who are pleasure-seeking will take the whole thing over. That is the danger. If you continually provide entertainment, you will draw that kind of people. I am in favor of keeping things a little on the dry side. Without a background of strength, the right kind of people just won't come.

With strength, there comes a joy in the struggle, in wrestling with your mind. It is as though you had climbed a steep mountain—you breathe pure air and see vast views all around.

I have a horror of this watering down just to make everyone feel comfortable. There is a trap there. We fall for the obvious and we miss the deeper thing.

Always struggle—the struggle of a hero, not of a coward—a conquering struggle, without even a thought there could be defeat in that struggle. It is not as though you can take an easy path and find that good meditation comes. There is no easy path. When the mind is difficult, you have to rise up and battle it. Outside troubles may come; inside troubles may come—but rise up and be a conquering hero. There is no other way.

September 24, 1962

It was Swami Ashokananda's birthday today in Lake Tahoe. Jo, Helen, Marilyn Pearce, and I had arranged a picnic at Mount Rose in celebration. Marilyn had a special gift for him—a polished box with a fitted lid that she had carved out of a block of incense cedar. But this morning Swami received the news that

Swami Akhilananda had died last night at 5:00 p.m. Swami Ashokananda debated whether or not to go on the picnic and decided not to cancel the arrangements. During the picnic he said, "I am talking with all of you, but my mind is with Swami Akhilananda." In the evening, Swami spoke only of his friend, Swami Akhilananda, and so lovingly.

During the mid-1960s, Swami continued to spend a month or six weeks each year at the Vedanta Society's monastic retreat at Lake Tahoe. Although the altitude and quiet days no longer refreshed him, he still loved the piney fragrance and the expansive view of still, blue water. My journal for 1964 gives a glimpse of the atmosphere with Swami at Lake Tahoe, beginning just after John Varrentzoff's tragic death as the victim of a freak accident. Found in John's coat pocket were cards on which he had written things Swami had said to him. One of these was "Whatever your experiences are—reject them!" Another was "Do you want to stay forever in your miserable, miserable, miserable mud puddle? You don't have to keep checking and rechecking mistakes. That is not a spiritual way of life. Many times a mistake is just left behind. Plunge into the thought of God."

September 8, 1964

Virginia Varrentzoff and her daughter Chela drove to Tahoe this morning with John's ashes. Jo took the grieving mother and daughter to a spot at the north end of the lake in Nevada, where the water is a clear turquoise and rocks string out from the shore. Chela climbed out to the last rock and there poured the ashes into the water. When they returned to the car, they were crying.

Tonight Virginia and Chela had dinner at Jo and Helen's cabin and then saw Swami alone in his cabin for some forty-five minutes before the rest of us (Kathleen, Ediben, Jo, Helen, and me) came in. Swami seemed so tired and ill that he could hardly speak, yet he tried to talk cheerfully for the sake of Virginia and Chela and served us ice cream and cake.

Swami said that the soul after death resolves to think only of God in its next life, but as soon as it emerges from the mother's womb and breathes the air of this world, it forgets all its good resolutions.

Swami: But Chela shouldn't hear these things. She is young and should enjoy life.

Chela (laughing): What are you trying to do? (She meant, I think, "Are you advising me to enjoy worldly life?")

Swami: There is a right time for everything. In youth one should have enjoyment. If one does everything at the right time, then in each period of one's life one will feel fulfilled. There is a way of life for each period: youth, middle age, and old age.

(Virginia and Chela stayed overnight in a motel and had lunch the next day with Jo and Helen before returning to San Francisco.)

September 11, 1964

Swami's blood pressure is still high. I have never seen him look worse than he has in the past few days. Yet he notices each little thing—a Band-Aid on someone's finger, a new piece of jewelry, a missing button, a new pair of slacks, and whether or not one is dressed warmly enough—small things that indicate states of mind, body, or soul. Nothing escapes him that concerns the welfare of his disciples. His mind is never on himself.

He is worried about Swami Vividishananda, the head of the Vedanta Society in Seattle, who has failing eyesight. It seems that the optic nerve is affected. Swami Ashokananda looks so tragic when he thinks about it. If Swami Vividishananda should go blind, his work in Seattle will collapse because the center does not have enough real workers to carry on.

Later that day

Swami: In ten years you will change your opinion about me; then how will you write a book about me? All of you [his students] will change your opinion.

Me: If that is true, you are surrounded by worthless people.

Swami: I am surrounded by normal people. It is natural that one's sense of values should change. It is human. What seems good now might not seem good later.

Me: I don't understand why you talk this way.

Swami (with an amused gleam): To warn you—so the jolt of disillusionment won't be so great.

September 1964

Since the first stormy days after our arrival at Lake Tahoe, every day has been warm, clear, and still—day after day of wonderful, golden weather. Swami looks better now, though he has become sad and tired worrying about Swami Vividishananda's eyesight and financial problems. Perhaps Ediben and Doug also weigh upon his mind; Doug, who has prostate cancer, grows worse and worse.

September 16, 1964

Swami: Sri Ramakrishna's and Swamiji's work is a power in itself. It will go ahead of itself. It is that power that draws people and makes them want to serve. Even if one should decide to shut down the Society, there would be an opposing force. A group of people would keep the work going; the power would work through them.

September 17, 1964

Kathleen and I were sitting in Swami's cabin.

Swami (to Kathleen, referring to me): Don't imitate her; you will get into a mess if you do. Her path is different from yours. You have your own way. You are channel 7 and she is channel 5, or vice versa. Each life has its own channel.

September 18, 1964

Swami: Swamiji sowed the seeds of Vedanta in San Francisco. He left a power there.

Me: Where are the seeds? After the people whom he knew or who saw him and heard him died, then where are the seeds, or power, located?

Swami: They are not only in the hearts of people; they are in the very air. Those who live in San Francisco are affected by them. The atmosphere he created is a force.

Me: It is an esoteric thing.

Swami: We are speaking of esoteric things, not of material forces.

September 19, 1964

Swami was sleeping when I went as usual to his cabin at 1:30 this afternoon. He had not, of course, slept all night. He sleeps in the afternoons.

This evening he seemed to be well and his eyes were shining, lustrous—his face full. His blood pressure was lower, and he no longer looked so deeply worried since there is hope that Swami Vividishananda's eyesight may recover.

He spoke of my writing a book about him and seemed pleased. Now and then he told me stories of his early life. I write down all I can remember as soon as I can.

September 20, 1964

Except for the time he walked over to Ediben's, where I was staying, Swami has not stepped out of his own cabin. Though his health has improved since we arrived at Lake Tahoe, he is still weak and thin. God knows how he will lecture in San Francisco a week from today!

I go every day to work with Swami at 1:30 p.m. Generally he is asleep and I tiptoe away. He hasn't been able to work at all. Sometimes (as in earlier years) he gives me lunch in his kitchen. We stand at his sink, he on the left and I on the right, and look out on a parklike forest. He eats, almost always cottage cheese, yogurt, and canned pears, and I have something similar. Then he washes the dishes.

IN SUMMERS PAST, Swami would sometimes bring one or two young men from the monastery to stay in his cabin at the lake. But he would never let them serve him. He made his own bed and washed his own dishes; he did his laundry in a bucket and hung his clothes out to dry on the porch railing, securing them with large, pancake-shaped rocks that Jo had gathered by the lake. He even did outdoor tasks.

Once, when the fire in his living room smoked, he came outside, wearing bedroom slippers and a coat over his dressing gown. He got a ladder from under the porch, set it against the house by the chimney, and (ignoring Ediben's panicky protests) proceeded to climb the ladder carrying a long broom. When he reached the roof, he tossed aside the screen that covered the chimney and thrust the broom down the opening as far as it could reach. The broom was not long enough to do a thorough job, but the maneuver helped because smoke came out of the chimney. He then climbed down the ladder, returned the broom to its place under the porch, and went inside.

Many years ago, one of the young men fortunate enough to come to Tahoe for the summer with Swami was the youngest of Edna Zulch's three sons, Fred, who was thinking in those days of becoming a monk and was living in the monastery in San

Francisco. Fred told the story of how he and another young novice knocked down a wasps' nest from the eaves of the porch. The dispossessed wasps were angrily buzzing around when Swami deliberately enticed one of them to sting him on his bare arm (in order, he said, to know what a sting felt like). When the wasp obliged, a look of sheer ecstasy came into Swami's face as though he, like the Hindu saint Pavhari Baba, had received "a message from the Beloved" when bitten by a cobra.

I was sometimes aghast at how Swami dealt with the wildlife at Lake Tahoe—often with a vision beyond the ordinary. One day during our kitchen lunch, I was horrified to see a big, black, long-legged spider in the sink. Swami summarily washed it down the drain. When I made a cry of protest, he said, surprised, and with total conviction, "Don't you see? It is just the form."

He usually took a very practical and commonsense view of the forest creatures. Aside from providing a salt lick for the deer, he did not accommodate them. On the contrary, he discouraged familiarity, for he knew from his experience with rodents at Mayavati that they could be highly destructive. He gave them no quarter. Once, I inadvertently let a mouse into Ediben's cabin when I was staying there alone. I put out food and water for its comfort. Swami insisted, instead, that I set a trap. Reluctantly I did so, and the little mouse, accustomed to my offerings, was betrayed. The next day, Jo, Helen, and I gave it a decent burial. Another time, walking along the path between Ediben's house and his own, Swami, Jo, and I came upon a sick or disabled bat, lying helpless in the open. With his cane Swami gently nudged the little creature into the bushes, where it would not be visible to a hawk. "Let it recover," he said.

And there was the memorable time when the long tail of a mouse dangled between the boards of his bedroom ceiling. He grasped it firmly and maneuvered the attached mouse toward a knothole, from where it fell into his hands. He then drowned it without ceremony.

All that was in the days when he had his health. Now, although he still washed his clothes in a bucket and sometimes padded into the kitchen at lunchtime wearing a many-layered combination of jersey pajamas, sweaters, and ski jacket, I found him most often reclining on his lounge in the living room gazing at the wide, blue water of the lake, which reminded him—as an expanse of quiet water always did—of infinity.

Here my journal ends. It ends not because there weren't many more spiritual gems to record after 1964, but because I was given innumerable small writing and editing tasks in addition to one big, all-consuming job. I had little time left to jot down my conversations with Swami Ashokananda.

My big job was to write the second book of *New Discoveries*. I began working on it at the close of 1964 and finished it toward the end of 1969. I did the research as I went along, by correspondence and sometimes by actual fieldwork—or, I should say, by pleasure jaunts to see the places and to meet the people that had loomed large in Swami Vivekananda's second visit to the West (which was what this new book was all about). Actually, Swami Vivekananda's first visit to the West had not been fully covered in the first book, which had been based entirely on my research, for I had not included what was already known. Moreover, I had followed Swamiji's trail only up to the middle of 1894, whereas his first visit to the West had not closed until the end of 1896.

Nevertheless, in 1964 I jumped ahead to his second visit, which began in 1899. I am not sure why Swami Ashokananda wanted the story to take that leap. Perhaps he felt that Swami Vivekananda's work in California in 1899 and 1900 was of great importance and wanted to be sure I recorded it correctly, or perhaps it was just because he wanted to see that period written before he died.

As had been the case with the first book, a great deal of research took place by miracle, as though Swami Vivekananda were closely watching the work and guiding it—or so I liked to think. For instance, in regard to the Hales (who played the role of Swamiji's family in the West), I found the McKindley sisters' niece (a relative who I had not known existed) by writing to a man for some unrelated data. In reply, he included the incidental information that there had been a third McKindley sister named Mary, whose daughter was still living; and, in an act of good will and generosity, he gave me the daughter's current address.

It turned out that she was not only still living but resided in Salinas, California, a town within easy driving distance of San Francisco. Her name was Mrs. Louise Baker Hyde. I, of course, wrote to her and received a warm and enthusiastic reply, along with an invitation to lunch. I spent a memorable afternoon with Mrs. Hyde, who had known and the entire Hale family and remembered them well. She lent me many precious photographs to have copied for the book. I had no doubt that Swamiji himself had led me to her.

The research often went like that, but there were also disappointments. I found John Fox's address, for instance, only a week or two after he had died. John Fox had been secretary to Mrs. Ole Bull (Swamiji's close friend and supporter) and was with Swami Vivekananda in London in 1896. His widow told me that he would have loved to talk with me about his memories of those wonderful days (she herself knew nothing of them). That was one of the times I kicked myself for being too slow. For the most part, though, research material seemed to drop into my lap from the sky.

In June of 1965, Kathleen Davis and I flew to southern California, where Swami Vivekananda had lived and worked in December of 1899 and the early part of 1900. We visited the tiny Victorian house in South Pasadena that had belonged to the Mead sisters, where Swamiji and seven other grown people and one small child had lived—presumably in comfort—for about a month. That small gem of a house is today a place of pilgrimage and the room that Swamiji had to himself has been made into a shrine. Kathleen and I visited every other place in southern California where Swamiji had lived or lectured, and I spent a full day gathering information in the Huntington Library, to which I had temporary access. All in all, we spent a full, rewarding, and very pleasant week.

In October of 1969, Bobbie Day and I flew to New York City where we rented a car and took off into the spectacular October countryside of upstate New York. When it was Bobbie's turn to drive, I, to whom this fantastic splurge of nature was a new experience, took dozens of photographs in an attempt to capture the splendor of the scarlet and golden trees. We drove first to the estate of Ridgely in the Hudson River valley, where Mrs. Frances Leggett (the daughter of Mr. and Mrs. Francis H. Leggett, Swamiji's hosts in 1899) had invited us to spend a day and a night. Frances Leggett, a gracious and warm hostess, took time to show us Ridgely and its various houses.

Then Bobbie and I went on a grand pilgrimage tour to visit the other places where Swamiji had lectured or stayed: Thousand Island Park in the St. Lawrence River; Camp Percy in New Hampshire; Mrs. Bull's house in Cambridge, and Breezy Meadows in Farmington, Massachusetts; and Greenacre near Elliot, Maine. Finally we returned to New York City.

From New York we flew back to San Francisco—I with much new information and many overexposed snapshots, some of which were of the empty sky and others of Bobbie's hands on the steering wheel. There was only one good photograph of a flaming autumn tree. In late October of that year, I finished writing the second book, entitled *Swami Vivekananda, His Second Visit to the West: New Discoveries*.

By then, Swami Ashokananda had had a cerebral stroke that paralyzed his left side. He had also become very ill with a kidney infection. His mind, however, was unaffected and he wanted me to read the new book to him. So, chapter by chapter, I read to him every night, at first sitting on a chair, which proved to be so uncomfortable that I took to kneeling on a cushion by his bedside, the manuscript open on the bed itself. Every now and then Swami would fall asleep and I would stop reading. After a few minutes of silence, he would abruptly open his eyes, fully awake. "Why have you stopped?" he would say. "Read on."

"You were asleep," I would reply. He would simply say again, "Read on." Once he replied incredulously, "Do you think I listen only with my surface mind?"

Though he often seemed to be asleep, I learned that he was, indeed, listening to every word. If there was something in the text he did not like or something that was not exactly correct, his eyes would fly open and he would point out the fault or suggest a better way of putting what I was trying to say or a better way of organizing the chapter. He was a wonderful critic and editor. When I had read all the chapters to him, he said to the room at large, not hiding his pleasure, "Marie Louise has written a good book." There was nothing that could have supported me more strongly during the editorial struggles that were to come than those words. "This time," he said to me later, "you will have to fight your own battles." He had armed me, though, and given me the backup force of his approval.

Meanwhile, Marion Langerman, a devotee from Berkeley, who was just then between secretarial jobs, moved to San Francisco in order to type the manuscript at Swami's request. She settled into Mara Lane's apartment and typed daily for hours on end, until, at the very close of Swami Ashokananda's life, the work was finished, and I could tell him so.

Swami left his body on December 13, 1969. The drama of the last part of his life has been related in *A Heart Poured Out* and need not be repeated here. The blows his work received, his illnesses, his last struggles, and his victories were not a part of my journal, probably because I did not have the heart at the time to write any of it down. On the day of his departure from this world, I wrote in my journal only the words "My Beloved Swami."

EPILOGUE

After the first overbearing mountains of grief gradually flattened out into a featureless and seemingly endless bog in which I found no footing and no path, nor wanted any, I awoke one morning as though called by a compelling and familiar voice—Swami Ashokananda's—asking me, "What are you doing? Finish your work!"

There was much work to finish. Although *Swami Vivekananda, His Second Visit to the West: New Discoveries* had been typed during 1969, I still had to write a preface, compile a list of illustrations, and copyedit the manuscript before it could be sent to India. On the evening of April 14, 1970, we offered the finished typescript in the shrine at the New Temple. Dorothy Murdock, Kathleen Davis, and I made a ceremony of it, performing a small worship at the altar. Afterward, we celebrated with chocolate ice cream and cookies at my new apartment in the convent building. We were moving back into life.

By 1970, Western civilization had reached the Xerox stage—though barely. Kathleen and I drove to the town of Burlingame fifteen miles south of San Francisco to have two xeroxed copies made of the typescript. I mailed the first copy to Swami Gambhirananda, general secretary of the Ramakrishna Order, on April 17, and a day or two later I sent the second copy to the publisher, Swami Budhananda, president of Advaita Ashrama. Swami Gambhirananda, who was known never to leave an unanswered letter on his desk overnight, replied at once with noncommittal brevity, "Advaita Ashrama can now think of taking up the task of arranging for publication."

At the end of 1969, the convent had moved into the building on the corner of Steiner and Vallejo Streets less than a block away from the New Temple. Edith Soulé, Martha Muirhead, her younger sister Mary, Luke Williams, and I had separate apartments in this same building. Kathleen Davis occupied a bedroom and a kitchen in the center of the convent quarters with the idea, which never materialized, that she would eventually be absorbed into the convent itself.

In the penthouse of this same building, a large room was devoted to the editing of Swami Ashokananda's lectures and classes, which consisted of over nine hundred recorded tapes, fifty or so already transcribed. Nancy Jackman, Kathleen, and I were in charge of the editing, which occasionally entailed some rousing arguments, primarily between Nancy and me.

After a trans-Pacific correspondence throughout 1971 and 1972 between Swami Budhananda and me over his editing of *Second Visit*—in which many points were battled over until the writing seemed to hang in shreds—the second book of *New Discoveries* was finally finished to our mutual satisfaction; it would be published in 1973.

In the meantime, I had been collecting material for the third book of *New Discoveries,* which would be subtitled *The World Teacher*. During 1971, I was deep in this work when Swami Budhananda wrote that he wanted me to edit those chapters of *The Life of Swami Vivekananda by His Eastern and Western Disciples* that dealt with Swamiji's life and work in the West, to bring them up to date in accord with the facts that had been brought to light in the first two *New Discoveries* books.

I was then fifty-nine years old and in good health but I felt that, at such an advanced age, I had only a few more years to live. I replied to Swami Budhananda that I could not, in my few remaining years, complete both my projected book and edit the *Life*. Swami Budhananda did not accept my reply. He persisted and eventually I acquiesced. I set aside my research for the third *New Discoveries* book and began to read the *Life* with the eye of an editor. In reply to my query about how far I could go in editing the book, Swami Budhananda wrote that I could make as many tentative alterations and additions as I wanted. With this go-ahead, I started serious work on the *Life* in November of 1971.

Swami Prabuddhananda was now in charge of the Vedanta Society of Northern California; he had come from Bangalore in June of 1970 and soon began to acquire students of his own. Among these were two fancy-free, hippielike young women from Kentucky who came one Wednesday night to a lecture at the New Temple on the recommendation of a friend. They were in a venturesome mood, for in those days a Hindu swami was still an object of mystery and curiosity and to attend a Hindu temple was a thrilling, convention-defying act. The giggling young women had no idea that a single flighty evening would change their lives forever. To the consternation and bewilderment of their Catholic parents, it wasn't long before they joined the convent. (Today, they are both ordained Vedantin nuns.)

One of these young women (Linda Winé, now Pravrajika Virajaprana) was a good typist and eager to be useful around the Vedanta Society. With Swami Prabuddhananda's consent, I asked her to help with the typing of my edited version of the *Life*. It was a difficult task even for an expert because, for the sake of clarity, I wanted the editorial changes typed with a red ribbon, which caused frequent interruptions in the rhythmical clacking into which every good typist falls. Nevertheless, Linda kept up with me, as did Kathleen, and the three of us soon produced a typescript of the *Life* to send to Swami Budhananda. It was aflame with red ink and must have raised the swami's labile blood pressure to the danger point. His monastic elders gave him permission to invite me to India to go over the text with him, word by word, at Advaita Ashrama (the editorial office of the Order's publications in the Himalayas, which was also an austere monastic retreat).

The invitation from Swami Budhananda, coming just then, was extremely fortuitous, for it coincided with another that I received from India one Sunday morning in late 1972. I was sitting in the back of the New Temple auditorium after a lecture when Mr. Warren, a monk who lived in the Vedanta Retreat at Olema, approached me. He had recently returned from India where he had taken *sannyas,* his final monastic vows (he was now Swami Sahajananda). He sat down on the chair next to mine—an alarming thing for him to do, considering that he was Swami Ashokananda's student and knew the rules separating the sexes as well as I did. I congratulated him on his *sannyas*. It was the first time I had ever spoken to him. He thanked me and, without further small talk, said, "I have a message for you from Swami Abhayananda. He asked me to say that he invites you to come to Belur Math."

Probably my mouth flew open. I knew that Swami Abhayananda was the famed and revered Bharat Maharaj, who had confronted tigers in the Himalayas and was a dear friend of Swami Ashokananda. Moreover, a visit to Belur Math, the monastic headquarters of the Order situated on the Ganges north of Calcutta and a place of pilgrimage in itself, had been my recent dream.

"When?" I asked.

Swami Sahajananda shrugged his shoulders. "He didn't say." Then he added, leaning slightly toward me for emphasis, "If I were you, I would accept." With that, he left the auditorium. It was many years before I was again near enough to him to thank him for having borne to me a message that would richly change the remaining thirty-odd years of my life (after all), giving them a color and a depth they could not otherwise have had.

I wrote to Swami Abhayananda at once to accept his invitation and to ask if Kathleen Davis, another devotee, might also come. The swami replied promptly that we were both welcome. The best time to come, he added, would be in December of 1973—almost a year away. While waiting, we edited a number of Swami Ashokananda's lectures and made substantive changes to the *Life* to make it both factually accurate and readable.

Most important, we prepared for what we looked upon as a trip to the darkest part of central Africa. We shopped in several sporting goods stores. Kathleen bought a mountaineering outfit, complete with climbing boots, which she later wore on the beach at Honolulu, sitting primly in meditation posture in the midst of sprawled, near-naked, sun-tanned bodies. I bought a heavy woolen pullover and ski pants, which I never wore at all, and a broad-brimmed sports hat, which I wore once or twice at Belur Math, much to the amusement of Bharat Maharaj and perhaps many others. Nothing we packed had much relationship to any of the circumstances in which we would find ourselves. The most important things, such as typewriters and manuscripts, we shipped separately. These critical items remained in Calcutta customs for months because I had not declared them, thinking that unaccompanied baggage was no one's business but our own.

At Belur Math a devotee provided us (at Bharat Maharaj's request) with saris, which another affable and quick-handed Bengali devotee showed us how to "tie," as they say. The complicated operation was dazzling. Left to ourselves, we gathered yards of excess material into a bunch that we stuffed inside a waistband, without the security of a safety pin. One evening while we were watching fireworks from Bharat Maharaj's veranda (it was Sri Ramakrishna's birthday), the skirt of my sari came loose and threatened to fall, taking with it the entire yardage. Not understanding the mechanics of the drapery, I did not know what end of it to secure and made a dash for a dark and secluded corner where I tore the sari off and started all over again to wrap it around.

I hated saris and soon settled upon a costume composed of a *lungi* (a colorful wraparound skirt such as workmen and servants habitually wore) with a Western shirt hanging loose over it. I was not at all aware that on a middle-aged woman this costume was hilariously incongruous to the Indians, who were too polite to mention it. Bharat Maharaj commented only on my hat. "You wear hat?" he said in his charmingly broken English, with a gleam deep in his eyes. At once, I removed the hat and never wore it again.

Bharat Maharaj, then in his eighties, welcomed Kathleen and me with love and kindness. He did everything to make us feel wanted and at home. He let us sit in his office at his round table for hours at a stretch and talked with us intermittently between his long conversations with Bengali devotees who came to him with their problems and their grief. Almost invariably these devotees, who approached him barely suppressing their sobs, left him with radiant faces, all sorrow removed. Although we could not understand the language, these small dramas were a joy to watch. Bharat Maharaj was clearly a healing ocean of love and concern as he greeted each of the devotees, most of whom he had known since their childhood. As we watched day after day, our own grief, which we still deeply felt, began to dissolve. Bharat Maharaj later told me that he knew our visit to

Belur Math would have that effect upon us, and that was why he had invited us.

Within a month of our arrival, Kathleen and I went on a pilgrimage tour of southern India, down to the windy tip of the continent, Cape Comorin, where we meditated in Swami Vivekananda's temple, which stands majestically on a rock beyond the shore. Traveling north, we became exhausted and cabled Belur Math to say we were returning immediately.

Back at Belur Math we found the company of Bharat Maharaj far more uplifting than the temples of south India. But this was not a restful time for me. A few days before Kathleen and I had left the Math for our tour of south India, Swami Lokeswarananda, newly designated to be the next secretary of the Ramakrishna Mission Institute of Culture in Calcutta, had come to Bharat Maharaj's office in the early evening to inform me that I would have to give two lectures at the Institute. My adrenaline level rose to overflowing and I launched an extensive and detailed explanation of why this was an impossible idea. During my earnest recitation, Swami Lokeswarananda looked with an impassive and stony face into a corner of the room. When I had quite finished and had fallen silent, certain that I had dissuaded him, the Swami turned to me and said unsmilingly, "Now, we must set the dates for your talks."

So, apart from visiting Bharat Maharaj and the president of the Order, Swami Vireswarananda, I spent this respite at Belur Math writing two papers. Delivering the first talk, I had a bad case of laryngitis but somehow managed to be heard by over a thousand people. The second talk at the Institute also went well, and I breathed a sigh of vast relief. But I was not off the hook; that stint was the beginning of what was to me a highly stressful career as a speaker—or rather as a reader of papers, for extraneous talks were truly out of my range. On many occasions in the years to come I would be asked (as though I had a choice) to "say a few words" to thousands of people who had assembled for reasons other than to hear me speak.

The climax of my life as a public speaker would come later, in 1982, when the Institute of Culture created the Vivekananda Award. I became the first recipient of this prize, which was presented to me before a large audience by Swami Vireswarananda on January 3, 1983, in recognition of my two *New Discoveries* books. I wanted to refuse the honor, but it was pressed upon me with such love and pleasure that a refusal would have been unthinkably churlish. And I of course knew myself to be not only honored but also blessed.

From our base at Belur Math, Kathleen and I set off again in March of 1974 to tour northern India. In April we reached Almora in the Himalayan foothills, where we had an invitation to visit Gertrude Emerson Sen, the well-known author of books about India. I had written to Mrs. Sen in regard to her large collection of Swami Vivekananda's many unpublished letters to his disciple from Detroit, Christina Greenstidel. These letters were understandably precious to her. Because of some earlier and now forgotten misunderstanding with the authorities of Belur Math, she had refused them access to her collection; but she had agreed to let me see it.

Kathleen and I immediately became friends with Gertrude Sen, a warm hostess and a fascinating conversationalist. Not only did she let me read her treasure of Swamiji's letters to Christina and to others, but she permitted a photostatist from Lucknow to come and copy them. She even converted a small bathroom into a darkroom for his use.

From Almora we drove deeper and higher into the Himalayas to Advaita Ashrama at Mayavati, escorted in a small car up the winding road by two swamis from Lucknow. Almost immediately, a daily editorial battle began between Swami Budhananda and me.

It was not until after Swami Budhananda had given me free rein to edit the *Life* as I pleased that he was instructed by the Belur Math authorities not to make *any* change unless such change was absolutely necessary; to Swami Budhananda, this was an unbreachable order. He was now caught between a radical bit-in-teeth editor and the conservative elders at Belur Math, to whom the *Life* was holy writ, not to be altered. Swami Budhananda never explained his dilemma to me and my ignorance of it would cause endless difficulty between us—I could not understand, for instance, his innumerable objections to my corrections of factual material.

We worked in the mornings and, it seemed to me, debated every word that I had changed in the text and every fact of Swami Vivekananda's life that I had set straight. Since Swami Budhananda had not informed me during our correspondence that each editorial change would require verification, I had left my voluminous research notes in San Francisco. I had no way, other than raising my voice to higher and yet higher levels, to substantiate the changes I had made. At lunchtime, exhausted and in a fury, I wended my way down the hill to the guesthouse where Kathleen listened to my account of the morning's strife, which I gave at first close to tears, then with laughter.

In the afternoons Kathleen and I enjoyed the serene, deeply silent forests of Mayavati, walking along the road until the sun set with a spectacular farewell. Generally, the snow peaks were not visible through the haze that arose from the plains; but when the towering white mountains were now and then revealed, we caught our breath in disbelief at their majesty. Our stay in the Himalayas lasted for six months, with our visas periodically extended.

In October of 1974, the editorial task force (consisting of Swami Budhananda, Swami Balaramananda, Kathleen, and me) finally returned to the plains. One of the first things Swami

Budhananda did was to take the much-scrawled-over manuscript to Swami Gambhirananda; with trepidation, he offered to read it aloud to him, since the general secretary's eyesight was poor. But to Swami Budhananda's immense relief Swami Gambhirananda said, somewhat crossly, "No! Why should you read it to me? You and Gargi have edited it. That's enough!"

Unfortunately, it wasn't enough. We hadn't finished. I worked on at Belur Math, now and then traveling by car through traffic-clogged, pothole-ridden, and fume-choked roads to Calcutta, where the editorial battle, now toned down, continued.

At the beginning of 1975, Kathleen returned to San Francisco by way of Ireland, where she visited an elderly and ailing aunt. A trip that she would not have ventured to make alone a year before, she now braved with assurance and aplomb. After six lonely months of holding our own in the spiritual fastness of the Himalayas, both Kathleen and I had changed.

As the summer climate grew stifling, Swami Budhananda suggested that I move into an air-conditioned room at the Ramakrishna Mission Institute of Culture, which was convenient to the Advaita Ashrama office in Calcutta, where we continued to edit the *Life*. I wrote in my journal on May 18, 1975,

> The sittings are now often entirely pleasant and good, with united, cooperative, concentrated work. I like it very much! SBU [Swami Budhananda's cable name, which Swami Balaramananda, Kathleen, and I always used among ourselves] is much more civil to me nowadays.
>
> I told this to Bharat Maharaj. He said, "Yes, because he is afraid of what we would say. At Mayavati he is the lion; here he is nothing."

In the sweltering heat of Calcutta my right arm, resting on a notebook, made the page wet with perspiration. The air conditioner in my room was of no help because I never turned it on, preferring the heat to its banging noise. In any case, the work was coming to completion. Although my relationship with Swami Budhananda was still punctuated by impenetrable misunderstandings, he and I were now on friendlier terms. My visa was again extended before we finally finished editing the *Life* at the close of 1975.

Swami Budhananda's eyesight was beginning to fail, so it was no longer possible for him to remain in charge of the Order's publishing department. By the end of December 1975, he was prepared to leave the Calcutta office of Advaita Ashrama. I went there from Belur Math to say good-bye. He was very friendly that day—and made the longest speech he had ever spoken to me.

"I have felt," he said, "that the Divine Mother took up two clumps of earth, two egos, one in each hand, and smashed them together. A lot of dirt fell from both clumps. I benefited from it."

I was overwhelmed that he said such a kind thing to me and I could only mumble, "It was I who benefited." I sincerely meant it.

In January of 1976 I would leave India, which had been my home for over two years, and I would not return until 1980. By then, Swami Ananyananda had become the president of Advaita Ashrama—a roundish, genial, and gentle monk. My work with him would be to finish writing *New Discoveries*. Aware that another book was needed to make the history of Swami Vivekananda's visit to the West complete, Swami Ananyananda suggested that I revise the two books of *New Discoveries* already published and then write a third book; each of these bulky books would then be cut in half to create six volumes. (As it happened, the third book would end up in the middle of the series as volumes 3 and 4 because it covered the last part of Swami Vivekananda's first visit to the West, while the second book, *Second Visit*, would conclude the series as volumes 5 and 6.)

At times during the next four years of rewriting and writing, I felt that I was not merely climbing Mount Everest without a guide or oxygen, but that the whole of the Himalayan range was bearing down upon my head. Had it not been for my echoing memories of Swami Ashokananda's voice, "Hup! Push on!" I doubt that I could have completed the third book.

Kathleen Davis was of constant help throughout 1976–1980. She was a good and tireless typist and had some training in copyediting. With *The Chicago Manual of Style* (twelfth edition) as our bible, we produced a fairly presentable typescript of more than 1,100 pages that filled to bulging four thick, three-ring binders. By 1980 the manuscript was ready to send to Advaita Ashrama.

The only difficulty was that no one other than Kathleen had read the entire text. It was, after all, an extremely important thesis that had been written to interpret Swamiji's message to a rapidly approaching age. My knowledge of Swami Vivekananda stemmed from Swami Ashokananda's interpretation of his thought, yet I was unsure; how dare I presume to rightly comprehend my teacher's interpretation? I felt that at least one monk of the Order should read the manuscript and set his seal of approval on it. Swami Prabuddhananda was extremely busy stirring the Vedanta Society of Northern California out of the stagnation of grief into which it had been falling when he took charge in mid-1970. I could not ask him to go carefully through a manuscript of more than one thousand pages.

Swami Ananyananda, the publisher, was the logical person to read and approve the book, but I wanted to avoid the agonizing and protracted trans-Pacific correspondence that I suffered through with Swami Budhananda during the editing of *Second Visit*. It would be better, I reasoned, to go through the book with Swami Ananyananda on the spot—that is, in India. I left San Francisco in December of 1980, this time alone, for Kathleen had no particular desire or need to go. By now she had happily moved into her own apartment in the convent building.

It took three visits to India between 1980 and 1982 before anyone paid any attention to the manuscript. Finally Swami Vandanananda, the new general secretary, arranged for the ailing Swami Dhyanananda, who was a Sanskrit scholar (quite beside the point, I felt), to come to Belur Math and go through the four binders of typescript.

For some reason, which still puzzles me, Swami Dhyanananda assumed a highly rancorous tone in the many notes he made regarding the text of the two-volume work. Since I had not met him and had not been asked to work with him one-on-one, his attitude did not disturb me. Swami Vandanananda took an hour out of his busy schedule almost every day to go over Swami Dhyanananda's latest notes with me. Some of these we ignored as being merely cranky; others, which were scholarly and valid, we agreed with; still others were left up to my own judgment to accept or reject. Swami Vandanananda and I differed on the validity of only a few of Swami Dhyanananda's long and cantankerous remarks. It was not until I actually met the ailing swami and thanked him for the trouble he was taking that his tone softened.

Swami Ananyananda, who had been unwell, began to read the manuscript only in early 1983. Working with him was like walking through a verdant landscape, as opposed to climbing cliffs and fording torrential streams. "You are the writer," he would say when I asked his opinion. He did not know that such trusting words came as a shock to me, so different were they from the verbal challenges of Swami Budhananda. Together, Swami Ananyananda and I, with the help of Swami Dhyanananda, put volumes 3 and 4 of what was now a six-volume work into their final form. It was almost thirty years since Swami Ashokananda had first urged me to write about Swamiji.

I visited India almost every year after that, to spend ever longer times at Belur Math, which I began to think of as my other home. Bharat Maharaj and Swami Vireswarananda were my first local guardians, showering their affection upon me as they did upon all the Western devotees who stayed at the foreign guesthouse—a special breed, fragile and prone to stomach upset. Actually, I was seldom sick during my long stays in India. Everything agreed with me and that, of course, was because my guardians saw to it that everything would. In this respect, I cannot fail to mention Shibu, the chief servant of the foreign guesthouse, who was like a mother in caring for the guests. Though limited, my conversations with Shibu were sometimes unforgettable. One evening we together watched hundreds of small winged creatures dancing and darting in the air above the pond in front of the guesthouse. Amazed, I asked Shibu what they were—large insects or small birds? With a joyful smile, he said simply, "Brahman playing."

With the death of Swami Vireswarananda in 1985 and then of Bharat Maharaj in 1989, I thought that Belur Math would never again be so full of tangible spirituality. But it was not so—sad though I was at their absence, in time Swamis Bhuteshananda, Atmasthananda, and Gitananda, among others, became seniors and amply bestowed their blessings on the devotees. In all the winter and spring months that I spent at Belur Math, I never failed to experience an effortless lift of spirit within and an inpouring of deep affection from the monks. Sri Ramakrishna, Holy Mother, and Swamiji were unwaveringly present, coursing through everyone, monk or devotee, who happened to be there.

When in India I seldom left Belur Math, but in 1994 I flew to Dacca to visit Swami Ashokananda's birthplace in Bangladesh with the idea of writing his biography. After a day or two at the Ramakrishna Math in Dacca, during which I was inevitably asked to "say a few words," I was driven southward with two swamis through acres of tea plantations to Habiganj, a tree-shaded town where we spent the night at the Ramakrishna Ashrama. The following day we drove another seven or eight miles eastward to the erstwhile village of Durgapur, where Swami Ashokananda had lived during his childhood and early youth. The communal riots in Bangladesh during the preceding decade had left standing only one house in this Hindu village, which had once been a thriving oasis of some seventy extended families surrounded by undulating fields of grain. The existing house belonged to surviving members of Swami Ashokananda's family, who were joined that day by family members and friends from neighboring villages in order to greet us with garlands, gifts of saris, small urns of village soil, and cheers of welcome. They seated us in a row on the veranda and offered us fruit and sweets with an air of excitement; I felt like a long-absent daughter of the village who had returned from foreign lands.

Soon the music started. Women in colorful skirts and blouses formed a circle under the trees of the courtyard and began to dance. For a time I watched, enchanted. The rhythm of the tablas and *sirods*, the elated cries and claps of the dancers, the simple steps that I knew I could perform—all were irresistible, and without asking leave of the swamis or of anyone else, I entered the circle of the dancers, waving my arms in the air and hopping about as happily as they. I sensed their delight that I had joined them. Though the swamis were alarmed that I might drop dead, Swami Ashokananda's eighty-two-year-old daughter had been warmly welcomed!

On the drive back to Habiganj we crossed a river to reach the small village of Gosainagar, once inhabited by untouchable hide-tanners. As a young man, Swami Ashokananda, then Yogesh Datta, had befriended and served these illiterate, malnourished, and previously ignored outcastes. He had forded the river to bring them food, clothing, and textbooks. He taught school for them, fed them, and cured them of disease. Eventually, he saw them established in the cobbler's trade, to become relatively prosperous and respected members of the Hindu community. All this he did as worship of the Divine, and this selfless service raised his mind to a level in which he experienced the reality of the object of his worship. The outcastes never forgot him.

The villagers, now cobblers, were waiting for us with garlands and musical instruments. They led us in a parade down the main street of the village, shouting and dancing as they went. At the end of the street, the procession turned and danced back to what seemed to be the village's largest and noblest house. I was seated in a thronelike chair on the veranda and offered many cakes, sweets, and morsels of peeled fruit. The men, women, and children of the village stood facing me, expectant—but also perplexed, for by now tears were streaming down my face. These excited people, the children, grandchildren, and perhaps great grandchildren of the outcastes whom my guru had so lovingly served some seventy-five years earlier, were now honoring his aged daughter with an outpouring of devotion for his hallowed memory. I could barely utter the few words I was asked to speak. My English was incomprehensible to them, but I hoped that these childlike and loving people understood my tears to be those of reciprocated love and not of sorrow or pain.

We drove back to Habiganj, and the next day to Dacca, where I stayed a day or two before I flew back to Belur Math.

The work that Swami Ashokananda had given me to accomplish was finished; I could now write about him. I will never understand how so much grace, from start to finish, had fallen upon me—much of it, I am sure, from Swami Vivekananda himself. I don't think anyone can ever know how or why grace happens, but whether it comes as a harsh blow or as a gentle push, and whether what one does with it is good or bad, one can never deny its sure and ineluctable reality.

LIST OF ILLUSTRATIONS

Unless otherwise noted, the illustrations are courtesy of the Vedanta Society of Northern California.

SECOND PHOTO INSERT

Between pages 202 and 203

INDEX

Page numbers in italics indicate illustrations that appear within the photo inserts (*A* between pages 106 and 107, and *B* between pages 202 and 203). The following abbreviations are used throughout the index: *MLB* for Marie Louise Burke, *SA* for Swami Ashokananda, and *SV* for Swami Vivekananda.

ABOUT THE AUTHOR

Marie Louise Burke became Sister Gargi in 1974 when she took her first vows in India from the Ramakrishna Order. She was honored with the monastic name of Gargi after the renowned Vedic scholar in recognition of her brilliant accomplishments as a researcher and a writer—and later, in 1983, with the first Vivekananda Award given by the Ramakrishna Mission.

She is the well-known author of the monumental six-volume classic *Swami Vivekananda in the West: New Discoveries,* as well as other works. The *New Discoveries* books have become indispensable sourcebooks in India and in Vedanta circles worldwide, and the knowledge they have given of Swami Vivekananda's personality has changed the lives of many readers.

Ms. Burke met Swami Ashokananda in 1948 when he was in charge of the Vedanta Society of Northern California in San Francisco—with which she became closely associated and where she still lives. He encouraged her to write about Swami Vivekananda, and told her that she could write about Swami Ashokananda himself only when all her other work was finished. *A Heart Poured Out,* Sister Gargi's biography of Swami Ashokananda, was published in March 2003 to critical and popular acclaim. In *A Disciple's Journal,* Sister Gargi reveals for the first time her personal story of spiritual struggle in the company of Swami Ashokananda.